DYLAN THOMAS

By the same author

Caitlin: Life with Dylan Thomas (with Mrs Dylan Thomas), 1986

DYLAN THOMAS
In the Mercy of His Means

George Tremlett

St. Martin's Press
New York

TO

The people of Laugharne

DYLAN THOMAS—IN THE MERCY OF HIS MEANS. Copyright © 1991 by George Tremlett. All rights reserved. Printed in the United States of America. No part of this book may be used or reproduced in any manner whatsoever without written permission except in the case of brief quotations embodied in critical articles or reviews. For information, address St. Martin's Press, 175 Fifth Avenue, New York, N.Y. 10010.

Library of Congress Cataloging-in-Publication Data

Tremlett, George.
    Dylan Thomas : in the mercy of his means / George Tremlett.
    p.   cm.
    ISBN 0-312-06957-X
    1. Thomas, Dylan, 1914–1953—Biography.   2. Poets, Welsh—20th century—
Biography. I. Title.
    PR6039.H52Z88 1992
    821'.912—dc20
    [B]
                                     91-33219
                                     CIP

First published in Great Britain by Constable and Company, Limited.

First U.S. Edition: February 1992

10 9 8 7 6 5 4 3 2 1

CONTENTS

ILLUSTRATIONS

ACKNOWLEDGEMENTS

Anyone wishing to write about Dylan Thomas has to make acknowledgements carefully for many are the curious tensions that lie between those who met, knew, loved or respected this strangely intriguing man. One previous writer played safe, mentioning nearly every available source including those with secrets left to tell and at least one person who routinely slammed down the 'phone as soon as the name Dylan Thomas was mentioned. My problem is especially difficult for I have known members of the Thomas family in varying situations for fifteen years, including Caitlin, her sisters Brigid and Nicolette, and the Thomas children Llewelyn, Aeronwy and Colm, and yet I would not wish it to be thought that this biography was authorised by them in any way.

Likewise through being a member of the Dylan Thomas Society, the Committees that oversaw erection of the Westminster Abbey and Laugharne Memorial Plaques, the Dylan Thomas Literary Award Committee, and also by living in Laugharne these past eight years, I have come to know many people intimately associated with Dylan Thomas without them suspecting (or me then intending) that I would write this biography. I have been particularly fortunate in knowing or meeting John Ackerman, Douglas Cleverdon, Alan Davies (Laugharne), Professor Walford Davies, Dr Mike Duggan, Mrs Mary Evans (Laugharne), Rob Gittins, Fred and Mary Janes, D.M. and Megan Jenkins, Glyn Jones, Gwyn Jones, Mervyn Levy, Miss Anna Lewis (Laugharne), Professor Ralph Maud, Leslie Norris, John Ormond, Lynette Roberts, R.D. Smith, Miss Anne Starke (Laugharne), Clem Thomas, Stuart Thomas, Wynford Vaughan-Thomas, Tommy Watts (Laugharne), Colin and Douglas Williams (Laugharne), and Robert Coleman Williams, but I would not wish any of them to think I had betrayed a confidence, or quoted them unfairly, nor do I think I have done so. Rather, it has been a case of many friendships (and some casual meetings) helping to mould a perspective over a period of years.

I am especially grateful to David Higham Associates Ltd and the Trustees of The Dylan Thomas Estate for permission to quote from Thomas's short story *The Fight*, his radio talk *Living in Wales*, his answers to a student's questionnaire which were published in *Texas Quarterly* (Winter 1961) and for extensive quotations from *Dylan Thomas: The Collected Letters*, edited by Paul Ferris and published by J.M. Dent & Sons Ltd. I have hesitated in my use of Thomas's poems out of respect for the form in which they were written, but have quoted from *Author's Prologue* to *The Collected Poems*, published by J.M. Dent & Sons Ltd., and some individual poems namely *Fern Hill*, *Poem in October*, *Poem on his birthday*, *Elegy* and *In the white giant's thigh*. My wish to be sparing lies in the belief that Thomas's work was crafted like the rarest timepiece or the finest porcelain and should always be handled with care.

My other debt is to the New York lawyer Eric Corbett Williams, whom I have never met. I heard that he was gathering material for a study of Thomas's experiences in the United States, and when I wrote to him regarding this he kindly sent me two parcels of letters and press cuttings with permission to use them if I wished. These contained many useful fragments of information. I have made full acknowledgement of these within the annotation, but would particularly mention his letter from the sculptor John CuRoi which contained one piece of eye witness information that might have been lost for ever since CuRoi was killed in a car accident shortly after writing this letter. Its impact was all the more horrifying for my realising how this description fell into place like the last brush of paint on a canvas or the keystone of an arch.

I also acknowledge with gratitude *Dylan Thomas in America* by John Malcolm Brinnin (published by Dent in Britain in 1956, although its influence was already felt with U.S. publication by Little Brown the previous year; *Dylan Thomas* by Derek Stanford (Neville Spearman, 1954), *Dylan Thomas: A Bibliography* by J. Alexander Rolph (Dent, 1956), *Dylan Thomas: His Life and Work* by John Ackerman (Oxford University Press, 1964), *Welsh Dylan* by John Ackerman (John Jones Ltd, 1979), *The Life of Dylan Thomas* by Constantine Fitzgibbon (Dent, 1965), *Two Flamboyant Fathers* by Nicolette Devas (Collins, 1966), *Dylan Thomas* by Paul Ferris (Hodder and Stoughton, 1977), *Laugharne and Dylan Thomas* by Min Lewis (Dennis Dobson, 1967), *Dylan Thomas: Early Prose Writings*, edited by Walford Davies (Dent, 1971), *The Days of Dylan Thomas* by Bill Read (Weidenfeld & Nicolson, 1964), *Leftover Life to Kill* by Caitlin Thomas (Putnam, 1957), *Poet in the Making: The Notebooks of Dylan Thomas*, edited by Ralph Maud (Dent, 1968), *A Concordance to the Collected Poems of Dylan Thomas* by Robert Coleman Williams (University of Nebraska Press, 1967), *The Magical Dilemma of Victor Neuburg* by Jean Overton Fuller (W.H. Allen, 1965), *Llaregub Revisited* by David Holbrook (Bowes & Bowes, 1962),

The Craft and Art of Dylan Thomas by William T. Moynihan (Cornell University Press, 1966), *My Friend Dylan Thomas* by Daniel Jones (Dent, 1977), *Dylan: Druid of the Broken Body* by Aneirin Talfan Davies (Dent, 1964), *The Last Days of Dylan Thomas* by Rob Gittins (Macdonald, 1986), *Under Siege: Literary Life in London 1939–45* by Robert Hewison (Weidenfeld & Nicolson, 1977), *The Poetry of Dylan Thomas* by Elder Olson (University of Chicago Press, 1954), *Dylan Thomas in Print: A bibliographical history* by Ralph Maud (Dent, 1970), *Important to Me* by Pamela Hansford Johnson (Macmillan, 1974), *The Dragon has Two Tongues* by Glyn Jones (Dent, 1968). *A Reader's Guide to Dylan Thomas* by William York Tindall (Thames & Hudson, 1962), *Dylan Thomas* by Andrew Sinclair (Holt, Rinehart & Winston, 1975), *A Pilgrim Soul: The Life and Work of Elisabeth Lutyens* by Meirion and Susie Harries (Michael Joseph, 1989), *Dylan Thomas: Dog among the Fairies* by Henry Treece (Lindsay Drummond, 1949), *Conversations with Stravinsky* by Robert Craft (Faber & Faber, 1959), *The Eye of the Beholder* by Lance Sieveking (Hulton, 1957), *A Personal History* by A.J.P. Taylor (Hamish Hamilton, 1983), *Conversations with Capote* by Lawrence Grobel (New American Library, 1985), *Sextet* by John Malcolm Brinnin (André Deutsch, 1982), *Basingstoke Boy* by John Arlott (Willow Books & Harper Collins, 1990), *Soho in the Fifties* by Daniel Farson (Michael Joseph, 1987), *The Fitzrovians* by Hugh David (Michael Joseph, 1988), *Four Absentees* by Rayner Heppenstall (Barrie & Rockcliff, 1960), *The Growth of Milk Wood* by Douglas Cleverdon (Dent, 1969), *The Religious Sonnets of Dylan Thomas* by H.H. Kleinman (Crescent Press, 1964), *Portrait of a Friend* by Gwen Watkins (Gomer, 1983), *Dylan Thomas: The Legend and the Poet*, edited by E.W. Tedlock (Heinemann, 1960), *Portrait of Dylan* by Rollie McKenna (Dent, 1982), and *Best of Times, Worst of Times* by Shelley Winters (Muller, 1990).

I have sought to annotate all references to the poems, short stories and radio talks of Dylan and likewise my quotations from essays and reviews in *Adelphi, The South Wales Evening Post, New Statesman, Time and Tide, The Sunday Times, The Times Literary Supplement, The National & English Review, The Daily Herald, The Spectator, The Observer, The Listener, The Western Mail, The Anglo Welsh Review*, the *Swansea Grammar School Magazine, Spread Eagle, The Herald of Wales, Country Quest, The London Magazine, Adam, Encounter, Horizon, Poetry London, The Welsh Gazette, The New York Times, Centaur, The Los Angeles Times, The Point, The British Journal of Medical Psychology, Botteghe Oscure* and *The World Review* as they occur within the text, and wish to express my gratitude to the editors, publishers and all concerned therewith.

I am grateful to my friends Jack Lane (Chicago) and Robert Coleman Williams (County Limerick) for several fine illustrations. Lane visited Laugharne as a young student in 1955 and photographed Granny Thomas, Gosport Street, The Boat House (front, rear & through the window), and the workshed (inside & out), capturing Thomas's shadows. Williams was walking past a bookshop in Greenwich Village when he spotted a signed copy of *In Country Sleep* for sale in the window. Loosely inserted within its pages he found Thomas's sketch of 'my house in Wales' and his brief few words on Words, both drawn for the book's previous owner, the American writer David Markson. I also thank Eric Corbett Williams (New York), whose name appears in both the Acknowledgements and the text, for the photograph of Thomas relaxing after a reading at the University of Vermont. These illustrations have added much to the atmosphere of this book.

Lastly, the people of Laugharne to whom this book is dedicated: They have had much to bear these past fifty years with poets wandering drunk in the night, thesis-writers treading their doorsteps, film crews arriving every other month hoping to find a missing witness, ghosts whispering in the trees and portreeves trying to direct the traffic. Most recently they have had to put up with me and I thank them for my solitude.

GEORGE TREMLETT

Oh as I was young and easy in the mercy of his means,
   Time held me green and dying
Though I sang in my chains like the sea.

Fern Hill,
Dylan Thomas

Dylan Thomas was like a jackdaw. He knew exactly what he wanted to steal.

Vernon Watkins

People were important in Dylan's life only as far as they gave him what he needed.

Gwen Watkins

Dylan's moral courage was as strong as that of all but the most exceptional people; that is, it was weak.

Daniel Jones

Dylan was a shit.

Caitlin Thomas

CHRONOLOGY

1914

27 October — Dylan Marlais Thomas born at 5 Cwmdonkin Drive, Uplands, Swansea.

1925

September — Enters Swansea Grammar School, where his father was senior English teacher.

1927

14 January — His plagiarised poem *His Requiem* published in *The Western Mail* (Thomas had pinched it from *Boy's Own Paper*).

February — *Boy's Own Paper* publish his poem *The Second Best.*

1931

July — Leaves Swansea Grammar School to begin work as a junior reporter on the *South Wales Daily Post.*

1932

Autumn — Joins the Swansea Little Theatre.

December — Leaves the *Swansea Evening Post* (as it had since been renamed).

1933

7 February — Death of his aunt Anna [Ann] Jones.

10 February — Attending her funeral inspires the famous poem *After the Funeral.*

18 May — *And Death shall have no Dominion* published in *New English Weekly.*

August — Visits London for the first time, staying with his sister Nancy and her husband on their houseboat at Chertsey.

September — *Adelphi* publishes *No man believes who, when a star falls shot.*

3 September — *Sunday Referee* publishes *That sanity be kept.* Pamela Hansford Johnson sees the poem and writes to him; their correspondence begins.

September/ October — His father has treatment for cancer of the tongue at London University Hospital and recovers.

29 October	*The force that through the green fuse drives the flower* published in the *Sunday Referee*.
1934	More magazines publish his poems, including *Sunday Referee*, *New English Weekly*, *Adelphi*, *New Verse* (in five issues), *Criterion* and *The Listener*.
23 February	Visits London for the second time, meeting Pamela Hansford Johnson and staying with her and her mother at Battersea Rise.
March	Publication of his poem *The Woman Speaks* in *Adelphi* prompts a letter from Glyn Jones, who becomes a personal friend.
14 March	Publication of the poem *Light breaks where no sun shines* sparks off a controversy in *The Listener*. Readers say the phrase 'A candle in the thighs' is obscene. The magazine, owned by the BBC, makes a public apology.
March/April	Spends Easter with Pamela Hansford Johnson and her mother.
22 April	*Sunday Referee* announces that Thomas has been awarded their Poetry Book Prize, which means they will publish his first book. He is the second writer to win the prize. The first was Pamela Hansford Johnson.
20/21 May	Spends Whitsun in West Wales with Glyn Jones. They both had relatives in Llanstephan and visit Laugharne.
27 May	Thomas writes to Pamela Hansford Johnson confessing that he has slept with another woman (which was probably untrue).
mid June	Stays in London for a fortnight.
1 July	Hears Oswald Mosley speaking at a fascist rally at the Plaza Cinema, Swansea. He goes with his friend Bert Trick, and afterwards writes to Pamela Hansford Johnson saying he has 'just left the Socialist Party and offered my services to the Communists'.
10 August/ 15 September	Stays with the Johnsons at Battersea Rise and then returns with them to Swansea – where Pamela is shocked to discover that Thomas is two years younger than he has said.
13 November	Moves into flat at 5 Redcliffe Street, Fulham, with Fred Janes and Mervyn Levy.
4 December	His work appears in book form for the first time; *Light breaks where no sun shines* is published in *The Year's Poetry*.
18 December	His first volume of poetry *18 Poems* is published jointly by the *Sunday Referee* and The Parton Bookshop.
1935 1 January	The first review of *18 Poems* appears in *The Morning Post*.

xiv

	During this year his poems continue to appear in *Sunday Referee*, *Programme*, *Scottish Bookman*, *New Verse* and *Life and Letters Today* and he begins reviewing regularly for *Adelphi* and *The Morning Post*.
February	Vernon Watkins sees *18 Poems* in a Swansea bookshop window, buys a copy and visits Thomas.
April	Stays in Llanstephan and visits Richard Hughes at Castle House, Laugharne.
April/May	Spends a month with the historian A.J.P. Taylor and his wife at their cottage in Higher Disley on the Derbyshire/Cheshire borders.
July/August	Stays at Glen Lough, Meenacross, Lifford, County Donegal, with Geoffrey Grigson, and then returns to Cwmdonkin Drive.
1936	This year his work is published in *Comment*, *Caravel* (Majorca), *Purpose*, *The New English Weekly*, *Criterion*, *The Morning Post* (regular reviews), *Life and Letters Today*, *Janus*, *Contemporary Poetry and Prose*, *Transition*, with reviews of his second book *Twenty-five Poems* appearing in most Sunday papers and literary magazines.
17 January	Writes to Dame Edith Sitwell after she decides belatedly to review *18 Poems* for *London Mercury*.
21 February	Second issue of *18 Poems*, with changed binding but using original printed sheets.
12 April	Meets Caitlin Macnamara at The Wheatsheaf and then spends five nights with her at the Eiffel Tower Hotel.
April/May	Stays at Wyn Henderson's cottage at Polgigga, Porthcurno, near Penzance; Caitlin has returned to her home in Hampshire where she is sitting for a portrait by Augustus John.
28 April	Richard Church writes to say that J.M. Dent will publish his next book, which becomes *Twenty-five Poems*.
26 June	Takes part in the Poetry Reading at the International Surrealist Exhibition at the New Burlington Galleries with Paul Eluard and David Gascoyne.
15 July	Fred Janes drives Thomas over to Laugharne after he hears that Caitlin will be staying at Castle House with Augustus John; they all go off on a pub crawl after attending the National Eisteddfod – and Augustus knocks Dylan to the ground when he sees him paying too much attention to Caitlin.
10 September	*Twenty-five Poems* published by Dent.

15 November	Dame Edith Sitwell reviews *Twenty-five Poems* in *The Sunday Times*, saying that no other poet of his generation 'shows so great a promise, and even so great an achievement'.
December	Thomas's father retires from Swansea Grammar School, and shortly thereafter sells 5 Cwmdonkin Drive to move to Bishopston.

1937

21 April	First radio broadcast – *Life and the Modern Poet* (BBC Welsh Service).
May/August	Dylan and Caitlin go to Cornwall, staying first at Lamorna and then Mousehole, in a cottage adjoining the Lobster Pot restaurant; later they move to a studio at Newlyn.
11 July	Dylan Thomas marries Caitlin Macnamara at Penzance register office, without telling her that his parents are opposed to him marrying so young and without resources.
September/ October	The couple go to stay with his parents at Bishopston. After a month, they move to Blashford near Ringwood, Hampshire, living with Caitlin's mother until the following April.

1938

January	George Reavey of the Europa Press (Paris) agrees to publish his collection of short stories *The Burning Baby*; this is later cancelled, and instead Dent agree to publish a collection in 1939 with the title *The Map of Love*.
April	The couple return to Bishopston.
April	James Laughlin of New Directions offers to be Thomas's publisher in the United States – Thomas is impressed because Laughlin has already published Jean Cocteau, Henry Miller, Gertrude Stein and William Saroyan.
1 May	Move to fisherman's cottage in Gosport Street, Laugharne, found for them by Richard Hughes.
August	Move to a larger house in Laugharne, Sea View, which they rent for ten shillings a week, furnishing it comfortably when Caitlin's aunt dies and they receive all her furniture.
28 August	Thomas makes his first appeal for a grant to the Royal Literary Fund, supported by T.S. Eliot, Cyril Connolly, Richard Hughes, Edith Sitwell, W.H. Auden, John Masefield and Walter de la Mare. The appeal does not succeed.
18 October	Takes part in the radio broadcast *The Modern Muse* with Louis MacNeice, W.H. Auden, Kathleen Raine and Stephen Spender (BBC Home Service).

November	With Caitlin seven months pregnant, the Thomases return to Caitlin's mother at Blashford to await the baby's birth; Augustus John drives them down there.
November	Wins the Oscar Blumenthal Prize for Poetry in the United States.
December	The London Verse Speaking Choir records *And Death shall have no Dominion* (HMV).

1939

January	Thomas travels to London to meet Henry Miller and Lawrence Durrell, who are staying at an apartment belonging to Hugo Guyler, husband of Anais Nin.
30 January	Llewelyn Edouard Thomas born at the Cornelia Hospital, Poole. Caitlin's mother provides her with a nurse.
24 August	*Map of Love* published by Dent.
20 November	Publication of Thomas's first book in the United States – *The World I Breathe*, which includes 40 poems taken from *18 Poems*, *Twenty-five poems* and *The Map of Love* and eleven short stories.
December/ February	The Thomases return to Blashford.

1940

4 April	*Portrait of the Artist as a Young Dog* published by Dent.
May	After faking illness to fail his Army medical, Thomas sneaks away from Sea View to Bishopston, claiming that creditors are pressing him.
June/August	They return to Laugharne briefly, but then go to Marshfield near Chippenham, Wiltshire, where John Davenport and his wife are inviting artists, writers and musicians to stay with them while London is under threat of bombing. The Thomases leave hurriedly when Dylan learns that Caitlin has been planning an affair with William Glock.
24 September	*Portrait of the Artist as a Young Dog* published in the United States.
September/ April	The Thomases stay with Dylan's parents in Bishopston, but for much of this time he is in London, saying that he is looking for work.

1941

January	Appeals again to the Royal Literary Fund for a grant saying that 'we are quite homeless and haven't one penny'. This time his application is supported by J.B. Priestley, Sir Hugh Walpole and Frank Swinnerton. He is awarded a £50 grant.

April	Asks the London bookseller Bertram Rota to sell his four remaining notebooks. These go to the State University of New York's Lockwood Library in Buffalo.
May/June	Stay with Frances Hughes at Castle House, Laugharne.
August	Move to London, leaving Llewelyn with Caitlin's mother at Blashford.
Autumn	Joins staff of Strand Films. Paid £8 a week as a scriptwriter working on films for the Ministry of Information. These include *The Conquest of a Germ*, *These Are The Men* (with a verse commentary), *This Is Colour*, *New Towns for Old*, *Balloon Site 586*, *Green Mountain Black Mountain*, *Where Are They Now?* and *Is Your Ernie Really Necessary?* (All produced in 1942 and 1943)

1942

March	Move to Hammersmith Terrace.
June	Publication of the Caseg poetry broadsheet version of *In Memory of Ann Jones*, illustrated by Brenda Chamberlain.
July	*Horizon* publishes Norman Cameron's poem *The Dirty Little Accuser*, attacking Thomas.
July	Fortune Press publish second edition of *18 Poems*.
Autumn	Rents studio apartment – 8 Wentworth Studios, Manresa Road, London SW3.

1943

February	*New Poems* published in the United States by New Directions.
15 February	*Reminiscences of Childhood* broadcast by the BBC Welsh Service; the first of his scripted-and-narrated programmes.
3 March	Aeronwy Bryn Thomas born in London during an air raid.

1944

April/June	To avoid the air raids on London, the Thomases move first to Far End, Old Bosham, Sussex, and then to stay with Donald Taylor at Hedgerley Dean where Thomas and Taylor work together on *The Doctor and The Devils*.
July/August	Move to Llangain to stay with Dylan's parents who have now left Bishopston to live at Blaen Cwm.
September	Move to the bungalow Majoda at New Quay, where Thomas begins one of the most productive periods of his life – writing poems, the radio script *Quite Early One Morning* and the adaptation of Maurice O'Sullivan's *Twenty Years A'Growing*.
2 October	Although due to be best man, Thomas fails to attend Vernon Watkins' wedding.

1945	Continues scriptwriting with work on *Suffer Little Children* and film biographies of Robert Burns and Dr Crippen (none of which were produced, although part of the script for *Suffer Little Children* is later used for the Diana Dors film *Good Time Girl*). Thomas's poems *Vision and Prayer*, *Holy Spring*, *Poem in October*, *Fern Hill* and *A Refusal to Mourn the Death, by Fire, of A Child in London* are all published in *Horizon* during the year, earning him an award from the magazine.
6 March	The shooting incident at Majoda. An ex-commando officer with a machine gun shoots at the bungalow suspecting that his wife has been living in a *menage à trois* with Dylan and Caitlin.
June	The ex-commando officer is accused of attempted murder – and acquitted. The story apears in the *News of the World*, and the Thomases leave New Quay to return to Llangain where they stay until September.
31 August	*Quite Early One Morning* broadcast by the BBC Welsh Home Service.
October/ December	After several months in a flat in Markham Square, Chelsea, the Thomases leave hurriedly – and arrive homeless on the doorstep of A.J.P. Taylor's home at Holywell Ford, Oxford. The Taylors let the Thomases live in their wooden summerhouse for the next 15 months.
16 December	*Memories of Christmas* broadcast by the BBC Welsh Home Service.
1946 7 February	*Deaths and Entrances* published by Dent. The book is highly acclaimed and leads to Thomas appearing regularly on BBC radio. He appears as a narrator in many productions.
25 October	*Holiday Memory* broadcast by the BBC Welsh Home Service.
8 November	*Selected Writings* published in the United States by New Directions.
17 December	*The Crumbs of One Man's Year* broadcast by the BBC Home Service.
1947 26 March	The Society of Authors awards him a £150 Travelling Scholarship with a recommendation that this be spent visiting Italy.
April/ 13 August	Goes to Italy with Caitlin and their children; her sister Brigid and her son, staying first near Rapallo before moving to a villa in the hills outside Florence and then Elba.

15 June	First broadcast of *Return Journey*, his radio documentary describing his return to Swansea after much of the city had been destroyed in the war.
September	Move to The Manor House, South Leigh, Oxfordshire, which had been bought for them by the Taylors.
October/ November	Narrates a ten-part serialisation of Milton's *Paradise Lost* for the BBC Third Programme.
Autumn	Begins writing scripts for British National Pictures, *Three Weird Sisters* and *No Room At The Inn* and also contracts to write three scripts for Gainsborough, *Me and My Bike*, *Rebecca's Daughters* and *The Beach of Falesa* which occupy him through 1948, although he also continues to work regularly for the BBC.

1948

March/April	Stays at Blaen Cwm, Llangain, with his parents while house-hunting again in Laugharne. His mother breaks her leg and he decides to take his parents back to live in South Leigh.
April/May	Narrates serial version of W.H. Davies's *Autobiography of a Super-tramp* for the BBC Home Service.
October	With the Thomases now determined to return to Laugharne, Margaret Taylor goes down there and tries to lease Castle House for them; she fails – but manages to buy The Boat House instead.

1949

March	Guild Books publish paperback edition of *Portrait of the Artist as a Young Dog*.
4 March	Goes to Prague as a guest of the Czechoslovak Writers Union.
May	Moves to The Boat House and within days receives letter from Brinnin inviting him to present a poetry reading in New York.
24 July	Colm Garan Thomas born.

1950

21 February	Arrives in New York for first US reading tour, appearing first for Brinnin at the Kaufmann Auditorium. Thomas presents forty readings over the next three months, mostly in universities and colleges.
May	*26 Poems* published jointly by New Direction (US) and Dent (Britain) in a limited signed edition of 150 copies.
4 September	'Sarah', a woman that Thomas had met in New York, arrives in London – Caitlin finds out and their marriage is threatened.
November	Thomas makes his third application to the Royal Literary Fund, this time supported by Harold Nicolson who says 'he is a very

heavy drinker . . . I gather that his wife is almost equally unreliable. On the other hand, he is one of our best poets.' The application is supported by Augustus John and Lord David Cecil. Thomas is awarded £300.

1951 January/ February	With the marriage still in trouble, Thomas goes off to Iran for six weeks to script a documentary for the Anglo Iranian Oil Co. While he is there, Caitlin writes to him saying that the marriage is finished.
February	They are reconciled.
July	Brinnin stays with them in Laugharne.
Summer/ Autumn	Thomas writes *Lament, Poem on His Birthday, Do Not Go Gentle Into That Good Night* and the *Author's Prologue* for his *Collected Poems*. He also writes half of *Under Milk Wood*.
Autumn	Caitlin has her first abortion.
1952 20 January/ 16 May	Caitlin accompanies him on his second US reading tour, which is even more successful than the first with Thomas fêted as he presents 45 readings of his and other poets' work.
22 February	Makes his first recordings for Caedmon Records.
28 February	Publication in the United States of *In Country Sleep* with a limited edition of 100 copies on hand-made paper as well as the trade edition.
November	On its publication, *Collected Poems* is acclaimed as the work of a great poet – and sells 30,000 copies in hardback in Britain in less than two years.
16 December	D.J. Thomas dies at the age of 76.
1953 31 March	Publication of *Collected Poems* in the United States.
9 April	Makes his television debut on *Home Town Swansea* for BBC TV, appearing with Fred Janes, Daniel Jones and Wynford Vaughan-Thomas.
16 April	His sister Nancy dies of liver cancer in Bombay.
21 April	Begins his third US reading tour.
14 May	*The Doctor and The Devils* published by Dent.
14 May	Thomas presents *Under Milk Wood* for the first time at the Kaufmann Auditorium in New York.
2 June	Records again for Caedmon Records.

3 June	Arrives back in London, the day after the Coronation.
10 August	Makes his first and only BBC TV solo appearance reading *A Story* – which has since become known as *The Outing*.
September	Brinnin visits Laugharne with Professor Bill Read and the photographer Rollie McKenna.
8 October	Publication in the United States of *The Doctor and The Devils*.
9 October	Leaves Laugharne for the last time, meets Daniel Jones in Swansea, and then goes on to London where he and Caitlin stay with Harry and Cordelia Locke.
19 October	Arrives in New York to begin fourth US reading tour and to begin work with Stravinsky.
29 October	Last public engagement; a lunchtime reading at the City College, New York.
5 November	Collapses at the Chelsea Hotel, and is taken to St Vincent's Hospital.
	Caitlin receives a telegram from Brinnin that her husband has been 'hospitalised'. She leaves to join him, and arrives on 8 November to find Dylan still in a coma.
9 November	Dylan Thomas dies at 12.40 a.m. while a nurse is bathing him. The only other person present was the poet John Berryman. Caitlin returns to Wales with the body and he is buried in Laugharne on 24 November.

PREFACE

OR almost as long as I can remember, Dylan Thomas has been part of
my everyday life. It's not an obsession, but a presence. Much of his
writing does not appeal to me, but a core of some twenty poems, the
autobiographical short stories, three or four radio scripts and his play for
voices *Under Milk Wood* is lodged away in my memory, likely to resurface at
any time. I can hear their sound in my head. Something happens with his use
of language that lifts his words from the printed page; he works through the
ear.

Now I have known that, without knowing why, for nearly forty years since
a teacher first urged me to read him aloud. Other people are affected the
same way. Thousands make a private pilgrimage to Thomas's home each
year, and I have observed them carefully. They want to see where he worked
and what surrounded him; not the place he was born. When I was writing
about rock 'n' roll and the musicians who make it, I found many of them also
fascinated by this intangible Thomas. Bob Dylan chose his name. Lennon &
McCartney, David Bowie and Van Morrison all acknowledged their debt.
The Beatles included his photograph on the sleeve of their *Sgt Pepper's
Lonely Hearts Club Band* LP. Marc Bolan and Phil Lynott went further,
publishing books of poems in which Thomas's influence was laid bare for all
to see. There's a kind of freemasonry binding us all; shared in the wholeness
of his craft.

Dylan Thomas learned technique at his father's knee and applied it
precisely. He kept returning to his parents' small corner of West Wales and
wrote within its boundaries, looking out at the world in all its mystery. But
Dylan Thomas is no more a local writer than James Joyce, D.H. Lawrence,
John Steinbeck or Gabriel Garcia Marquez, who all set their work within
such a unified frame. Dylan Thomas was in their league; a highly
accomplished world writer who died in his prime.

However, he was also something else: a performer whose reputation was
made mainly through sound in the age of radio. People *heard* more of him
than they do of many writers and he, in turn, had to lead a more public life.
Many famous men have private weaknesses, but as they rise they usually

learn to conceal them with a winning smile. Dylan Thomas had that gift as well – to a point. He was a natural charmer. At parties or in pubs, he would rattle off anecdotes and funny poems, tell zany stories, flatter the ladies and captivate his friends. He was such a genuinely funny, entertaining man that they tended to overlook his peccadillos – to a point.

These qualifications might never have been known had he not died on the brink of world fame. After his fourth U.S. lecture tour Thomas was due to start work with Stravinsky. He had plans for a stage play and cinema scripts; his *Collected Poems* had been rapturously acclaimed, and with his skills as a live performer, television was just opening up for him. Honours would have come cascading down upon his head, the Nobel Prize or the Order of Merit . . . had he been able to handle success. The trouble was he could not. Dylan Thomas may have known that. He was in the mercy of his means.

I had been aware of Dylan Thomas since my teens, without studying him seriously, until my wife suggested we might go to Wales. Her family came from his part of West Wales, and she felt like going home. We went to Laugharne for a day. This was fifteen years ago. As we walked its streets, around the Castle, across the foreshore and through the woods, many of Thomas's words and phrases kept coming to mind. There and then, I realised that his landscape lay all around me. His sense of place was almost tangible. It was as if one had read *Ulysses* without knowing that Dublin existed. After that first visit, I re-read the various biographies and found them lacking. Their authors seemed unaffected by sight or sound. I realised, too, that common threads ran through them. Assertions in one became assumptions in another. For some reason that I could not quite understand, then, these books had been written with little recourse to Thomas's family. Some sources were relied upon strongly, but others barely mentioned. This made me more interested in the Thomas legend. I could see that the pieces did not fit.

Over the years, we became active in the Dylan Thomas Society, played our part in the erection of the memorial plaques in Westminster Abbey and St Martin's Church, Laugharne and upon the wall of Thomas's former London home at Delancey Street, Camden Town, and helped to launch the Dylan Thomas Literary Award. At one stage, I thought of bringing together all the various Thomas tangents under the umbrella of a Dylan Thomas Memorial Trust that would organise lectures, scholarships and the annual Award, and even became its chairman, but that proved a bad idea. The pieces did not fit any better than the legend. However, through these activities we came to know Caitlin, their children and many of the family's closer friends.

By then we had decided to live in Laugharne ourselves, not for any reasons especially connected with Dylan Thomas but simply because we wanted to begin a new life, well away from London. We planned to build a house and open a bookshop, with me resuming my career as a writer after coming all too close to the political vortex. We thought of emigrating, but chose Laugharne instead although, living here, one cannot escape Thomas's presence. Gradually, my belief hardened that there was much that needed explanation in the Thomas legend as I understood more and more that the man known to his family and neighbours must have been far more vulnerable than the caricature of myth and biography.

Initially, I thought Caitlin might provide most of the answers. She refused to co-operate with previous biographers. As the only surviving member of his immediate adult family, I thought she must hold the key. At one time she wanted to write a personal account of their marriage, but found this difficult. Eventually, after several years' discussion, she and I agreed to write her memoirs together. I spent a year researching all that was known about their life and then a month out in Sicily, staying at her home, recording fifty hours of taped reminiscences. I then spent five months editing the tapes into a flowing first person narrative, returning to Sicily in March 1986 for another two weeks' intensive work, going through every line of the manuscript, word by word, for any errors of fact or emphasis. We called our book *Caitlin: A Warring Absence*. The day we finished, walking in her garden in Catania between lemon trees and prickly pear with Mount Etna in the distance, I told her, 'You do realise that all the biographies now have to be re-written?' We continued to discuss this point, with me saying where her recollections differed from the biographies of Constantine Fitzgibbon, Bill Read, Andrew Sinclair, John Ackerman and Paul Ferris. 'You'd better do it yourself,' she said, advising me to wait five years (which indeed I have, almost to the day) to avoid being too influenced by what she had told me.

Caitlin was essentially a study of their marriage, observed through her eyes, subjectively rather than objectively. This book takes a different standpoint, beginning with Thomas's death, reporting what happened thereafter with the creation of the Trust that controls his Estate, and then studying the way the Thomas Legend began taking shape with the lurid allegations contained in John Malcolm Brinnin's *Dylan Thomas in America* (1955). In the early chapters I suggest why the Legend may be partially false, and then go back over the evidence arguing that it is possible to look at

Thomas's life in other ways. Professor Ralph Maud advised me to annotate my sources and I have done so. Most are clearly identified within the text. Some are not named, not for any evasive reasons but simply because constant conversation helps form an opinion without necessarily being quotable. I have also deleted much extraneous detail concerning the events of Thomas's life, being more concerned with those that shaped him.

One delicate matter needs prior explanation and that is the relationship between the Trustees of the Estate and his widow, since it is my opinion that this lies at the heart of many misunderstandings about Thomas's life and reputation. This will be examined further in the next chapter, but at this stage, considering the whole context within which this book is written, I would emphasise that the Trust is a separate entity.

The circumstances need stating.

Dylan Thomas went to New York to begin his fourth U.S. tour on 19 October 1953. He collapsed a few days later and was admitted to St Vincent's Hospital. Caitlin flew there to join him, but he died without regaining consciousness. She was in a highly emotional state (see Chapter One), but insisted on taking his body back to Wales for burial.

Less than twelve months before, his father had died and Thomas, as the only son, had made arrangements for the funeral. This had been deeply distressing. D.J. Thomas was dourly atheistic, and made a pact with his wife and his brother Arthur that all three of them would be cremated without religious ceremony when their time came. Thomas complied with his father's wishes, as any son would, but on the day of the funeral in Pontypridd was given details of the cremation that made him vomit. When he returned home that evening, he begged his wife to ensure that 'nothing like that ever happens to me.' She kept her word.

His body was taken back to Laugharne where the funeral was held at St Martin's Church on November 24th. Many of Thomas's friends travelled there to pay their last respects. It was a disturbing occasion that turned some poets to verse. Louis MacNeice, who dropped a packet of sandwiches into the grave in his nervousness, felt compelled to write his *Canto in Memoriam Dylan Thomas*. George Barker composed *At the Wake of Dylan Thomas*, and Vernon Watkins, always a gentle soul, wrote of *Peace in the Welsh Hills*. As with many West Wales funerals, there was laughter and sorrow, heavy drinking and some hysteria. Caitlin wanted to throw herself into her husband's grave and later became very drunk. Her grief was harrowing, all the more so when she began to dance frenetically. This gave the funeral a primal air that is talked of still in whispers.

And yet, during this same day, it is said that she set in train the series of events that led to her losing control of her husband's estate. First, she consulted Dr Daniel Jones who had been a friend of her husband's since their teens and had taken charge of the funeral arrangements, and then she talked to the literary agent David Higham, who had represented Dylan Thomas. They suggested that a Trust should be created with them as Trustees together with Stuart Thomas, a Swansea solicitor.

Now, it should be understood that Dylan Thomas was widely believed to have died in poverty leaving his family penniless. There were certainly many unpaid debts, and there was much concern for his widow and children. Three separate appeals were launched to help them. Few people appreciated how successful he had become, least of all his family, for Thomas borrowed wherever he could, begging and wheedling when there was no real need, even leaving his wife short of money for food and clothing when he had cash in his pocket. Hardly anyone knew this. In public, he was another man; the charmer with a magic gift for words.

It was this public figure that became so symbolic: the poet who died of drink without his worth being fully appreciated. Sympathy for his family ran deep. Richard Burton and the cast of *Under Milk Wood* gave their fees and royalties to one of the appeal funds. Two memorial concerts were staged with the support of Burton, Emlyn Williams, Sir Hugh Casson, Dame Sybil Thorndike, Hugh Griffith, Dame Edith Sitwell and Louis MacNeice, and all the proceeds (together with record royalties) went into the funds, together with donations big and small.

In such a situation, it was understandable that those closest to Dylan Thomas should wish to help the family put their finances on a firm footing. The arrangements to establish the Trust were made with some speed. On November 30th, Mrs Thomas applied for Letters of Administration at the District Probate Registry in Carmarthen accompanied by Stuart Thomas and Dr Jones. Letters of Administration were granted on December 7th wherein it was certified that 'an affidavit for Inland Revenue has been delivered wherein it is shown that the gross value of the said estate in Great Britain so far as at present can be ascertained ... amounts to £100 and that the net value of the estate amounts to £100.' This was duly reported in *The Daily Telegraph* (December 24th 1953) as –

DYLAN THOMAS LEAVES £100

On December 28th 1953, Caitlin Thomas signed the Settlement Deed whereby she transferred the handling of

'all copyrights and interests in copyrights in respect of the literary works of the late husband of the Settlor Dylan Marlais Thomas . . .'

together with £100 in cash deposited at Lloyds Bank, St Helens Road, Swansea, to the Trustees, namely Stuart Thomas, Daniel Jones and David Higham.

By signing this Deed and a subsequent Deed of Variation dated October 1st 1957, Mrs Thomas ceased to have any control over her husband's copyrights. Thereafter it was the Trustees who decided how his short stories, scripts and poems might be published, recorded, broadcast, filmed or televised; it was they who decided upon the publication of his letters and chose his official biographer.

For many years, ever since she lost a High Court case in 1966 over ownership of the original manuscript of *Under Milk Wood*, Mrs Thomas has been at loggerheads with the Estate (although Stuart Thomas continues to act as solicitor for the Thomas children). Intermittently, she has taken legal action against the Trustees. One of her main concerns has been that the Trustees would not make financial provision for her fourth child Francesco who was born when she was 49. Her youngest son's father is Giuseppe Fazio, a Sicilian, with whom she has lived for nearly thirty-five years. I know them all extremely well, and in writing this book have been careful not to say anything more than is necessary to prove my point. All I wish to say in this preface is that, in my opinion, Caitlin has been well cared for by Giuseppe, who has stood by her in good times and bad, giving her the love and support that she has needed in coping with the consequences of her husband's posthumous fame. It has been a difficult role for him and Giuseppe Fazio has my respect.

Whether or not the Trustees have treated Mrs Thomas fairly is not my immediate concern. I have no wish to know any more than I do already about her relationship with her first three children, who are also beneficiaries of the Estate, or of the estrangement that has occurred between her and the

Trustees. I am aware of the Court proceedings that she has initiated against the Trustees, and do not consider them to be suitable subject matter for this book other than to point out that, in my opinion, these factors have all tended to exacerbate the manner in which the Trustees have handled the Estate. In my view, they have been unduly secretive (possibly fearing the consequences of any public statement), with the result that little is actually known about the scale of Dylan Thomas's literary achievement. In death, Dylan Thomas has gained world recognition on a par with Milton, Shelley, Goethe or Dante without the London literary establishment realising the scale of his accomplishment.

In its first four years, the Estate handled income totalling £47,234 16s 1d. These were high earnings for a writer in the mid-Fifties. By comparison, when I joined an evening newspaper in 1957 members of the editorial staff used to talk dreamily of the day when they might earn £1,000 a year. By the late Eighties, the Estate was handling a gross income of around £100,000 a year. Figures like these have not been publicised. Likewise, the press were not informed that Dylan Thomas's works were being translated into many languages (see page 4), or that his poems were constantly quoted around the world. Down in Wales, Dylan Thomas is still regarded as 'a bit of a boyo' rather than a literary figure of world importance; they treat him as a useful tool of the tourist trade, quite unaware that he has out-grown them all.

I suspect that the trouble has been that the Trustees have never thought Dylan Thomas a world figure themselves. His success seems to have surprised them, and I have the impression that they have done their best in all the circumstances without ever sharing that feeling of grandeur that Thomas brought to his work.

Initially, Caitlin seems to have gone along quite happily with the Trustees' decisions. For reasons that I have never been able to understand, Dr Jones became the 'literary trustee' and in this capacity exercised editorial judgement over Thomas's work. However, Jones soon withdrew, writing later that in its early days the Estate 'consisted solely of debts' and that 'all who were closely concerned with Dylan, his work and his family, seemed to suffer in varying degrees from a kind of hysteria' and that he had shown 'excessive punctiliousness in the execution of what I considered my duties, jealousy in the preservation of texts, suspicion of others, and irritability in my relations with them . . . I quarreled with all around me on the slightest cause, not realising that they too were suffering from nerves and were really exercising some restraint in dealing with me' (*My Friend Dylan Thomas*, p. 83).

Jones resigned as a Trustee on May 24th 1955 and was succeeded that same day by the broadcaster Wynford Vaughan-Thomas, who – like Jones and Stuart Thomas – had also gone to Swansea Grammar School, where they had been taught by Dylan Thomas's father. Around the same time, Brinnin's book was published and Caitlin left Laugharne to live in Rome, partially to avoid embarrassment.

Ever since, the Estate has been largely run from Stuart Thomas's office in Swansea with David Higham Associates Ltd acting as agents for the Estate. Over the years, the relationship between the Estate and Highams seems to have subtly changed. Initially, David Higham was a Trustee but no-one from his company replaced him when he died on March 30th 1978. My impression is that Highams now tend to refer to the Trustees rather than act for them (and I have good reason for thinking that as they well know). I have no criticism whatever to make of Highams. They are one of London's best-known literary agents and in all my dealings with them I have found them courteous and helpful.

My criticism is directed against the Trustees. For many years, this has meant in practice Stuart Thomas and Wynford Vaughan-Thomas. I do not believe either man ever fully understood the importance of Dylan Thomas's work or the significance that it holds for my generation. Caitlin has written to me about Stuart Thomas in the most abusive terms, although less critically of Wynford. I have no wish to mention matters that are not necessary in proving my point. Suffice it to say that Stuart Thomas's stepdaughter married Caitlin's eldest son, and this marriage did not last. However, there was a child of the marriage and there are thus complex bonds within all these relationships that cannot be cast asunder no matter how the parties may disagree. The family call Stuart Thomas by the nickname 'Stewbags'. Vaughan-Thomas, always 'Wynford', became famous for his wartime radio broadcasts and wrote one good book about the battle of Anzio. He was a splendid raconteur whose TV wanderings were much enjoyed, but he lacked ballast and ended up a middling fish in a small pond writing guide books to Wales and minor books about Royalty. He told some good stories about Dylan Thomas, but they tended to vary a bit with the telling and I once asked him what he did as a Trustee of the Dylan Thomas Estate. His eyes crinkled up as he smiled in his impish way, 'I leave all that to Stuart' (which may well have been another exaggeration, although I suspect it was close to the truth).

This, then, was the situation during the years that I was trying to persuade

Caitlin to co-operate with me in writing her memoirs. Two old school chums were running her husband's estate with little reference to her, and she had been out in Italy for thirty years, virtually incommunicado. There were no other contemporary relatives of Dylan Thomas still alive, apart from his children, nor had there been since Granny Thomas (his mother Florence) died in August 1958. To put it discreetly, I sensed some disquiet. Caitlin told me that if she made enough money from our book she would 'have another crack' at the Estate. (She did. And she did, in 1988).

The Trustees seemed to sense the need for defensive action. With publication of *Caitlin* looming, and Wynford Vaughan-Thomas in the final stages of a terminal illness, they decided to strengthen the Trust. Without telling Caitlin or her children, Stuart Thomas and Wynford Vaughan-Thomas co-opted two further Trustees. These were the author Kingsley Amis and another solicitor Michael Edward John Rush, then Chief Executive of West Glamorgan County Council. Their co-option was confirmed by Deed of Appointment dated May 6th 1986. News of their appointment did not leak out until after the death of Wynford Vaughan-Thomas on February 4th 1987.

It was the appointment of Kingsley Amis that caused most surprise. His familiarity with the works of Dylan Thomas and the history of the Estate is beyond dispute. Sir Kingsley (as we now must call him) began his literary career while working as a lecturer in English at the University College of Swansea between 1949 and 1961. *Lucky Jim* (1954) was one of the most acclaimed novels of its generation, and he followed this with *That Uncertain Feeling* (1955), *I Like It Here* (1958) and *Take A Girl Like You* (1960) before his career went into a sort of tail-spin for some years. He was writing about whisky, James Bond and even science fiction between studies of Tennyson, Jane Austen and Rudyard Kipling, producing columns for *The Daily Mirror* and books with unfortunate titles like *Jake's Thing* (1978).

In 1986, Amis emerged from the shadows with *The Old Devils* which earned him The Booker Prize. Literary critics seemed unaware that its central characters bore a striking resemblance to the Trustees of The Dylan Thomas Estate. As it happens, he wrote the book in Laugharne, staying at Cliff Cottage, just a few yards away from The Boat House, sometimes popping into the bookshop that my wife runs and drinking occasionally at The Three Mariners, before moving to Swansea where he stayed with his old friend Stuart Thomas. There are many references to a dead poet called Brydan, who is clearly Dylan; descriptive passages that can be easily located by those familiar with the landscape of West Wales, and waspish portraits of one or two people in Swansea 'literary circles' that were quickly identified by friends and enemies alike.

The problem with his appointment as a Trustee was that *The Old Devils*, along with many other writings, made it all too clear that Sir Kingsley Amis dislikes Dylan Thomas, both as a man and as a writer – and his co-option tends to confirm my suggestion that the Trustees have never fully understood the significance of Thomas's work. They do not take him seriously enough. If they did, one of the last men whom they would wish to co-opt is Sir Kingsley William Amis (although I will admit that the Old Devil wrote a welcome review of *Caitlin*).

I say this because Amis has disparaged Thomas over many years. Writing for *The Spectator* (August 12th, 1955), Amis dismissed 'ranting, canting Thomas the Rhymer' as a man who 'wasted his talent and integrity'. Writing again for *The Spectator* (November 29th 1957), he recalled a tipsy Thomas reading to the English Society at the University College of Swansea six years earlier, his coats bulging with bottles of beer. The overall tone is baleful, noting how well Thomas read *Fern Hill* –

His voice was magnificent, and his belief in what he read was so patent as to be immediately infectious, yet there was something vaguely discomforting about it too, not only to me. Although obviously without all charlatanry, he did here and there sound or behave like a charlatan.

Over the years that initial impression has hardened into something deeper. In his novel *That Uncertain Feeling*, Amis portrayed Thomas a drunken lecher and professional Welshman. In his volume of poems *A Case of Samples* (1956), Amis wrote insultingly –

They call you 'drunk with words'; but when we drink
And fetch it up, we sluice it down the sink.
You should have stuck to spewing beer, not ink.

In his review of *Caitlin*, which I found personally generous, Amis wrote that 'what held them together was devotion not only to booze but also to criminality, minor fraud, stealing from friends and messing up their houses, cheating, cadging, above all a shared conviction that rich, complacent people, i.e. those living on their own earnings, deserved to have anything movable taken off them by footloose creative souls like Mr and Mrs Dylan

Thomas. I suppose that seems more or less all right if you admire his work enough. I don't myself.' (*The Mail on Sunday*, October 26th 1986).

When a reader wrote to challenge him, Amis replied: 'Whether or not he was a good or great poet, which you think he was, and I think he was not, he remains a rotten man. Unless you think it is all right to neglect your children, lie to your closest friends and cheat them, steal from them and vandalise their houses. Perhaps you do: I do not' (*The Observer*, February 1987).

And then, writing in his *Memoirs* (1991), Amis described Thomas as an 'outstandingly unpleasant man' and 'a pernicious figure, one who has helped to get Wales and Welsh poetry a bad name and generally done lasting harm to both . . . (he) cheated and stole from his friends and peed on their carpets. At the start he boozed a lot because it fitted his image as a poet.'

Many of the personal comments that Amis makes about Dylan Thomas are not ones that I would disagree with. Indeed, later in this book, the reader will find much to substantiate them. But should the author's estate be in the hands of a man who thinks like this? And is it not strange that Stuart Thomas and Wynford Vaughan-Thomas should wish to hoist aboard a fellow with such opinions? When I wrote to Caitlin to tell her of Amis's appointment, enclosing the press cuttings that related to it, she replied that she had heard 'absolutely nothing' about this before and thought Amis highly unsuitable, adding that 'Between him and Stuart Thomas there is not much to choose: they are birds of a feather . . . . I am horrified to learn that the worst man possible, the grossest vulgarian in the world who presumptuously booms on every occasion his loathing for Dylan and his writing, has been actually appointed . . . It is not only a perfectly ludicrous, but a quite disgusting choice for a Trustee. He is the dead opposite of everything that Dylan believed in. But Dylan is in no position to answer him back. Had he been, he would have torn his envious and spiteful accuser to verbal shreds . . . .' (personal letter from Caitlin Thomas dated March 29th 1987).

The way the Trustees behave is no great concern of mine. As an author who wishes to write upon the musicians and writers who have influenced the times in which we live, I am anxious only to be objective. Much more could have been said, but I have been discreet. These matters are laid before the reader so that it may be seen that I have sought to test the strength of each piece of information, and its origin, balancing one against another to form an overall judgement, having formed the opinion long ago that previous biographies relied too much upon Swansea sources, giving insufficient weight to other influences that helped mould Dylan Thomas's perspective. His breadth of vision intrigues me still. I believe that he wrote some twenty great poems that will live for as long as the English language is spoken, using his own life and background as his stanchion. I still cannot understand how such a compassionate man cared so little for the feelings and well-being of those around him. That does not belittle the scale of his achievement, although it does diminish the man.

George Tremlett
Laugharne
June 1991

A LEGEND IN THE MAKING

THE lights go dim. Coughing and rustling in the audience quietens. A stout but broad, podgy figure, dressed in a crumpled suit, with tousled, unwashed hair, walks out from the wings with a stride in his step, looking ahead to a rostrum where he stands for a moment, gazing out over waves of shining faces caught briefly in the stage lights, gripping its sides with both hands, drinking from a glass of water, pausing, sweat pouring from his brow as he begins to apologise. This was Dylan Thomas 40 years ago, reaching out to an audience touched by sound, through radio and the rhythms of his spoken word, a gathering that had come from all parts of America, from common rooms and green rooms, university senates and Mid-West suburbs, students and tutors, writers and dons, actors, painters and girls, always plenty of girls, leaning forward in their seats, chins cupped in their hands, hanging on his every phrase.

They expected so much. Word had travelled that Thomas was wild and uninhibited, drank too much and chased women. Some had travelled hundreds of miles to be there, sleeping rough or staying overnight with friends, a tingling excitement running through their veins. I have talked to some of those who saw him all those years ago, and strangely the image that Dylan Thomas left in their minds remains sharp and vivid. Now, in their 6os and 7os, they come by plane, bus, train or hired car to Laugharne to stand by his grave with its plain wooden cross, to drink where he sat in Brown's Hotel, to visit the post office where he posted his poems and stories, to see the house named Pelican where he rented the ground floor flat for his parents, and finished *The Times* crossword most mornings with his father, to call in at the butcher's, baker's and general store where he collected bones for the stewpot, bread still hot from the oven, matches, cigarettes or bags of boiled sweets (which he loved), dropping them all in his bicycle basket before pedalling off along Victoria Street and over The Cliff to his home, The Boat

House, which is now a museum.

There's another strange thing. Tourists come in their tens of thousands to visit The Boat House where Thomas snored and trembled, fought with his wife and dreaded the crunching sound of the postman's feet as he walked down a path of cockle shells bringing bills in the morning mail. The visitors' books (there have been dozens of them) give their names and addresses. Like the stars of rock music, Thomas found and kept an audience that does not usually read poetry, buy books of short stories, or 'quality' papers. He was a people's poet who caught the ear of the people through radio in that brief post-war period when wireless was the main form of family entertainment. Men and women of all ages somehow identify with him as they do not identify with the Eliots and Audens. They talk of his voice. And it is impressive to observe their emotional reactions to this humble, shy, confused, fearful and in many ways objectionable man who was great fun in a smoky pub on a winter's night but neglectful of his family and a poor lover; a selfish man who believed himself touched by angels, one of the chosen ones.

Throughout his adult life others shared that belief. For nearly 20 years they saved his letters, sought signed copies of his work, recorded their memories. Everything about the man, from his well-honed vowels and childhood memories to the bar stories and abandoned scripts, was saved for some future day, mostly destined to end up in the archives of American universities. One family kept his tin bath; another, his kitchen table. Thomas himself marketed his waste paper, which he called 'work-sheets'. Signed first editions of his early books now fetch £1,500–£2,000 at auction. A presentation copy of his first slim volume *18 Poems* was sold privately for £8,000. The tiniest scraps of paper bearing his doodles are worth hundreds of pounds. One woman treasured for 40 years a tablecloth on which he had scrawled a cartoon and signed his name – then sold it for a fine price.

There is little of Dylan Thomas left in Wales. His family have gone. Most of his friends are dead. A few minor letters have been acquired by the National Library of Wales in Aberystwyth, but the important archives have been established by the University libraries in Texas, New York, Harvard, Delaware, Indiana and Southern Illinois, the New York Public Library and the British Museum. A few personal letters remain in private hands. His love letters to Caitlin are owned by a collector in California. His family have nothing. It has all been sold.

This posthumous acclaim would have been no surprise to Dylan Thomas. Illusions never troubled him. Craft, trade, skill or profession: Poet. That was what he believed, neither more nor less. Explanations were seldom given, for he sensed that his marbled phrases would withstand the test of time. As he perfected all his stylistic tricks, Thomas made extra cash by selling those 'work-sheets' as soon as he had finished a poem.

Genius was his, or so he suggested, and many have accepted him at his own evaluation. This is not easy, for such qualities seldom come in any expected shape or form. Thomas noted in an essay he wrote in 1933 that the thinkers of the world often trod a boundary where it was 'difficult to differentiate, with any sureness, between insanity and eccentricity'.[1]

In that early essay, written for the local newspaper in Swansea where he was training to be a journalist, the poet observed that Blake sat naked in his garden, not caring what his neighbours thought; that blowing bubbles brought Newton lifelong pleasure, and that Poe, Clare, Verlaine and Baudelaire all died through drugs, drink or madness. He was making that point in his late teens and convinced Caitlin, on the night they met that he, too, carried their burden of genius. He talked about this throughout their marriage, wondering whether it was inevitable that he might face an early death. Others could perceive something special, a hidden well of thoughts that could be disciplined through language and the use of sound. Verbs, vowels and shafts of comic wordplay seemed to dance upon his lips so that his glass would be refilled to keep him talking, while others wondered at his artistry. In the frailty of his innocence he could not resist temptation.

Some saw this. Caitlin did, for sure, though jealously came between them. Dame Edith Sitwell recognised 'great warmth, charm and touching funniness' and 'had never known anyone with a more holy and childlike innocence of mind'.[2] This never changed. Towards the end Stravinsky realised, 'As soon as I saw him that the only thing to do was to love him'.[3] By then, as Stravinsky noted, Thomas's face and skin had a colour and a swelling that came from too much drinking. 'He was a shorter man than I expected, not more than five feet five or six, with a large protuberant behind and belly. His nose was a red bulb and his eyes were glazed. He drank a glass of whisky with me which made him more at ease, though he kept worrying about his wife, saying he had to hurry home to Wales, "or it would be too late."'

The only thing to do was love him. It takes an artist to know that for, as Thomas observed 'the borderline of insanity is more difficult to trace than the majority of people, comparatively safe within the barriers of their own common-sensibility, can realise'.[4]

To balance art against the artist is difficult for biographers scraping away at family trees or knocking gently at the doors of memory. Everyone has their recollection of the famous. Their angelic childhood faces, Sunday School devotions, playground battles, classroom wit, early sexual fumbles or

3

escapades in small town bars. The greater their fame, the more such stories multiply. In the background of every artist lie minor figures whose own stature rests on early acquaintance. So it was with Dylan Thomas. Here was an actor playing many parts, convinced of his genius but never quite at ease with it, and from every crowd scene come these accounts of the liar, plagiarist, drunkard, comedian, thief, friend, husband, son, fraud, womaniser, hero, coward and master of both the written and the spoken word. By such anecdotes are legends made, which makes it all the more important to treat them with suspicion, and to assess with care the evidence of those who do not know what Stravinsky meant.

Over 40 books have been written about Dylan Thomas since his death in November 1953, some pictorial, some part-biographical, some critical. There have also been television and radio documentaries, produced in many languages, and mostly drawn from the published material – there are literally thousands of newspaper articles.

Dylan Thomas has become a legend. A plaque in his memory was installed in Westminster Abbey, partly at the request of US President Jimmy Carter. Richard Burton and Elizabeth Taylor helped raise funds for it; both appeared in the film version of *Under Milk Wood*. Two thousand people turned up for the dedication ceremony without being invited. Some had flown from far corners of the world. Prince Charles later complained that he had not received a ticket. The Boat House has been renovated with funds provided by the EEC. Rock musicians avow their debt to him.

Pilgrims from many countries travel to Wales to see where he lived. His works have been translated into Arabic, Japanese, Russian, Hungarian, Swedish, Czechoslovakian, Serbo Croat, German, Danish, Spanish, French, Italian, Norwegian, Finnish, Hebrew and Dutch.

This enthusiasm has made the poet wealthy in death. His writings generate an income of around £120,000 a year. This will continue until the year 2003 when his works go out of copyright. Until then, those who write about Dylan Thomas are inhibited by the Trustees of The Dylan Thomas Estate.

The origins and role of these Trustees has been barely explained in the two main biographies, Constantine Fitzgibbon's *The Life of Dylan Thomas* (1965), which was authorised by them, and Paul Ferris's *Dylan Thomas* (1977), which was not. For many years these two books, alongside John Malcolm Brinnin's *Dylan Thomas in America* (1955), have been accepted as definitive judgements on the poet's life. I believe all three to be defective. To

4

assess this opinion one needs to know more about the books written on Dylan Thomas, his family and the workings of the Estate.

Thomas's biographers have tended to repeat each other. Dylan co-operated with the first, Henry Treece, inviting him to Laugharne in August 1938 and answering his letters, but by the time *Dylan Thomas: Dog Among the Fairies* (1949) was published ten years later, they barely knew each other. A muddled book of little consequence, it annoyed Thomas intensely. The second, *Dylan Thomas: A Literary Study* (1954) was written by Derek Stanford without apparently realising what a vast body of work the poet had left behind him, or the extent of his private correspondence.

The first books of substance were Brinnin's, Caitlin Thomas's *Leftover Life to Kill* (1957), Rayner Heppenstall's *Four Absentees* (1961), John Ackerman's *Dylan Thomas: His Life and Work* (1964) and Bill Read's *The Days of Dylan Thomas* (1964). Brinnin's was to prove the most influential.

Caitlin's memoir mostly concerned her own emotions with little reference to Dylan. The book was written on Elba where she escaped in distress in the early days of widowhood. The manuscript was cobbled together in great passion, written in longhand at high speed, almost as a form of therapy, and then knocked into shape by an editor. The book became a bestseller. Heppenstall's work, which also included recollections of George Orwell, Eric Gill and J. Middleton Murry, contained several anecdotes which reappeared in subsequent biographies. Ackerman and Read both attempted serious character studies, with *Dylan Thomas: His Life and Work* particularly good in its explanation of the poet's Welsh background, and *The Days of Dylan Thomas* evoking a fine sense of atmosphere. Both writers were handicapped by having little access to Thomas's family, and the Trustees refused them permission to quote from Thomas's letters which were then unpublished.

Bit by bit, the many conflicting facets of Thomas's personality were emerging but each new portrait was essentially one-sided. This was also true of Brinnin's *Dylan Thomas in America*, another bestseller, which portrayed him in his final days as a drunken adulterer, losing his grip on life. The revelations that followed built upon this premise. Initially, the Trustees wanted Ruthven Todd to be the poet's official biographer and signed a contract to this effect on 5 August 1959. Todd's book failed to materialise, so the biography was written instead by Constantine Fitzgibbon whose problems with Comrade Bottle were far worse than those of his subject. Fitzgibbon produced *The Life of Dylan Thomas* (1965) and edited *The Selected Letters of Dylan Thomas* (1966) with few critics realising how these books had come into being at the Trustees' behest. Twelve years later Paul

Ferris brought out his 'unauthorised' biography, drawing on similar sources to Fitzgibbon (and a few better ones), before he, too, turned to the poet's correspondence, editing *The Collected Letters of Dylan Thomas* (1985). This volume is so unwieldy, with 982 pages, that perhaps Ferris felt intimidated, for there was very little analysis or explanation. Eventually, one hopes, an American university may finance a more thorough study of Thomas's correspondence, published in three or more volumes with a scholarly annotation, although this may have to wait until the poet's work is no longer in copyright.

Certain dates become significant when one considers these matters, the role of the Trustees, and whether or not they have acted wisely in the years since Thomas's death.

It was not known at the time of his death, nor for many years thereafter, that Thomas and his wife were going through a crisis. Caitlin thought the marriage was finished, although she had no knowledge of her husband's relationship with Brinnin's assistant, Liz Reitell. Caitlin felt neglected. In many ways she was the dominant partner, but, in the space of three or four years, Dylan had become an international literary celebrity. He was a hero abroad, fêted and funded, but not at home where she constantly complained of their lack of money. They fought like drunken alley cats, rolling home late at night from Brown's Hotel (Laugharne had never been too worried about the licensing laws), with Dylan crawling backwards down the garden steps to The Boat House on his hands and knees to avoid falling into the sea. Once inside the cottage, she would attack him with both fists and anything she could lay her hands on, being always the stronger, and, if he didn't manage to flee upstairs fast enough to the refuge of their bed, would knock him down, straddle his chest, grab him by the hair and beat his head upon the floor. This violence had gone on for years. Many friends had witnessed it. Some (especially those who had been close to him in his Swansea days), blamed her for all their problems, not knowing of the coarser side to Thomas's character, and her feeling of impoverishment. Caitlin also felt betrayed, believing that he had been unfaithful, but until she read Brinnin's book she had never known for sure how her husband behaved when far from home. That book was the final straw. In his death she became embittered. 'He was a bastard', she told me with feeling that was all the more touching for my sensing that she doesn't really believe it and, in her heart of hearts, loves him still.

* * *

6

The last time Caitlin saw her husband alive and well was on 19 October 1953. They had travelled up from Laugharne together, via Swansea, and spent nearly ten days in London, staying with Harry and Cordelia Locke in Hammersmith, going out to dinner with friends, shopping, visiting the theatre (away from home the Thomases lived well, although often with someone else's money). Dylan delivered his *Under Milk Wood* manuscript to Douglas Cleverdon at the BBC, had a few drinks with Constantine Fitzgibbon, saw Philip Burton (all of which will be detailed later). They could see that he was unhappy. Drinking would take up part of every day. After a few whiskies, Caitlin's grievances rose back to the surface. 'You're only going for fornication and flattery,' was her constant gibe, for once she had a stinging phrase Caitlin used it well. What happened thereafter has been told many times, originally by Brinnin, whose description of Thomas's last days was based largely on information supplied by his assistant Liz Reitell.

Thomas stayed at the Chelsea Hotel, drank intermittently (but by no means constantly), stressing to friends that he was anxious to return home this time with more money than after his previous US tours. As a visiting celebrity, he had much to do. On the evening of Saturday 24 October, and again the following afternoon, Thomas appeared in *Under Milk Wood* at Brinnin's Poetry Centre, with audiences of over a thousand people, and three days later gave a poetry reading at City College, followed by a symposium on Film Art which he attended with Arthur Miller, teasing the audience with comic wordplay. The next weekend he attended one party on the Saturday and three on the Sunday, saying on the Monday afternoon that he had never been so drunk in his life.[5] He went out drinking again on the Tuesday night. What happened then is described in Chapter Twelve where these events are detailed more fully. On the Wednesday he collapsed and was taken to St Vincent's Hospital. When he heard of this, Brinnin sent a telegram to Caitlin.

It was then 5 November and a BBC outside broadcasting unit was in Laugharne, recording a programme on the town for which Thomas had written and recorded a segment in which he expressed his affection for Laugharne. Caitlin was sitting in the audience, listening to the programme being made, when the telegram was passed to her. The following day she left for London, determined to catch the next available plane, but had to wait for some hours while this was arranged. She started drinking in Soho, and when the photographer John Deakin tried to commiserate she went to crash a bottle down upon his head; had he not moved swiftly, the blow could have killed him.[6] She continued drinking on the flight to New York. No one had prepared her for the seriousness of Thomas's condition, and when she arrived at his bedside, Caitlin lost control. Her helplessness was pitiful. She threw herself upon him, clawing his face and ripping at the oxygen tubes fastened to his nose. Later, having tried to strangle Brinnin and after tearing a statue of the Virgin Mary from the wall and trampling it beneath her feet, she was restrained in a strait-jacket for her own protection and taken to the Rivercrest Sanatorium. It was there that she was told of her husband's death on Monday 9 November.

Caitlin was discharged on 10 November and moved in with her friends Dave and Rose Slivka. She attended the New York memorial service for Thomas with Tennessee Williams, e.e. cummings and William Faulkner, and then, after battling with the British Embassy, secured the necessary papers to take Thomas's body back to Britain aboard the SS *United States*. Caitlin was still distraught. Whenever she drank heavily, she started dancing. This horrified observers who did not realise that as a trained dancer who still practised daily, she always turned to dancing as a form of therapy when distressed. Their reactions only made matters worse. On board the liner she was again strapped in a strait-jacket and kept in the ship's hospital. When released, Caitlin joined the coffin in the hold and travelled back by its side.

The liner arrived back in Southampton in the early hours of Sunday 22 November. She was met by Ebie Williams, landlord of Brown's Hotel, who had driven from Laugharne to collect the coffin. He had been accompanied by Dr Daniel Jones, who had taken upon himself the 'self-appointed role of generalissimo'.[7] On the journey back to Wales, Ebie took a wrong turning and ended up in Dorset. They eventually arrived back in Laugharne at 5 a.m. on Monday 23 November, to find that six of Thomas's friends had stayed up overnight to receive his coffin and carry it into his parents' home, Pelican, in King Street, where the nails were removed and the lid opened so that townspeople and relatives could pay their last respects to his embalmed body.

The funeral was held on Tuesday 24 November, with Daniel Jones taking charge. In his book *My Friend Dylan Thomas*, Jones says that 'for some reason, the role seemed to be acknowledged by others. I used Mrs Florence Thomas's house as my "headquarters" and people "reported" to me there. Occasionally I went on a "tour of inspection", usually, of course, to Brown's Hotel . . .' There was mayhem in the township, some of which he describes, with Caitlin drunk, dancing and hurling drinks, and another woman making herself available to all comers. Jones describes it as a 'farcical nightmare'. Laugharne remembers it as a good funeral, for it wasn't their only one to end with mourners fighting; at one more recent funeral two brothers started fighting at the graveside, and one kicked the other in the testicles. No one moralises over incidents like these for it is understood that emotions are taut on such occasions; there is often heavy drinking after Laugharne funerals, and it is in no sense disrespectful. That night Caitlin was so distressed that she planned to commit suicide by throwing herself from The Cliff. Realising that she was in a bad way, her sister Nicolette and close friend Cordelia Locke suggested she go back to London with them, which she did the following day, having arranged for the children to be looked after.

For many weeks afterwards, Caitlin drank heavily and it was during this period that the Trust came into being. Her memory of the events that followed is hazy, but she has long disputed being in Wales when Letters of Administration were formally applied for on 30 November. It seems unlikely that she was there on 7 December when these were granted, the District Probate Registry in Carmarthen having been provided with an affidavit testifying that Dylan's estate was worth only £100. The word 'unlikely' is used with some care since I have before me as I write photocopies of documents that establish that on 1 December Caitlin threw herself out of a window at Cordelia Locke's flat in Hammersmith, after attacking a man in a pub, and was then taken to the West London Hospital with a fractured collarbone.

The following day, 2 December, Caitlin was admitted as a voluntary patient to the Holloway Sanatorium at Virginia Water on the recommendation of Dr A.S. Paterson, Physician in Charge of the Department of Psychiatry at West London. In these reports she is described as 'a chronic alcoholic' who 'may be violent'. Dr Paterson suggested that Caitlin needed 'careful handling', was 'likely to be demanding' and would 'insist on leaving before long'. According to the Sanatorium records, Caitlin discharged herself on 7 December, the very day that she is supposed to have been in Carmarthen receiving the Letters of Administration.

This becomes important when one considers what happened next. On 28 December Caitlin signed a Deed of Settlement whereby a Trust was created to handle income from 'all copyrights and interests in copyrights in respect of the literary works of the late husband of the Settlor Dylan Marlais Thomas'. Caitlin has long claimed that she received no independent legal advice before signing away her inheritance to this Trust. Equally, it must be said in fairness to the original Trustees that she was in no fit state to deal with complex legal matters. They must have realised that large sums of money might derive from Thomas's copyrights, and that this rightly belonged to his family. The trust deed provided that half the net income would go to Caitlin with the other half divided among her children Llewelyn, Aeronwy and Colm. This seems a wholly fair arrangement and few would argue with it.

However, the effect of this deed and the formation of the Trust was to create a situation in which control of Dylan Thomas's copyrights – and thus his letters, personal documents relating to his affairs and much information essential to any biographer – passed from his family to the Trustees.*

Literary estates are notoriously difficult to manage, especially when authors lead complicated lives and die intestate. One only has to study the fierce controversies that surround the estates of Sylvia Plath, Philip Larkin and T.S. Eliot to realise where the dangers lie for a would-be biographer. Anyone wishing to write about Dylan Thomas has to be equally cautious, with the added disadvantage that so much has been written already that one needs to know how each book came to be written and in what circumstances before placing it in its proper context.

To understand the background to the biographies one has to appreciate Thomas's family relationships and the complexities that surround the Estate. Dylan Thomas was only 39 years old when he died. He left no will. Llewelyn, Aeronwy and Colm were aged 14, 10 and 4. They were too young to form a mature perception of their father and, in any case, saw relatively little of him. Contrary to legend, the Thomases were not poor. Dylan earned large sums of money in his latter years but handled it carelessly. He was constantly borrowing and highly secretive about his finances, often claiming to be penniless (which caused Caitlin to develop the unpleasant habit of rifling his pockets when he was drunk. Since he could never remember where his money had gone, this created no problems between them and did, at least, provide her with cash for food, clothing and household essentials.) However, they always employed domestic help and Llewelyn and Aeronwy were both sent to private boarding schools. Colm was little more than a baby and, by all accounts, a happy one, wrapped up in a world of his own. Dylan's own father had died in December 1952, and his sister Nancy the following

---

*One argument in the Trustees' favour is that if the Trust had not been created, Dylan Thomas's copyrights might have fallen into other hands. It is said in Laugharne that a stranger offered Caitlin £100 in cash in the bar of Brown's Hotel if she would sign a piece of paper assigning the copyrights. She was tempted. At the time, the full scale of Thomas's literary achievement was unknown. *Under Milk Wood* had not been broadcast and his works not mass-marketed.

April. His mother, Mrs Florence Thomas, continued to live in Laugharne after Dylan's death, but she died in 1958. By the time the first biographers came along, Caitlin was the last surviving adult member of his family – and she had gone off to Elba and then to Rome, refusing to talk to any of them. This left the Trustees as the main source of information on the poet's life.

At the age of 49, Caitlin had a fourth child by a Sicilian lover, Giuseppe Fazio. This evidently scandalised the Trustees who rejected all her entreaties to regard the child, Francesco, equally with her other children. The family situation became even more complex when her elder son Llewelyn married the stepdaughter of the most active Trustee, Stuart Thomas. Intermittently over the past 25 years, since she lost the celebrated High Court case over ownership of the manuscript of *Under Milk Wood* (for which she blames the Trustees), Caitlin has been in a state of litigious warfare with them. I have many letters from her in which she expresses hatred and contempt for the Trustees. At times, she claims the Trustees have refused her money for household expenses or medical treatment. Periodically (most recently in 1988), Caitlin has commenced Court actions against the Trustees to extract sums of money that she claims have been due to her, although these disputes have rarely been discovered by the Press. It is my view that she has been misrepresented on many occasions, and of her relationship with Giuseppe Fazio I can only say that in the many long periods that I have spent with them, in their home and in this country, he has always been loving and attentive – and Caitlin would be the first to admit (and has!) that she can be a most demanding woman.

One needs to be aware of all this, without necessarily knowing all the details, to assess the background to each book written about Dylan Thomas.

John Malcolm Brinnin's famous book *Dylan Thomas in America* was first published in the United States in 1955 by Little, Brown & Co. Brinnin and Thomas had both written for the little magazines of the Thirties, with Brinnin recognising a rare talent in the Welsh poet. On being appointed Director of the Poetry Centre at the Young Men's and Young Women's Hebrew Association in New York, Brinnin immediately invited Thomas to lecture there and subsequently arranged many of his US readings. They first met on 21 February 1950, when the poet arrived to begin his first US tour, and shared occasional confidences thereafter. During that tour, Thomas leaned on Brinnin. Caitlin accompanied him on the second tour when Brinnin provided Thomas with a written schedule of his commitments and left them to it. On the third, such plans were largely handled by Liz Reitell. The fourth ended in disaster with Liz Reitell calling in the doctor who later prescribed Thomas's fatal overdose of morphine. Initially, Dr Milton

Feltenstein, who is now dead, prescribed cortisone for what he thought was a largely alcoholic condition. After two cortisone injections, Feltenstein gave the poet half a grain of morphine. As Dylan had been drinking whisky and taking benzedrine, the cocktail proved fatal and he went into the coma from which he never recovered.*

Thomas died five days later, and by then Brinnin was back in New York, endeavouring to comfort both Caitlin and Liz Reitell. It was an uncomfortable situation. Caitlin thought Brinnin was in love with her husband and was unaware of the mistress's existence. Brinnin kept the two women apart, and when he came to compile notes for *Dylan Thomas in America* relied on Liz Reitell for details of those occasions when he had not been present, without any real understanding of Dylan's psychological needs or the relationship between husband and wife.

Years later Brinnin wrote a biographical study of the American homosexual novelist Truman Capote, with whom he also suggested that he had had a close, trusting friendship. Unfortunately for Brinnin, Capote was still alive and able to retort:

He's never been a close friend of mine, he never really *was* a close friend of mine. I haven't seen him, to speak of, for twenty-five years . . . (the book) is very amusing. A great deal of untrue things are in it. I'd say seventy per cent of what he wrote in it isn't true at all . . . he's actually a good writer. He wrote that book which I thought was very good, called *Dylan Thomas in America*. But since reading this I have to think back. I wonder just exactly how much of this *Dylan Thomas in America* was true.[8]

So must any biographer approaching a life of Dylan Thomas, for Brinnin was the starting-point, the sensation that laid the origins of the myth, the author whose revelations brought an ever-deepening interest in both the writer and the man.

*Thomas's health will be described later. I have discussed the known medical facts with three doctors who confirm that morphine was the wrong drug to use in his situation. Half a grain would have been three times the normal dose, even if it had been the right drug to use. We may never know precisely why Dylan Thomas died. No one knows what other drugs Thomas was taking apart from benzedrine, although he had started to boast about his drug-taking. Caitlin has told me that when she arrived in New York 'there was a lot of talk about drugs'. He may have tried other drugs but she did not investigate this further thinking that it didn't matter now that Dylan was dead.

— 2 —
CHILD OF THE CHAPEL

THE Dylan Thomas myth began with his death. He was already a highly successful writer, although his constant wails of poverty made strangers think of him as the archetypal romantic poet struggling to stay true to his muse. This was largely a charade. He had become used to wheedling and sponging as a way of life, regularly touching friends for cash when he must have known that he earned more than they did.

Fame had come early. His first volume of verse, *18 Poems*, was published in December 1934, shortly after his 20th birthday, and his second, *Twenty-five Poems*, in September 1936. In the years leading up to the Second World War Thomas was a highly acclaimed young poet. His genius was acknowledged by influential critics of the day. His writings appeared in many leading literary magazines, with his collection of poems and stories *The Map of Love* published in August 1939, his first US selection *The World I Breathe* in December 1939, and his largely autobiographical short stories *Portrait of the Artist As A Young Dog* in April 1940. This had not happened casually. Thomas had taken the traditional Dick Whittington route for the young provincial in search of fame. He left Swansea at 18 and went to London, knocking on doors, meeting editors, making friends at the BBC, hanging around literary pubs in Fitzrovia, Soho and Chelsea, pushing himself with all the grace of a brush salesman.

Remarkably, he gained this recognition with little money or, as Caitlin puts it, wholly from within his own resources, and it is this achievement, barely traced by most biographers, that laid the foundation for his later career. Dylan Thomas's background was far more complex than most Englishmen could ever understand. Like so many of his Anglo-Welsh contemporaries, Welshmen writing in English, he came from a family firmly rooted in rural values and, more particularly, the Welsh-speaking chapel

13

communities of Carmarthenshire and Cardiganshire, which were far less puritanical than they outwardly appeared, bound together by a language, literature and music that gave them a sense of nationhood which is cherished still. His mother brought to the family home in the Swansea Uplands the habits and customs of an ancient past. She baked her own bread, bottled preserves, made cakes and jams, barely mixing with her suburban neighbours. Contrary to what has been written elsewhere, Florence and David John Thomas (who was known as Jack or 'D.J.') both came from large families with parents, aunts, uncles, nephews, nieces and cousins living either in the Swansea suburbs, or mostly, in the villages around Carmarthen. For several generations, Florence's family, the Williamses, had farmed on what is known locally as the Llanstephan Peninsula, the sparsely populated but richly fertile farmland bounded by the tidal rivers Taf and Towy. This area looked to Carmarthen as its market town. The Thomases came from Johnstown, then more a village than a suburb of Carmarthen, D.J. being the son of Evan Thomas who lived with his wife at The Poplars, overlooking Johnstown village green. Both were active members of the Heol Awst Congregational Church in Carmarthen.

Dylan may have been born in Swansea in the early months of the First World War, but it was in these small communities of West Wales that he felt his roots. This was a strange, remote, some say mystical land, rich in legend, that had somehow managed to retain its sense of self through many centuries. It was one part of Britain that neither the Romans nor the Normans ever really conquered, a region where folk lore survived through poem and song, with its ancient language still in daily use. Geographically, it was a tiny area of no great economic importance. The world could live without it, but this part of Wales could also live without the world, for it was rich in natural resources, a strip of farming land on the sea's edge, separated from the rest of Wales by natural river and mountain boundaries. When the Romans came, its people took to the hills until they had gone. They survived every English conquest, and there remained in the West a people with stockier physique, distinctive facial features, reddish hair and a culture that somehow remained intact.

Theirs was a difficult land to conquer, for these hills and river boundaries contained hundreds of tiny communities, some just groups of cottages at the end of a mountain track or down a wooded valley, where there happened to be a fresh water supply. What made them different was their independence which found a religious and a political form. With the Reformation, they became staunchly Protestant, embracing Calvinism, and then fragmenting through the centuries until each village might harbour three or four variations of faith, each centred around a preacher and his chapel. Having their own language, they established their own literature and printing presses. They were an ostensibly religious people who did not always practise all they preached.

This was only just beginning to change during the lifetime of Dylan's parents. D.J. and his wife could trace their ancestry back through generations of farmers and village tradesmen before the coming of the railways and the opening of mines and steelworks integrated this area more closely with the life of England and the rest of Wales. Before that, for centuries, these people had been remote, enjoying maritime contact with Ireland, Iceland, southern Europe and the Mediterranean. There was even a tradition that they discovered America before Columbus.

In their religious beliefs, political attitudes, choice of literature, music and social behaviour, they kept to themselves. In the more remote parts of Wales, this lifestyle still survives, despite the intrusions of television and the tourist trade. Two or three generations ago for someone like Dylan Thomas, with his natural innocence and poetic gift, the area was something akin to a Biblical land. This parallel is apt because the strongest influences were always the preachers. These were not dry, ascetic, learned scholars who dwelt in ivory towers, but parish bulls, bold men of powerful force who dominated their flock, driving them to prayer and sacrifice through fear of the wrath of the Lord. They were men of humble origin who combined their religious passion with daytime trades such as farming, carpentry or stone masonry. When Sunday came it was to the pulpit that they turned, Bible in hand, forefingers quivering towards Heaven, threatening damnation to those who flirted with temptations of the flesh, or the perils of Demon Drink.

There were scholars who saw their inspiration in ancient works of literature, teachers who believed that education was an end in itself,* hymnwriters,† and politicians who were invariably Liberal, believing that every problem would be solved if only the English would leave them alone.

A generation earlier, the Thomases had lived just a few miles the other side of Carmarthen, up in the hills around Brechfa, Llandyssul and Llanybydder, where an uncle, William Thomas, brother of Evan, achieved

---

*West Wales has long had high educational standards. It was here that Griffith Jones (1683–1761) established a network of village schools. By the time he died it was estimated that 158,000 pupils had been educated in his schools, all being taught the Welsh Bible and the Catechism.

† As Thomas said in *Under Milk Wood*, this was 'a musical nation' with many choirs and small orchestras. *The Dictionary of Welsh Biography* (1959) details hundreds of clergymen who were also hymnwriters, harpists and musicians.

local renown as a social reformer, schoolmaster, minister and writer. This uncle chose the bardic name Gwilym Marles. He embraced the Unitarian faith and the Liberal cause. This brought both him and his congregation into conflict with the local landowner who turned them out of their chapel at Llwynrhydowen. William Thomas established a new chapel and a school in Llandyssul. He wrote a novel, which was published in the magazine *Seren Gomer* (1855), and contributed regularly to the magazines *Yr Athraw* and *Ymofynydd*. One of his pupils, William Thomas, became a famous Welsh language poet, Islwyn.

Although the railways, newspapers and a nationally-imposed educational system that was English language-based brought new ideas to these areas of Wales, for some, the late Victorian age gave wider opportunities. The University of Wales was established at Aberystwyth in 1872 and bright young men from poor rural families were encouraged to believe that the world could be their oyster. This generation turned its back on the old values, searching for something new. D.J. Thomas was part of this cultural revolution; a working-class boy, a railwayman's son, who won a Queen's Scholarship to Aberystwyth, where he obtained a first class honours degree in English in 1899.

By the stricter conventions of his rural Welsh chapel background, D.J. became an advanced thinker. He studied *English* literature, rejected religion, enjoyed drink, and appears to have had tolerant views on sexual matters. Florence was pregnant when they married, although she lost the baby, and they evidently continued to have a happy sex life well into their 60s. Pamela Hansford Johnson, who stayed with the couple and remained friends with them after her romance with Dylan ended, recalled that Florence sometimes used to say to her after lunch, 'Excuse me, dear, but Jack likes me to go up on the bed with him', and off she would go.

In turning away from the narrower values, Jack held a philosophy similar to Caradoc Evans, who was the first Anglo-Welsh writer to speak out against the hypocrisy of the chapel elders. His first book *My People* (1913) caused a sensation in Wales. It was denounced in pulpits, banned by bookshops and libraries, burnt in public – and widely read, quickly going into six editions. Evans, who was born near Llandyssul and worked as a draper's assistant in Carmarthen before turning to journalism, went on writing short stories in *Capel Sion* (1916) and *My Neighbours* (1919), before writing the play *Taffy* (1924), which shocked the Welsh community when it was staged in London, and the novels *Nothing to Pay* (1930), *Wasps* (1933), *This Way to Heaven* (1934), *Morgan's Bible* (1943) and *Mother's Marvel* (1949). He was widely disliked in Wales for holding chapel followers up to ridicule, showing them to be no better than the rest of the community in their pursuit of sex, drink and gluttony, but he was clearly much respected by the Thomases, for Dylan praised him highly and visited him at his home in Aberystwyth.

But whereas Dylan Thomas would later portray the Welsh with affection in *Under Milk Wood*, Evans stabbed at their pride with a pen dipped in vitriol. Take this defence of *My People*:

My book is not unclean; it is an unsavoury book, for the people with whom it deals are very wicked, and they have learnt all manner of evil devices from their pastors. They are pagans, and they worship gods . . . . they have prospered above any of their congregation, and their abodes are the mansions of the land. They command offerings in the name of God, and fatten thereon. They see on all sides of them peasants – whose bodies are crooked from toil, and whose soils are sterile – labouring all the light hours to keep them in comfort. They make mischief in families, and cry aloud the name of the widow who fails in her dole to the capel . . . Wales would be brighter and more Christianlike if every chapel was burnt to the ground and a public-house raised on the ashes thereof.[1]

Jack Thomas possessed a rage like this, and had that been his only influence on the young Dylan it might have been harmful, but this was never so because the father clearly loved the very symbols that he professed to hate; the son grew up in a house where the old values were both cherished and scorned, but never forgotten. Jack may have gained his English degree, but in their home he and Florence spoke Welsh, and although they may have had to make their home in Swansea, because that was where he could find work as a teacher at a time when jobs were scarce, D.J. never settled there in his mind. He was always, until the end of his days, a frustrated man who had hoped for a better life but had never been able to put his past behind him. Likewise, Florence never lost her West Wales roots, and there are still distant relatives living in the area. One afternoon I was driven around the Llanstephan Peninsula by the poet's daughter Aeronwy and her husband Trefor and shown the many farms and cottages where aunts, uncles and cousins had lived.

Throughout his childhood, Dylan knew these lanes, hamlets and tidal waters well. Florence's sister Ann and her husband Jim Jones farmed at Pentowin, looking across the Taf towards The Boat House, before taking a tenancy at Fern Hill, just two or three miles across the fields at Llangain. Relatives farmed at Waunfwlchan, which had been Florence's grandparents' farm, between Llanybri and Llangain, and others lived in cottages nearby. In this area there came together all the different influences that gave Dylan his secure sense of place. When he moved back to Laugharne in 1949, he could see Pentowin every day from the window of his workshed on The Cliff, watching his neighbour, the deaf and dumb ferryman, taking his boat across the river from the rocks near Ferry House. Images of rivers, tides, sand, sea, herons, curlews and ferrymen occur throughout Thomas's writing, but so does a sense of faith, for this was a background rooted in belief as well as landscape. Dylan knew himself well, a parochial man who saw the world writ large in everyday incident, never losing that gift of observing deeper meaning in what otherwise might have been ordinary experiences. For him staying on those family farms was to be 'green and carefree, famous among the barns' (from *Fern Hill*). To visit such places again was to see

> ... the woods the river and sea
> Where a boy
> In the listening
> Summertime of the dead whispered the truth of his joy ...

These lines are from *Poem in October*, which is constructed around the Laugharne estuary landscape which Thomas would have known first as a boy staying with his aunt and uncle on the other bank of the River Taf.

That such visions were set in Wales just happened to be his life. They could have been anywhere for this gift gave him the ability to see all mankind in a moment and translate that image. Such feats required deep confidence for he took words used in everyday speech, and seemingly ordinary events, and then showed us what we had missed. This is where his biblical influences are also found. He was not a holy-rolling, bible-punching zealot of the type that the Welsh know all too well, but there were simple beliefs in his family background that transcend all the usual boundaries. Both the Thomas and Williams families were active Nonconformists. The Thomas side of the family had produced the famous Gwilym Marles. On his mother's side, there was the Rev. Thomas Williams (her brother) who became minister at Nicholston Hall Chapel, Gower, Swansea, and the Rev. David Rees (who married her sister Theodosia), minister first at Canaan Chapel, Swansea, and then at Paraclete Chapel, Newton, Mumbles, Swansea.

Florence was just as much a child of the chapel as they were, and although D.J. may have turned away to embrace a wider culture he left her to bring up their children in her own way. Florence was gentle, simple and loving, with no obvious intellectual attainments. She was talkative, a busy gossip among her women friends, and shrewd. She gave her children a secure home, fussing and fretting over them both in the parlour at 5 Cwmdonkin Drive in a manner familiar to anyone who has known Welsh family life.*

Florence was convinced that ill health ran in the family, and she may have been right. D.J. did not have a strong constitution, although he survived cancer of the mouth in his fifties and lived for another 20 years. Nancy and Dylan were both 'chesty'. Florence mollycoddled them, insisting on extra layers of winter clothing, warm vests, good solid Welsh home cooking, and seasonal vitamin pills. Whenever Dylan got into any childhood scrapes, Florence could be relied upon to insist that it was someone else's fault, defending him in the playground and Cwmdonkin Park, or doing battles with teachers, thus giving her son a lifelong reputation for being 'spoilt'. There was truth in that. He was, being the only boy in the house with an elder sister, a nanny-cum-housekeeper and Florence, who was never happier than when a group of women were sitting around her kitchen table. But with all that smothering affection there also came an introduction to those chapel values. Dylan was packed off to Sunday School every week, and also accompanied his mother to the nearby Congregational Chapel in Walter Road, and the chapels where the uncles officiated or were preaching that weekend. It was not considered unusual to attend chapel two or three times on Sundays. That was all part of the old Welsh way of life.

Biographers have tended to play down this religious background. Ferris goes further and argues that 'religion was a stage-prop of his poetry; he used its language and myths, which he had learnt in childhood, without ever absorbing or caring much about its central beliefs'.[2] I prefer Thomas's own account:

> the things that first made me love language & want to work *in* it and *for* it were nursery rhymes and folk tales, the Scottish ballads a few lines of hymns, the most famous Bible stories and the rhythms of the Bible . . . the great rhythms that rolled over me from the Welsh pulpits; and I had read for myself, from Job and Ecclesiastes, and the story of the New Testament is part of my life.[3]

*This is written on the authority of Aeronwy, who remembers her grandmother well and says she retained all these distinctive qualities of the Welsh 'mam' until her death in August 1958. In her latter years, Granny Thomas would show visitors around The Boat House, always calling herself 'Dylan's Mam'. Aeronwy believes that her influence has been underestimated, 'she was no fool and much more intelligent than people thought'.

Central assumptions lay at the core of his upbringing, and although he was not a devout man Thomas ensured that his children were duly christened. Aneirin Talfan Davies[4] argues that Thomas was close to embracing Catholicism towards the end of his life; this theory is not wholly convincing, for father and son both discarded many of the outward trappings of a religious life, and yet there is a constant use of biblical phrases, particularly from Job and Ecclesiastes, in Thomas's poetry, and one can see that he drew from his childhood a personal view of man's place within a wider universe.

For him, Wales was the key, but this was never the familiar Wales of miners' choirs, rugby battles and costumed ladies going to market in their tall black hats. Thomas mostly ignored these conventional images. On those occasions when he even mentioned them, he did so dismissively. For him, such preoccupations were absurd. He loved a wider world, but the prism through which he observed it was Wales. What he saw in his own country was an older Wales, pre-dating its towns and cities, where trout and salmon swam up its tidal waters, corn and apples grew, seasons changed, the weather turned, and women conceived as they had done since the world began (cf. *The force that through the green fuse drives the flower*). It was a vision as simple or profound as the Book of Genesis, born of a background where there was a family Bible in every home, usually in the Peter Williams translation, and where values retained a constancy.

By the time Dylan was born, D.J. and Florence had been married almost eleven years. Their daughter Nancy was eight years old. The family had settled for a quiet, respectable life in the Swansea suburbs with D.J. already firmly set in what was to become a working lifetime spent teaching English Literature to the boys at Swansea Grammar School. It has been generally assumed that this was not the life he wanted, but it was the one D.J. chose. No evidence survives of him attempting any other career, although he was 27 years old by the time he took up the post. His only other known job was a few months spent at Pontypridd County School.

D.J. became an embittered man with no religious faith (he would stand at the window blaming God when it rained), but he retained a knowledge of the Bible and used its phrases in conversation. I have in my possession D.J.'s own copy of Handel's sacred oratorio, the *Messiah*, with his signature, which suggests that he retained feeling for religious music. It has also been said, mainly by those who knew him as a teacher, that D.J. was a failed poet who achieved success through his son; that he was a sour man whose prospects had been blighted by drink, nursing a poisonous envy of those with better and more highly-paid jobs, but these stories are not corroborated.

His father, Evan Thomas, was a guard with the Great Western Railway, the company that provided the passenger service between West Wales and London and carried coal and steel from the South Wales valleys to the Swansea deep sea port. D.J.'s brother Arthur also spent a lifetime on the railways, and although Evan died before Dylan was born, his wife Ann lived on for many years thereafter. She was a frequent visitor to the family home during the poet's childhood.

Many years later, after both D.J. and their children had died, Florence was to say that she first met her husband at a fair in Johnstown. They married on 30 December 1903, when D.J. was 27 and his bride six years younger. He was by then employed at the Grammar School, she was a seamstress at a Swansea draper's store. Their first home was a terraced cottage in Sketty, then a village surrounded by farmland on the outskirts of Swansea. Later they moved to Montpelier Street, nearer the town centre, and it was there that Nancy was born. By the time their son arrived, D.J. was approaching middle age. He was 38 years old and had become rather stiff and formal in his ways, always neat and clipped in appearance, walking to school each morning dressed in dark grey, wearing a hat, daily paper under one arm, an umbrella in his other hand. He could have been going off to work in a solicitor's office or behind the counter of a local bank.

This sense of maintaining appearances was more than just a suburban whim. It was also very Welsh. Schoolmasters were respected and expected to show an example, exercising authority. This he did. D.J. would not tolerate schoolboy sloppiness and was a strict disciplinarian, employing wit, ridicule, sarcasm and occasional bursts of violent temper as he led his charges through the wonders of literature. This aspect of his character has been well documented by Fitzgibbon and Ferris. Wynford Vaughan-Thomas, who was also taught by D.J., told me that D.J. was feared at Swansea Grammar School for his occasional bursts of physical rage, but gained respect because he clearly loved literature and had a fine fruity booming voice similar to his son's, with which he would proclaim the classics. Another pupil described him as 'a tetchy, irritable little man'.[5]

On the day that he retired, and was presented with the usual farewell gifts, D.J. recited Lamb's essay on *The Old and New Schoolmaster*:

Rest to the souls of those fine old Pedagogues: the breed, long since extinct, of the Lilys, and the Linacres: who believing that all learning was contained in the languages which they taught, and despising every other acquirement as superficial and useless, came to their task as to a sport!

Passing from infancy to age, they dreamed away all their days in a grammar school. Revolving in a perpetual cycle of declensions, conjugations, syntaxes and prosodies; renewing constantly the occupations which had charmed their studious childhood; rehearsing continually the part of the past; life must have slipped from them at last like one day.

and

Boys are capital fellows in their own way, among their own mates; but they are unwholesome companions for grown people. The restraint is felt no less on the one side, than on the other.

It would have been only natural for such a teacher, spending his working days with boys, to have sought other company in the evenings. This D.J. did, especially in the years after Dylan was born. The family had moved to 5 Cwmdonkin Drive. Its extra size gave D.J. a room of his own where he could read quietly, undisturbed and surrounded by books, while Florence busied herself cleaning, washing dishes, ironing clothes, and baking, sharing the household chores with their nanny-cum-housekeeper. After his evening meal D.J. would leave them to it and go down to his local, The Uplands Hotel, where he was known as 'The Professor' because of his academic air.

From the outside, the house is deceptive. Like so many suburban homes built in the years leading up to the First World War, No. 5 Cwmdonkin Drive had a narrow frontage and a substantial depth. There was a front parlour facing the street, which was entered from a hallway and set aside for more formal family occasions or entertaining visitors. Behind that there was a middle-room, a book-lined study for D.J., the kitchen and scullery. For D.J., life revolved around his study; for Florence, the kitchen.

By the time their son was born, the couple were happily living together but leading separate lives. By that I am not suggesting that there was any underlying tension or unhappiness between them, but they clearly had very different values. Although D.J. had become atheistic, Florence still clung to her chapel attitudes. The present owner of the house, Frank Jones, told me that when removing the original linoleum in the couple's bedroom he found a row of Welsh prayers neatly laid out beneath what would have been the marital bed, presumably put there by Florence when the Thomases bought the house on its completion in 1914.

D.J. found her habits tiresome, and would sometimes come home from school to find her women friends sitting around the kitchen table nattering over cups of tea, which was enough to make him grumble and even rage, before shutting himself away in that inner room where he could be alone with Shakespeare or D.H. Lawrence. There, the gas fire would be already lit, with his carpet slippers warming by the grate (this was a simple pleasure which D.J. came to expect, and which Caitlin later provided for Dylan; father and son enjoyed such creature comforts). He would retire until early evening, still formally dressed with collar and tie, wearing his hat. (This became an obsession. D.J. was over-conscious of his baldness and wore his hat in the house until it was time to go to bed.) He would sit reading, and before going down to The Uplands Hotel usually invited Nancy or Dylan to sit by his knee, listening to nursery rhymes or short stories, sharing the mysteries of his bookshelves. In this private sanctum, D.J. reigned supreme, for his voice had the timbre, pitch and resonance of a Shakespearean actor. Here, in the privacy of this little room, there were no boys mocking his baldness, pretending to burp or fart or otherwise slight his values; just two children enjoying bedtime in an age when there was no radio or television, and old customs retained their magic.

As a child, Dylan had angelic features, with round, wondrous eyes, and a mass of curly blond hair. Being spoilt, he was naturally naughty, often thieved, doing all the slightly wicked things that children do if not taught otherwise, but who can doubt that at bedtimes, sitting at his father's knee, he captivated D.J. by his receptive ear, a boy warming to the very things that brought the teacher joy – words:

> I did not care what the words said, overmuch, nor what happened to Jack & Jill & the Mother Goose rest of them; I cared for the shapes of sound that their names, and the words describing their actions, made in my ears; I cared for the colours the words cast on my eyes. I realise that I may be, as I think back all that way, romanticising my reactions to the simple and beautiful words of those pure poems; but that is all I can honestly remember, however much time might have falsified my memory. I fell in love – that is the only expression I can think of – at once, and am still at the mercy of words, though sometimes now, knowing a little of their behaviour very well, I think I can influence them slightly and have even learned to beat them now and then, which they appear to enjoy.[6]

Father and son developed a bond during those childhood years that was to form the thread of Thomas's writing life. This relationship remained private to the end, something that neither Florence nor Caitlin could share, and yet both women helped sustain it in loving Dylan with a rare tolerance. He was over-indulged, but this was what the child and the man needed to get through life. He was only looking for comfort, and always had that to go home to, with Florence turning a blind eye when anything went wrong, puffing him up with vests and woolly jumpers, while he ran free in Cwmdonkin Park, with its vast acres of grass, tennis courts, boating lake and summer bandstand. His pleasures were those of any child, enjoying life without too tight a parental hand – staying out too late if he could get away with it, playing cowboys and Indians with his wooden rifle, spying on courting couples, creeping into the local cinema without paying for his ticket, stealing small sums from his mother's handbag or sister's pocket, posing in Nancy's clothes, smoking cigarettes behind the bushes, swearing mightily, yet always turning on that cherubic smile if any adult caught him out. In school holidays, he would be sent to stay with aunts and uncles at Llangain; at weekends, chapel. All this may have been ordinary enough in one sense, but for Florence always letting him get away with far too much. She was convinced of her son's frailty and perhaps over-anxious, having lost the child she was expecting at the time she married.

Dylan was far less sickly than she thought, although he had brittle bones, the weak chest that ran in the family and also, possibly, a weak liver because he never had a high tolerance to alcohol.* Childhood illnesses became family dramas, with Florence happily keeping him away from school, propping him up in bed with pillows, extra blankets, hot water bottles, and an endless supply of boiled sweets, bottles of pop, and dishes of bread and milk with the bread always neatly cut into squares† and whatever he wanted to read.

With Florence's over-indulgence and D.J.'s stress on the power of language, Dylan was acquiring a strange attitude to life. Words meant everything. Literature was studied with joy, everything else neglected. When he failed exams, or just didn't bother to go to school, his parents seemed unconcerned, as though something was happening beyond their control. He first went to a privately run school in Mirador Crescent. The painter Mervyn Levy, who was there at the same time and became a lifelong

---

*Stories of Thomas's heavy drinking have to be treated with caution. He did drink far too much, but had such a low tolerance that he would often be drunk when friends were just getting started. From many discussions with his widow, children and family friends, I believe that Thomas may have suffered from some form of sugar-deficiency. He also had a craving for sweets. Thomas was possibly asthmatic. He wheezed and coughed, complained of pains, and smoked at least 40 cigarettes a day, usually Woodbines. When this worried an onlooker, he invariably said he would never reach 40 years, although this was largely an affectation.

†This craving for maternal affection lasted until the end of his life. Whenever he had a hangover, Caitlin would pack him off to bed and take him his bowl of milk with bread cut into squares.

friend, has told me that Florence would often keep Dylan at home for the flimsiest reasons, although he later had more serious mishaps, breaking his nose when he fell downstairs, and being kept in hospital for two operations after a bus ran over him when he was 12.* Dylan also had a bronchitic illness in his mid-teens which necessitated convalescence.

Each new drama enabled him to spend more and more time at home, avoiding most forms of exercise. The only sport he seemed to enjoy was running† although he later acquired an armchair passion for cricket. In his father's study, another world lay at his fingertips, for this was no ordinary library. D.J. was one of those natural scholars who had to understand the origin of words as well as their meaning, knowing that behind each work of literature lay formative influences. His library included encyclopaedias, sets of Shakespeare, Dickens, Trollope, Hardy, Meredith, Moore and the Brontë sisters, with a wide range of English, Welsh and some European literature from Chaucer to Henry James, its strongest emphasis being on nineteenth and twentieth century poets. Wordsworth, Tennyson, Keats, Byron and Shelley were all well represented, along with the Romantics and Georgians. In a letter to Pamela Hansford Johnson, Dylan wrote that his father had 'nearly everything that a respectable highbrow library should contain', whereas his own books included Gerard Manley Hopkins, Stephen Crane, Yeats, Walter de la Mare, Osbert Sitwell, Wilfred Owen, W.H. Auden, T.S. Eliot, Aldous Huxley, Edith Sitwell, D.H. Lawrence, Humbert Wolfe, Siegfried Sassoon, various anthologies, most of James Joyce, all Gilbert Murray's Greek translations, some Shaw, a little Virginia Woolf and some E.M. Forster. 'This is inadequate, really, but added to Dad's, it makes a really comprehensive selection of literature,' he wrote.[7]

Even that gives only a broad outline of the influences in the home, for one knows from other references in Thomas's letters, and the fact that the young Dylan was familiar with all the usual children's stories, Billy Bunter, *Just William*, children's comics and detective fiction, that this was a house with wide perceptions.

Within it, the mischievious little boy with angelic features was listening to

---

*This accident happened in June 1926 on the day of the Swansea Regatta. Thomas was on his way there, having borrowed a bicycle, and was knocked down by a bus at Derwen Fawr. The bus ran over him. A childhood friend, Armel Diverres, who walked to school with Thomas every morning, recalled that Florence was very upset, believing her son might die. Thereafter she became even more lax. *Dylan Thomas Remembered, idem.*

†Thomas won the school cross-country race at the age of 12. His photo appeared in the local paper. He carried that cutting with him in his wallet for the rest of his life, and it was found in his pocket when he died in New York.

poetry at the age of two, and reciting Shakespearean speeches by the time he was four. Florence would say, 'Oh, Daddy, don't read Shakespeare to a child only four years old' to which D.J. would reply, 'He'll understand it. It'll be just the same as if he were reading ordinary things.'[8] Attending school in Mirador Crescent, Dylan was proclaiming Shakespearean orations at the age of seven – and would then go running to his teacher, Mrs Hole, sitting on her lap for what seemed like hours on end, complaining that he had a pain in his tummy if there was anything he didn't want to do. 'He wasn't a normal child, if you know what I mean,' says Mervyn Levy 'There was something distinctly odd about his repertoire, for he could recite whole speeches from *Richard II*, which he had learned by heart, and yet he was still very dependent . . .'

Dylan duly turned into a sickly, introspective teenager, given to wandering alone along the shore of Swansea Bay, or over the Gower cliffs, learning to write at his father's suggestion, and rapidly acquiring a facility with words beyond his years. Long before entering Grammar School in September 1925, he was writing poems, and avoiding the more muscular games that boys of his age enjoyed. Sitting at his new classroom desk he was 'so quiet that one hardly noticed him'[9] and yet it is clear that he wanted recognition and was so keen to be a poet that he plagiarised other people's work and passed it off as his own. He stole one poem, *His Requiem*, from a magazine and sent it off to the Welsh daily paper, *The Western Mail*, under his own name[10] but there were others.[11] Latterly, it has been suggested that Thomas was a shameless literary thief, but this recollection in his short story *The Fight* hints otherwise:

A poem I had had printed in the 'Wales Day by Day' column of *The Western Mail* was pasted on the mirror to make me blush, but the shame of the poem had died. Across the poem I had written, with a stolen quill and in flourishes, 'Homer Nods'. I was always waiting for the opportunity to bring someone into my bedroom . . . But nobody ever came in, except my mother.[12]

From that self-revealing comment, one pictures a lonely child, anxious to see his name in print, desperate for some acknowledgement. Whereas other teenagers might have idolised sporting heroes, as today's collect posters of TV stars or rock musicians, the young Dylan surrounded himself with books and photographs of his favourite authors, which he pinned to his bedroom wall alongside pictures taken from the works of Shakespeare, a portrait of Walter de la Mare torn from his father's Christmas issue of *Bookman*, and other illustrations of Robert Browning, Rupert Brooke, Stacy Aumonier and Whittier.[13] He was becoming a strange young man to whom being a poet was every bit as important as writing poetry, isolating himself from the world around him, and yet watching it carefully, a spectator within his own home. Even in his late teens he was only 8st. 10lbs. in weight, and less than 5ft. 6in. tall, or so he said in a letter to Pamela Hansford Johnson. This may have been an exaggeration, for Caitlin tells me that he was extremely self-conscious about his height, wearing the thickest heels he could find to add an extra inch or two, which suggests that he may have been nearer 5ft. 2in. or 5ft. 3in., with effeminate mannerisms. He had read his Keats, Shelley and Byron, their lives as much as their works, and understood the social impact of Wilde, Beardsley and Baudelaire. He wore colourful shirts and floppy scarves, 'borrowed' from his sister, and carried a hat by a loop on his little finger, calling himself 'the Rimbaud of Cwmdonkin Drive', a phrase that told everyone what he thought of himself.

— 3 —
FRIENDS AND STRANGERS

YLAN Thomas made hardly any friends outside his home until he
had left school at 16 and joined the staff of the *South Wales Daily
Post*, as it was then called. (The newspaper's title was changed to
the *South Wales Evening Post* in March 1932.) His work as a junior reporter
seemed to give him confidence. Before he had been lonely and solitary,
leading an almost reclusive life, seldom encouraged to bring anyone back to
Cwmdonkin Drive. His parents had never truly settled in Swansea, joining
in none of the town's activities, and inviting few people into their home other
than those aunts, uncles and cousins whom Dylan was to immortalise in his
short stories and radio talks.

In this, as in so much else, the Thomases remained true to their traditional
values. When rural families moved away from home, they tended to stick
together, forming Carmarthenshire and Cardiganshire societies in the cities,
patronising each other's shops and businesses, like immigrants from a far-off
land, often returning 'home' to West Wales for holidays or to retire. This has
not changed. There is still a strong sense of kinship in West Wales, with tiny
villages welcoming 'family' back from many parts of the world. When work
is scarce, as it has been in recent years, men go off to work in the cities,
leaving their wives and children at home, returning to be back in the village
pub for Friday darts nights and out on the rugby field on Saturday
afternoon. This sense of family, of being *Welsh*, has survived all the
economic changes of the past hundred years, and is something easily
misunderstood by academics searching for deeper meanings.

Those last years of the 19th century, when D.J. was studying English
Literature at Aberystwyth, were a period when the population was
expanding fast, with men moving around the country to take up jobs in
the coalfields and steelworks that adjoined this rural landscape. Llanelli
and Port Talbot had their boom years while Swansea became a busy

international deep sea port shipping coal and coke, steel rails, ironwork, tinplate and cement, a town with an economic importance out of all proportion to its size. Swansea grew fast, spawning a professional class, and for the young Aberystwyth graduate a post at the town's main Grammar School was one of the best to be had. But it did not bring him contentment. Daniel Jones, who became one of Dylan's closer friends, said of D.J. Thomas

The cause of his discontent and self-pity was never put into words, but was explicit in other ways. He considered that his abilities earned him in justice at least an 'Oxbridge' chair rather than his 'humbler' position of schoolmaster. He despised his profession, regarded his charges as little animals, and looked down upon those who were more or less content to be schoolteachers and tried to be good at the job. He was therefore feared by the boys and shunned by his colleagues. The arrogance of the man needed no words to make itself felt, but occasionally it did find words. Often, after a long and thoughtful silence and a propos of nothing that had been said or done, he would announce to the class: 'I have forgotten more than all of you put together will ever know.'[1]

It clearly troubled Jones that he was rarely welcome at Cwmdonkin Drive, until one day his mother met Florence, who explained: 'Mr Thomas is very nervous, and has enough to do with boys during the day.' D.J. partly resolved his inner problems by separating the different levels of his life. The Grammar School was at one end of his spectrum; Cwmdonkin Drive at the other. The two worlds did not meet, and this habit of compartmentalising himself was something that Dylan also inherited, learning to shut himself away in his bedroom for hours on end, writing, smoking endlessly (another habit he shared with his father), cultivating separate and contrasting relationships with his parents. Another visitor to the house, Thomas Taig, noticed 'his deep respect for his father's intellectual standards and a profound emotional bond with his mother'.[2]

Always a keen walker, D.J. would stride from one world to another in just a few minutes, dressed in those formal clothes that he thought he should wear. His only friend among the other teachers was the classics master, 'Soapy' Davies. They used to drink at lunchtimes at The Mountain Dew,[3] sharing an enthusiasm for literature and beer. Some afternoons they would return to their classrooms flushed and excitable. On Wednesdays, which was half-day in this grammar school as in many others, these sessions were known to last longer, with D.J. rolling home a little the worse for wear.

When that happened, D.J., a short man with a large beer belly (which he lost in later life), would curse his wife, children and any women friends she happened to have in her kitchen, complaining about his fate, his lack of money, or whatever else might have temporarily touched his quick. These rows were always one-sided. Florence was not a natural fighter. Since D.J. recoiled from any physical expressions of love, never kissing or hugging his children, their relationship with him was restrained, whereas Florence was kind, loving, warmly smothering. Later still Florence loved to cuddle her grandchildren in her bed. Caitlin confirms that Dylan always saw this as the woman's role, however much he might pretend otherwise in a crowded bar. It was not sexual adventure that he was searching for in his adult life, but yet another warm bed in an otherwise cold and austere world. However, to earn his father's respect, Dylan had to be good at the one skill D.J. admired: a facility with words.

Only three of D.J. Thomas's letters survive,[4] but it is clear from the few remaining letters from Dylan to his parents and the intense emotion that underlies the poem written as D.J. came close to death, *Do Not Go Gentle Into That Good Night*, that an intellectual bond of rare intimacy developed between them. Daniel Jones noted that Dylan 'respected his father and was proud of him, and that any would-be detractor would be wise to remain silent about him in his presence'.[5] Fitzgibbon met them together only once, when D.J. was visiting London in 1945, and was 'struck then by how much Dylan was on his best behaviour with his father, how anxious that his friends too should make a good impression. And the pride that the old man took in his famous son was quietly apparent.'[6] Those filial letters show a man with a proper concern for his father's well-being, beyond the mere dutiful. Pamela Hansford Johnson, the only woman friend of Dylan's to be invited to stay at Cwmdonkin Drive, observed that D.J. was his 'best friend'.[7]

There came a point in Thomas's late teens when other relationships became important. These were mostly with men older than himself, and were essentially one-sided, usually beginning with the person showing respect for Dylan's writing. They would have to be good listeners with something useful to say. After the poet had gleaned all he could from the relationship, the friendship would taper off, but seldom end completely. By the time these relationships had entered their final phase, Thomas would have observed the other person's weaknesses with an acuteness that often proved embarrassing.

Mervyn Levy, born in the same year as Thomas, and a fellow-pupil at that school in Mirador Crescent, enjoyed the friendship of small boys which remained important to Thomas, who would become maudlin and sentimental in Levy's company in later years, remembering their games and pranks, telling endless stories about mice and cats like a child who had never totally grown up. Thomas's friendship with Daniel Jones came much later, with Thomas dating it around July 1928 in his short story, *The Fight*, in which he says that he was 14 years and nine months old when their relationship began with that famous bout of fisticuffs. Jones's own memoir, *My Friend Dylan Thomas*, is elusive on facts and dates, and my belief (having met Levy, Fred Janes and others of their circle and read Thomas's letters to them) is that Jones may never have been as influential as he thought he was.

For reasons already explained, Jones seldom visited Cwmdonkin Drive, but Thomas regularly walked to the Jones family home, a large, semi-detached house where Dan lived with his parents, brother Jim and a cousin of his mother's whom they called Aunt Alice. It was a happy home, 'unconventional and easy-going in the extreme, and unselfconsciously so', with much noise and laughter, word games and music. There they would experiment with sounds, constructing their own studio, linked up to a radio loud-speaker, reciting scripts and poems, on which they would sometimes co-operate, writing alternate lines under the pen-name Walter Bram, which Jones suggests was 'a name probably borrowed from Bram Stoker'.[8] The friendship continued, off and on, until Dylan's death. Jones had natural bombast, and an extraordinarily wide range of cultural interests. He claimed to have written seven historical novels before he was 12, and has since composed many symphonies. As with most relationships, Thomas was fairly dry-eyed about this one:

> He reads all the time, and is cleverer than ever. But his mind's in a mess, for he doesn't know any direction, he isn't sure either of music or writing, though he does both competently and often brilliantly.[9]

My suspicion is that Jones played a crucial role in Thomas's development, but of a different kind to the one he supposed. By the time they met, Dylan was writing vigorously, but his only real critic was his father and his only outlet, apart from that poem sent to the *Western Mail* and others offered to the *Boy's Own Paper* and *Everyman*, was in the *Swansea Grammar School Magazine*, which his father had established and oversaw.[10]

From the time he entered the school in September 1925 until he left nearly six years later, three months before his 17th birthday, having spent an extra year at school to make up for time lost through illness. Dylan was a frequent contributor to the school magazine and was latterly described as its editor. The magazine appeared three times a year and like most similar publications was mostly concerned with the day-to-day life of the school. Nevertheless, this tiny magazine gave Thomas the chance to parody other writers, publicise his appearances in school plays, print his own poems, or give vent to his views on the present state of literature[11] or cinema.[12] For a young poet of Thomas's striking self-confidence, this was whetting his appetite, which was where Dan Jones came in. Whatever his own abilities might be, Dan Jones

> listened wisely, like a boy aged a hundred, his head on one side and his spectacles shaking on his swollen nose . . . . Nobody had ever listened like that before.[13]

And so it was with most of Thomas's new friends, as he emerged from that Cwmdonkin chrysalis, his early poems neatly tucked away in his notebooks.[14] If you listened carefully, he enjoyed your company. Dylan Thomas was always selfish, but accompanied this trait with another rarely found in people of such egotism, and that was an easy-going charm. This would make those who barely knew him believe themselves intimate friends. As he travelled out into the world, this charm drew people to him, for he naturally responded to their affection, entertained them with an endless flow of funny stories, showing concern for their minor woes; always meeting them on their territory because he had none of his own to share. It was a virtuoso performance, as compelling in suburban Swansea as it was to prove later in the drinking dens of Soho and Fitzrovia – and totally deceiving, for Thomas ruthlessly discarded anything and anyone not essential to his purpose.

The deception lay in the fact that no one was ever told. People were just abandoned. Sometimes his selfishness was cruel. He could be punctilious in his work, yet neglectful in his personal life, for they were wholly separate. He never shared himself with anyone. Caitlin came to understand this, although she found it painful. His male friends never did, because once he was in a pub or a restaurant, surrounded by an audience, Thomas seemed to be the closest friend they had ever had.

After Dan Jones, there were many more. They all gave the poet something, but their intimacy continued only if *they* made the effort. Thomas never kept a diary and seldom much more than an appointments book (and only that towards the end of his life). He usually failed to keep the addresses and telephone numbers of his friends, and would read their letters cursorily, dropping them in the waste bin. However, if he did write to someone his letters would sparkle with charm because he knew what they wanted, and tailored each letter to the recipient's need, or his own perception of their character. This was skilful, for whenever he needed encouragement, help or money, Thomas would wheedle and twist in games of verbal ballet, knowing precisely the effect his words achieved.

Dan Jones would get soft, silly letters steaming in sentiment.[15] Vernon Watkins, the Swansea poet eight years his senior who lacked the self-confidence to give up his safe, steady job with Lloyds Bank and devote himself to literature, received strong reassuring letters that were kind and attentive and belied their author's true opinion of his work. Bert Trick, a Swansea grocer 15 years his senior who supplied Thomas with a stern vision of socialist ideals that had never been available in the family home, received long, detailed intellectual letters. Trevor Hughes and Glyn Jones, who both approached him with words of praise and were likewise older men, were suitably encouraged. Pamela Hansford Johnson found herself burdened with all the baggage that Dylan Thomas thought a highbrow bride should carry.

Thomas remembered his letters as though they were poems. He would refer to them subsequently, even though he kept no copies, and barely concealed his belief that his letters should be kept by their recipients. He knew what he meant when he wrote to Wynford Vaughan-Thomas for the first time, and advised him to 'treasure the paper'. It wasn't just a joke. And, yes, Wynford kept it! Years later, Thomas might write to someone again, picking up the threads as though no time had passed, which was part of his charm, but still a deception; he was changing when they were not, and always knew when he was leaving them behind.

These friendships mainly began in his mid-teens. After his extra year at the Grammar Schoool,[16] Thomas began appearing in amateur theatrical productions and also began working as a junior reporter for the *South Wales Daily Post*. His father found him the job and Dylan worked there for 18 months, from July 1931 until January 1933. Thomas recalled this period in his short story *Old Garbo*, but it is clear from the recollections of his editor, Mr J.D. Williams, that he was an unsatisfactory recruit. Williams also edited the Saturday newspaper *Herald of Wales*, and still enjoyed reviewing amateur plays. Shortly before he died, Williams reviewed Thomas's second book *Twenty-five Poems* for the *Herald of Wales*, recalling

I saw him first on the stage, a schoolboy playing in the annual drama show of the Grammar School, *Cromwell*, I think, in Drinkwater's pageant. It was obvious to the most dense person in the Llewelyn Hall that here was a clean-cut personality. He stood out shoulder high above the rest of the

33

cast: . . . . because of a certain distinction of voice and bearing . . . . he was a beginner in Swansea journalism, under strict injunctions to learn shorthand within a definite time. It was good discipline, I thought, as I saw him moving about amid the inquests, the police courts, the district council meetings; 'making the calls' at those places where newspapers gather their news. But Dylan Thomas never mastered shorthand – did he ever try! – and his career in the reporting room of the *Evening Post* was entertaining, but a sore trial to the chief reporter, who had to see that all the engagements on the 'Book' were covered[17] . . . .

Thomas's over-critical comments on local chapel concerts, and his opinions of other local poets, had to be trimmed down to avoid giving offence. To avoid being prosecuted for libel, the paper was forced to apologise after he had suggested in another review that the book *Laughing Torso* by Nina Hamnett had been banned, and Williams describes him as

an irreverent youth who, week after week, turned in articles in which all that one felt to be established in art was knocked roughly over. Once or twice I persuaded the young iconoclast to moderate a judgement here and there . . . there was also a short story which the poet submitted for publication in the *Herald of Wales*. All that I can recall about it now is that it was sited in a mining valley, and that it ended with a head in a gas stove. This never would have done for the *Herald*; laughingly we agreed that it would not . . . . Dylan Thomas's press career ended. His shorthand did not become efficient enough to help him at a mothers' meeting.

From this it would appear that Thomas was either sacked, or left 'by mutual agreement', returning to his bedroom at Cwmdonkin Drive, where thereafter he worked alone in his bedroom, writing short stories and poems, with just his bed and a well-worn chair, surrounded by books, papers, beer bottles and the stale smell of old cigarettes, developing a routine that continued for the rest of his life. He would stay in bed until late morning, potter about for an hour or two, read newspapers or light fiction, pop down to the pub at lunchtime, and then return to what he later called his 'work-sheets'. Each time he changed a word or a comma in a poem he would write it out again, with each poem thus passing through as many as a couple of hundred different versions before he finally settled on the one he preferred. After a poem had appeared in print, he would often change it again before it was published a second or third time. In his later years, he carefully kept these work-sheets, selling them to collectors for cash, but then would write a poem on innumerable sheets of scrap paper, write it on both sides of the paper, often upside down and criss cross ways, unpunctuated surrounded by drawings of lamp posts and boiled eggs, in a very dirty mess; bit by bit I copy out the slowly developing poem into an exercise book; and, when it is completed, I type it out. The scrap sheets I burn, for there are such a lot of them that they clutter up my room and get mixed in the beer and the butter.[18]

It was a lonely life, as a writer's often can be, broken only by rehearsals with the Swansea Little Theatre which met three miles down the coast in Mumbles, half-way between two favourite pubs, The Mermaid and The Antelope, or meeting friends that he had made while working as a reporter, either in the Kardomah coffee bar or in Ralph's Bookshop in Alexandra Road. By night, Thomas would go pubbing, but never had the money for serious drinking. His mother might slip him a pound, but there was only his father's salary coming into the house so, perforce, he wrote more then, than in any other subsequent period of his life.

Through Daniel Jones he became friendly with another musician, Tom Warner, and also the artist Fred Janes, who was to become especially close. Janes was, and is, a quiet but self-sufficient man who could be supportive without making demands. Janes and Thomas shared rooms in Redcliffe Street, Fulham, with Mervyn Levy when Thomas moved to London in 1934. At one stage, like his sister Nancy, Dylan had hopes of a career in theatre. He enjoyed performing and after making his first appearances with the school dramatic society[19] went on to join the local YMCA Players,[20] and then the Swansea Little Theatre, which Nancy had already joined. Its plays were mostly produced by Thomas Taig, who first met the 'podgy young reporter with prominent eyes and rather full lips'[21] when Thomas arrived at the theatre one night offering a play that he had written. Taig later recalled in an article for *The Anglo Welsh Review* (Summer 1968), that he

met Dylan many times: in Swansea, London and Laugharne; in rehearsal frequently and in convivial bar-parlours; at his various homes and when he came with Caitlin to visit at my place. Yet I hesitate to say that I knew him really well. I doubt whether anyone – with the possible exceptions of a few close companions – knew the real Dylan. I think of him as infinitely vulnerable, living from moment to moment in a heightened awareness of sense-impressions and emotional tensions, the victim rather than the master of his environment. One of my most vivid memories is of the day that war broke out, a Sunday morning when I drove over with Vernon

Watkins to visit the Thomas family in Laugharne. By the time we arrived the declaration of war had become known and we found Dylan distraught and for once almost speechless at the news. From the few ferocious comments that he let drop I sensed that he was suffering acutely, suffering in advance, I imagine, all the horrors of the coming slaughter. At any rate he was like a wounded animal caught in a trap and there was nothing one could do about it. When I hear anyone speak disparagingly of Dylan's excesses in his public character of the 'roaring boy' I feel like asking, 'How would you like to live with all your nerve-ends exposed?' As I see it, anyone so constituted, so sensitive to every pin-prick of human experience (as his poems show), must have been forced from earliest childhood to protect himself as best he could. Dylan's way was to adopt the character most suitable for the occasion – to play up instinctively. Impersonation was as natural to him as breathing. With me, for instance, he was always most co-operative – unassuming and almost punctiliously correct in his behaviour. This was not putting on an act in the usual sense. He was simply living directly the relationship between us – unlike Shelley, unlike Wordsworth, probably nearer to Blake – there was no gulf between inner and outer reality. The spirit was present in the flesh.

To call this behaviour acting in any strict sense is to confuse the values of both life and art. Although he enjoyed taking part in a play occasionally, he soon grew tired of stage make-believe and preferred to have his creations accepted not as true-to-life but as life itself. Had this been deliberately undertaken it might have bordered on deception; with him it was like a reflex action, which could make life complicated at times. I recall a scene in the long bar of The Fitzroy, Bloomsbury; I was talking to an academic friend at one end, some of Dylan's close contemporaries were in the middle, and at a table further off two or three showy young women with whom he was on bantering terms. The chameleon act which ensued as he circulated from one group to another was a sight never to be forgotten . . . There were times when he could appear to be ruthless and even callous, because he detested any trace of self-importance or hypocrisy in others and considered the lion-hunters fair game for the lion. But concealed behind the bravura of his public image was one of the rarest and least corruptible spirits . . . . My guess is that what we call life was for him a hectic dream in which he took an active part.

Few observed Thomas as perceptively as this, for his charm was such that most people believed they knew him by what they saw, which was usually just the face he happened to choose for performing in pubs or maintaining friendships with those who did not share his deep literary interests. This is what makes his letters so revealing. When his *Letters to Vernon Watkins* were published in 1957, friends who had known him on a lighter level were astonished to find that he and Vernon exchanged deeply personal letters discussing the use of words in all their intricacy. Caitlin has told me that when the two men met, they would disappear for hours on end, solemnly discussing language and the ways it could be employed. Others saw only what Thomas wanted them to see, as is clear from this delightful anecdote told by Wynford Vaughan-Thomas in a BBC radio talk,[22] in which he recalled them visiting the Swansea Empire after Dylan

had just become a reporter on the local newspaper at the age of sixteen, and was therefore our oracle on everything that concerned the gayer, more rakish side of life. 'Care to meet an actress tonight?' he said with studied unconcern. 'I've got the entree back-stage.' Dylan made it sound as if he was making me free of the whole romantic world of grease-paint, dazzling young stars, stage-door johnnies, and champagne suppers. We arrived breathless at the dressing-room. A voice as cracked as the pane on the door called out, 'Come in, dearie', and we found ourselves in the presence of none other than dear old Nellie Wallace – who could not, at that time, have been less than sixty-five. Dylan rose to the occasion.

'Miss Wallace', he said, 'we bring you the homage of the artists of the future for the artists of the past.'

'Variety or legit?' enquired Miss Wallace.

'Legit,' we replied. We didn't know what it meant but it sounded better.

'In that case, boys, you've got a hell of a road to travel! Have some gin?' Miss Wallace produced a bottle from behind a pile of cosmetics and poured out the first and the strongest gin that I'd tasted in my life. It exploded in Dylan and myself with devastating effect. 'Take it easy, boys. Take it easy,' Miss Wallace chuckled. 'All you want is a bit of practice. Here's one thing at any rate in which the artists of the past can wipe the floor with the artists of the future.' And she dealt with the rest of the gin in one quick gulp.

Then off she went on stage to prance out from the wings, with a feather waving from the grotesque pile of red hair and an impossible hunting costume, singing about a gallant young huntsman: 'I was after the fox, me boys – but *he* was after *me*.'

'This,' said Dylan, 'must never be told to the boys. We'll keep it for our memoirs.'

Thomas was clearly such fun in company like this, and so solemn within, that his friends, as well as his biographers, have found him hard to assess. Those who came closest to the real man have often been reluctant to talk at all, or are now dead. Many met Thomas on Wynford's level, but few on Taig's. One who did was Bert Trick, whom Thomas met at Taig's suggestion. Trick was a skilled engineer who had lost his job in the slump. He then opened a grocer's shop. He and Thomas met in 1931 when Thomas was planning to launch his own magazine, *Prose and Verse*, having mentioned this fact to the *South Wales Daily Post*, where it had been reported that the new publication would cost two shillings and that it was 'necessary to sell at least two hundred copies at this price in order to cover the initial expenses'.[23] Not one single issue was ever produced, but through this newspaper story Thomas became friendly with Trevor Hughes,[24] who offered him a short story, and Taig told him that Trick had written some poems. Trick later recalled:

He brought his poems, written in a number of school exercise books rolled into a cylinder and stuffed into his already over-stuffed coat pocket. He said that Mr Taig of the Mumbles Little Theatre had suggested this to him. As I did not know Mr Taig, except by name, I suspect that Dylan had tracked me down because of a number of bad poems which had been printed in the *Swansea Evening Post* at various times. I was captivated by him at our first meeting. His cathedral voice, his biting wit and his superb poetry gave me the conviction that here was a youthful genius. The next ten years of close association confirmed that impression. Dylan as a person was greater than the sum of his parts.

Some time after our friendship had begun we acquired the habit of meeting at his home in Cwmdonkin Drive every Wednesday evening and at my home on Sundays. He was then as angelic-looking as in the Augustus John portrait of him, or the portrait painted by his friend Fred Janes which hangs in the National Museum of Wales. He always carried a trilby hat, a size too large, hooked by the ribbon to his little finger. In all the years I knew him I never saw it on his head. It may have been carried to balance the Woodbine which was always stuck to his lower lip. The round, wondering eyes, the curls and the pouting lips were all belied when he grinned, for then he looked impish and positively satyr-like. His sense of fun was infectious and at any pomposity he directed a shaft of wit as devastating as a bomb. Cant, humbug or piousness were always targets for his mordant wit and his blunt use of Anglo Saxon on these occasions could cause the uninitiated to blush.[25]

With Hughes and Trick, Thomas developed more intellectual friendships. The three of them contributed letters and articles to the *Swansea and West Wales Guardian*, and although their plans for *Prose and Verse* came to nothing, with Hughes in Harrow and Thomas moving to London, they kept in touch, writing periodically. By his late teens, with these broader friendships, Thomas had the beginnings of a rounded self-confidence. He was starting to live by his wits and for his writing, and to place his work at the centre of his life. In later years he was to remember this period fondly, although it is most unlikely that he was, as he sometimes claimed, drunk four nights a week, because he did not have enough money – drinking on credit came later. Nevertheless, there were nights, especially after performances at the Swansea Little Theatre, when he would draw a crowd around him in The Antelope or The Mermaid, telling bawdy stories, obscene limericks and scatalogical shaggy dog stories, which brought him his 'roaring boy' reputation. It was on one of these nights that he crawled into the bar of The Mermaid on his hands and knees, barking like a dog, and biting any ankle in reach – a party trick that was much misunderstood in later years when he tried it out at more solemn American literary parties.

In a sense, he was lucky. D.J. had wanted him to go to Oxford University, for the schoolmaster believed that was the path to literary success. Had Thomas done so, his rawness might have lost its edge. Instead, here he was, fussed and mollycoddled at home, indulged in all his whims; quietly intense with some friends and boisterous with others; wild, cheerful and apparently undisciplined, to those who did not know how seriously he spent his days. For those who knew him then, this was the formative period of his life. For many years thereafter, and especially when talking to biographers, they would recall those happy evenings spent together, his stage appearances and early poems, as though this was a golden age, which for them it was. They were unaware that Dylan was outgrowing Swansea with each visit to London, his acceptance by writers there and the very nature of his skill. He never lost touch completely, however, although he might describe Swansea as 'a dingy hell'[26] or refer to its 'North London stuffiness',[27] advising Pamela Hansford Johnson only to go there in summer because of its 'shabby, badly built streets' and the 'unutterable melancholy blowing along the tramlines'.

— 4 —
A SHARED INHERITANCE

A young provincial poet anxious to make his name quickly had limited outlets in the early Thirties, especially one living far from London who had missed out on all the opportunities that came from a university education. Radio was still a fairly new phenomenon. Television had only recently been invented. The press were largely interested in established authors. Literary magazines were dominated by a coterie of left-wing writers who had all been at Oxford together and spent much of their time acclaiming one another.

As a young man, just turning 20, Dylan Thomas broke through these barriers, and did so still living mainly in Swansea, tucked away in his bedroom, with his bottled beer and Woodbines, apparently under no great pressure 'to get a proper job' (although his parents were anxious about his drinking). His father continued to influence him in many ways, in what he read and how he wrote, although even then Dylan had decided that he wanted his poems to be heard rather than read; he was already writing with their sound in mind as much as their verbal content, and made this clear the first time he met Bert Trick. Twenty years later Trick recalled

I invited him into my sitting room and we sat and discussed all sorts of things, sizing each other up, and after an hour or so, I asked, 'Would you like now that I read your poems?' And he said, 'Oh, no, poems shouldn't be read; they should be spoken.' Whereupon, he pulled a rolled-up blue school exercise book out of his pocket, sat back in the easy chair, with his leg over one arm, and in an arresting voice started to read some of his early poems. I was astonished. It was clear that here was a poet singing in a new voice.[1]

Trick was so impressed that he went and fetched his wife, Nell, telling her,

'I've found a genius. You must come and hear this.'

Later still, when he married, Thomas would wander into the kitchen while Caitlin was washing, ironing or cooking and say, 'What do you think of this?' as he tried out the lines of a new poem, or even just a phrase, always asking her to listen rather than read. It seems more than probable that his parents were equally accommodating during his formative years, with his mother more influential than has been generally supposed (so Caitlin and Aeronwy tell me), and his father, as ever, willing to help him with the technical tricks that Dylan employed with his use of rhyme, metre and assonance. This filial relationship was hardly ever discussed outside the home, but my understanding is that Dylan continued to consult his father – checking the source of phrases, classical quotations, the use of words and other poets' work – right until the end of the elder man's life; this was observed and overheard when they were back together again in Laugharne, just a few minutes apart.

With backing like this, Dylan eyed those barriers with wary disdain. Fashions seldom bothered him, although he would curse the Audens, Spenders and Eliots, convinced that literary London was one big 'racket' (a word that occurs frequently in his letters). His confidence was remarkable, for he felt far more at home with Donne, Milton or Dryden than the latest slim volumes of self-conscious verse from this slightly older generation who had all been born just a few years before the First World War and so came together at Oxford in an age of freedom and frivolity that was a world away from Swansea's suburbs. Thomas read them all, but they passed him by. He had his own sense of purpose and a belief, owed to his father, that there was a private side to life, an inner world that the outer man could use, shape and occupy. These were ideas that he would share with his more intellectual friends, while still playing bar-room buffoon with others. To Trevor Hughes, he wrote:

You must *live* in the outer world, suffer in it & with it, enjoy its changes, despair at them, carry on ordinarily with moneymaking routines, fall in love, mate and die. You *have* to do that. Where the true artist differs from his fellow is that *that* for him is not the only world. He has the inner splendour ... You may think this philosophy – only, in fact, a very slight adaptation of the Roman Catholic religion – strange for me to believe in. I have always believed in it .... Perhaps the greatest works of art are those that reconcile, perfectly, inner & outer.[2]

Thomas was only 18 years old when he wrote that letter. None of his poems had been published in any important literary magazines, but he was writing constantly, devoting himself solely to poetry and entering at least 212 poems in those surviving notebooks, between April 1930 and April 1934 (which may be less than half his actual output since six other notebooks were lost). He was posting them off here, there and everywhere, in the hope of finding a kindly editor. Rejection slips arrived regularly in the morning post, but this did not discourage him unduly; no doubt his father told him that would-be professional writers had to take such setbacks in their stride. This was another facet of his private education in Cwmdonkin Drive, for D.J. subscribed to the leading literary magazines of the day and would have known of the difficulties writers had overcome; it was all part of the romance of being 'a man of letters'.

The first national magazine to publish Dylan's work was *The New English Weekly*, now long-forgotten, which claimed then to be 'A Review of Public Affairs, Literature and the Arts'. It was edited by A.R. Orage. The issue dated 18 May 1933, featured an early version of Thomas's famous poem, *And death shall have no dominion*. Proud though he may have been to see his work in print, Thomas complained that Orage

> though a very pleasant and very sincere man, is known to be almost entirely lacking in taste . . . He doesn't pay *at all*, and the standard he sets is so low that it's hardly flattering to be accepted by him.[3]

Much more exciting for Thomas, and no doubt for his father, was the acceptance of his work by Richard Rees, editor of *Adelphi*, and by Victor Neuburg who edited a 'Poet's Corner' in the London paper *The Sunday Referee*.

Adelphi was a pocket-size monthly literary magazine that had latterly embraced socialism. It had been established by John Middleton Murry, who was still associated with the magazine. This would have impressed D.J. for Murry and his wife, the short story writer Katherine Mansfield, had befriended D.H. Lawrence during his period of social ostracism, and D.J. had been an early Lawrence follower. Murry still wrote for *Adelphi* occasionally, and its other contributors included T.S. Eliot, Lawrence, Mansfield, A.E. Coppard, M.L. Skinner, George Santayana, Leo Tolstoy, H.M. Tomlinson and, among the younger writers, John Lehmann, James Thurber, Herbert Read and Rayner Heppenstall. In its September 1933 issue, Rees published the Thomas poem *No man believes who, when a star falls shot*, and asked him to send in some more. That same month *The Sunday Referee* published its first Thomas poem, *That Sanity Be Kept*, prompting Pamela Hansford Johnson to send him some of her poems, thus beginning a pen-friend correspondence that nearly ended in marriage.*

Initially, Thomas wrote rather formally, once or twice a week, talking about himself and his ambitions, clearly pleased to communicate with someone outside his Swansea circle. He led her to believe that they were the same age (which wasn't true; Dylan was two years younger), gradually wrote more intimately, until, as she said,[4] they were 'fully prepared to fall in love' before they had even met.

Pamela had left Clapham County Secondary School at 17 to work as a secretary in the London branch of an American bank. Her father died when she was eleven, leaving his family penniless. She and her mother lived in a large red-brick house in Battersea Rise that had been bought by her grandfather in the 1880s. That was where she first met Dylan in February 1934, having invited him to stay for a few days:

He arrived at the door, palpably nervous. After a brief exchange of courtesies, his first words to me were, 'Have you seen the Gauguins?' There was a Gauguin exhibition in London at the time. He afterwards told me that he had been rehearsing this query, which seemed an appropriate form of opening an exchange between artist and artist, all the way in the train from Swansea.

He was smallish and looked smaller than he was because his clothes were too big. A huge sweater exaggerated a boyish frame. His trousers were baggy (though a maudlin Welsh friend who saw them hanging on a clothes-line was once heard to drool – 'such *little* trousers!') He wore a pork-pie hat, revealing as he took it off, the most beautiful curling hair, parted in the middle, the colour in those days – when he washed it – of dark gold. But in the curiously-shaped face, wide and strong at the top, tapering to weakness at the mouth and chin, there were those marvellous eyes, dark brown, luminous, almost hypnotic.

Then, there was the magnificent organ voice. At that time, it had lost all the Welsh lilt; Dylan, like his father, spoke standard English. He was to recover the lilt later on, when it came in useful.

My mother was as enraptured when she met him as I was, and spoiled

*This correspondence has yet to be fully annotated. Her letters to him appear not to have survived, whereas many of his are included by Ferris in *Collected Letters*. These letters total over 60,000 words and are crucial in understanding the image that Thomas was trying to project to the world. They were mostly written from Cwmdonkin Drive or when he was staying at Llangain. However, it is a one-sided correspondence. Ferris suggests that 70 of his letters may have been lost – and, needless to say, Thomas did not keep hers!

him as though he had been a child. He didn't in the least appear to mind this; even, he welcomed it. He would offer no resistance when, going off to meet friends, she suggested that he might wash his neck.[5]

They sat up late into the night, discussing art, music and literature, with Pamela soon realising that 'he was inclined to stupendous bluffing . . . but he could hold forth, in that resounding voice, upon all these things, and he did.' They also played gramophone records and drank the beer that Dylan brought in from the local off-licence, although she stresses that he was not then, nor for some time afterwards, a habitual drinker, though this was what he pretended, since

> Drinking was, for him, one of the great necessities of the poet's image: he fantasticated his drinking. Later, tragically, the fantasy became the reality. The other two necessities were to become tubercular and – extremely oddly – to get fat.[6]

Later that year, Thomas returned to Battersea Rise and stayed six weeks with the Johnsons, calling on editors, trying to sell his work:

> We were deliriously happy. We talked of marriage, certainly we would marry some day, when Dylan had a job. He talked of becoming a bicycle salesman, doing his rounds in yellow rubber hood, cape and boots. 'When bicycles hang by the wall,' he would sing blithely.[7]

Some days they would cross the river to Chelsea, drinking in the garden of the Six Bells, or wander across Clapham Common, talking poetry, but Pamela was already noticing that

> Dylan did introduce me to one or two of his older Welsh friends; but to no-one else. He believed in keeping his friends in compartments, and the friends of his boyhood didn't like it. If we came out together into the King's Road, and he spotted a poet whose acquaintance he had recently made, he would leave me, cross the road for a conversation and join me later. It was a wounding habit.[8]

When he returned to Swansea, already finding that he could write better away from London, their letters would resume, but she sensed the less attractive sides to his character, which revealed themselves in one way the day that she and her mother were due to go down to Swansea to meet his parents for the first time, at their invitation. Dylan was against it – so he happily put them on the train to Torquay, 'where we remained until my mother realised this, and we raced to catch the Swansea one. I think he knew it was the wrong train in the first place, and was prepared to go to Torbay or anywhere, so long as it wasn't home.' Pamela realised that Dylan was 'thoughtless and unreliable', even though she says that he 'did have the wish to please'. She avoids mentioning the famous letter[9] in which Thomas claimed to have slept with another girl, and instead suggests that when visiting the flat that he was sharing with Fred Janes and Mervyn Levy:

at once I knew that I was not wanted. I was no longer of their kind. That I had written a successful book made it, for Dylan, worse: like Scott Fitzgerald, I don't think he wanted another writer in the family. I went away stunned with misery.[10]

Although often tedious, Thomas's letters to Pamela Hansford Johnson are important for they reveal how he was thinking, dividing his life between Swansea and London, trying so hard to find acceptance, meeting as many other writers as he could (particularly on the left), and coping with editors' reactions to his poems. From one letter, we learn that Richard Rees caused him some disquiet by commenting that his latest parcel had 'an insubstantiality, a dreamlike quality' which nonplussed him – with Rees going on to remark that they reminded him of automatic or trance-writing. One can just imagine the young poet sitting in his bedroom, reading Rees' letter over and over again, for he declares

Automatic writing is worthless as literature, however interesting it may be to the psychologist & pathologist. So, perhaps, after all I am nothing but a literary oddity, a little freak of nature whose madness runs into print rather than into ravings and illusions. It may be, too, an illusion that keeps me writing, the illusion of myself as some misunderstood poet of talent.[11]

Adelphi published another of his poems *The Woman Speaks* (March 1934), and then Rees invited him to become an occasional reviewer, which required other skills in which he proved surprisingly adept. Thomas reviewed the work of three poets in the September 1934 issue – *The Solitary Way*,

William Soutar; *Squared Circle*, William Montgomerie and *Thirty Pieces* by Sydney Salt – noting that Soutar

is too content to *incline* towards words and not to work *out* of them. But he is an authentic poet. His verse is dictated by his ear as well as by his creative intelligence . . . *The Death of the Ear* would be an apt subtitle for a book on the plight of modern poetry . . . most of the work of Mr Pound, much of Mr Auden and Mr Day Lewis, and the entire output of Mr Pound's disciples, Mr Ronald Bottrall, Mr Carlos Williams, etc., does sound abominable. It would be possible to explain this lack of aural value and this debasing of an art that is primarily dependent on the musical mingling of vowels and consonants by talking of the effects of a noisy, mechanical civilisation on the delicate mechanism of the human ear. But the reason is deeper than that. Too much poetry to-day is flat on the page, a black and white thing of words created by intelligences that no longer think it necessary for a poem to be read and understood by anything but eyes.

Thus, in reviewing the work of others, he became revealing about his own. Thomas always believed that the best poems grew when read aloud, acquiring extra shape and substance. Caitlin says that throughout their years together he always muttered, boomed, rattled and ranted, composing each phrase audibly (which was he always found somewhere else to work wherever they lived, once there were children in the house).

As Thomas started contributing to more and more magazines, he began making the most of each breakthrough, travelling to London whenever he could, first staying with his sister Nancy (now married and living on a houseboat at Chertsey), and then later with Trevor Hughes and Dan Jones (who had both moved to Harrow), the Johnsons, and, as time went by, anyone who would offer him a bed for the night. Briefly, he shared different flats in the Fulham/Earls Court area with Fred Janes and Mervyn Levy, but often vanished for several days at a time without either of them knowing where he had gone.[12] Levy has told me that they had great difficulty getting him to pay his share of the rent, and would do so by grabbing him, and then holding him upside down until the coins fell out of his pockets.

On the surface his life seemed chaotic. Thomas did little to allay that impression, although he was far more professional than has been generally supposed. An editor who accepted his work could be sure of receiving more poems or (later) short stories. Rejected work was quickly recycled. Editors who showed enthusiasm received a personal visit. Anyone who wrote acclaiming his work could be certain of a reply. And, as his circle of acquaintances grew, Thomas made the most of that, too, meeting them all on their own territory, at their offices, in their homes or in the pubs they used, keeping his own private inner world more secluded than ever, because this was always rooted far from London.

As a self-publicist, Thomas was indefatigible, keeping in touch with Swansea journalists whenever he returned from London with news of some achievement, receiving regular mentions in the *South Wales Evening Post*, and *Herald of Wales*, the *Swansea and West Wales Guardian*, a local left-wing paper to which he contributed letters, essays and occasional book reviews, and the *Western Express*. Bert Trick wrote regularly for the latter two weeklies, and he and Trevor Hughes could be relied upon to mention Thomas's work.*

Among the London magazines that published his poems and short stories were *The New English Weekly* (two short stories and one poem in 1934), *New Stories* (the short story *The Enemies*, June–July 1934), and *The Bookman* (book reviews in the November and Christmas issues, 1934). His work also appeared in *Scottish Bookman* (October 1935), the Oxford review *Programme* (23 October 1935), the magazines *Comment, Janus, Caravel* (published in Majorca), *Transition* (edited in Paris), *Purpose* and *Contemporary Poetry and Prose*, literary magazines that have long since vanished.

It was an impressive debut, made all the more spectacular by the acclaim for his first book *18 Poems*, which brought him the kind of reviews that young, unknown poets dreamed of mistily. The book was a long time coming. Seven of Thomas's poems had been published in *The Sunday Referee* during 1933 and 1934, and he clearly sent in others. These impressed Victor Neuburg, who ran 'Poet's Corner' with the assistance of Runia Sheila Macleod.[13] Initially, Thomas listened carefully to Neuburg, taking advice, even occasionally re-working a poem, but he later became dismissive of Neuburg's judgement.

His first poem to be published in *The Sunday Referee* was *That Sanity Be Kept* (3 September 1933). A fortnight later it was announced that Thomas had received a prize for a poem that was not printed, and the following month that 'good poems' had been received from Bert Trick, Dylan Thomas and Pamela Hansford Johnson (8 October). One of his finest early poems, *The force that through the green fuse drives the flower*, was published next (29 October), and the following month it was announced that Dylan Thomas had been awarded another prize (19 November). Further poems were mentioned in December, January, February and March and in April,

---

*This is all detailed in the Maud bibliography, with Rolph useful for further analysis.

Neuburg reported that Dylan Thomas would become their second poet to have his work published in book form (22 April 1934).*

Neuburg had difficulty finding a publisher who would share the financial risk involved in printing and binding a volume of verse by an unknown author. During the months that followed, it was reported that publication had been delayed. At one stage, Thomas asked them to send his poems back and T.S. Eliot came close to publishing them instead. This hiatus was resolved when David Archer of the Parton Bookshop agreed to co-publish the book, contributing £20 towards the initial costs with another £30 being allocated by Mark Goulden and *The Sunday Referee*.

Archer was a famous Soho eccentric who managed to dissipate a substantial inheritance, running an uneconomic bookshop, and providing a safe haven for the writers of the day. According to Dan Farson,[14] Archer held a party to celebrate the publication of *18 Poems*, which was launched initially with an issue of 250 copies, selling at 3s. 6d. each. The following day he met Dylan Thomas in the street and asked if he had enjoyed the party.

'I hear it was a very good party,' replied Thomas, 'but you forgot to invite me.'

'Oh, silly me,' said Archer.

Publication date was set for 18 December 1934, and Thomas returned home in time for Christmas in Cwmdonkin Drive, with a bundle of presentation copies for his friends.[15] The reviews started appearing, and it was then that Dylan Thomas was acknowledged as an important poet of surprising authority:

I recognise in Dylan Thomas a poet so free from embarrassment, sore throat, sulks and stutters, that I must formally declare his *18 Poems* the most hopeful thing in English poetry since Robert Graves's last volume . .
. . Dylan Thomas is both new and good (or will be, if, etc). In the first place, his use of language is Shakespearean, which nobody's has been since Milton, except Keats, Hopkins (v. Dr Leavis) and, more recently,

---

*Pamela Hansford Johnson was the first to have her poetry published in book form through the sponsorship of *The Sunday Referee*. This was the volume *Symphony for Full Orchestra* (1934). At first the staff of *The Sunday Referee* were deeply suspicious of the unknown Welsh poet. Before being told that his poems would be published in book form, Thomas was invited to London to meet the editor Mark Goulden, the literary editor Hayter Preston and Neuburg, and only then did they accept that they were not the victims of a literary hoax (Fitzgibbon, pp. 115–16). Thomas left no personal account of this incident, which may explain his reluctance ever to discuss his father's influence.

Graves . . . the same verbal exuberance, rich precision, rollick, refusal to apologise for what he is saying. And it all fits that grand organ, the human throat, like a Handel aria.

Rayner Heppenstall,
Adelphi, February 1935

A verse-critic may review 500 books in a decade. He will be fortunate if, in the same period, he discovers ten considerable poets . . . Mr Auden is already a landmark. His own poetry stands clear above fashion. But the Audenesque convention is nearly ended; and I credit Dylan Thomas with being the first considerable poet to break through fashionable limitation and speak an unborrowed language, without excluding anything that has preceded him . . . For a first book this is remarkably mature. Thomas's poetry is personal or universal, but not social . . . This is not merely a book of unusual promise: it is more probably the sort of bomb that bursts not more than once in three years.

Desmond Hawkins,
Time and Tide, 9 February 1935

Mr Thomas uses a complex and exotic vocabulary for the direct communication of simple, uncomplicated modes of feeling. So that where he is 'difficult' it is a purely verbal difficulty – a matter of finding any precise interpretation for the favourite images, the high-keyed epithets which characterise his verse. Indeed, Mr Thomas's danger, or so it seems to me, is that he is interested in the sound-pattern of words to the exclusion of other, and equally important values. Thus, for all its sonorousness, his poetry is always a little overloaded, a shade bombastic. This is generally an early fault, and easy to cure . . . Mr Thomas must cultivate a tougher, sparer use of language, must make himself more of an ascetic in words.

I.M. Parsons,
The Spectator, 26 April 1935

Other reviews appeared in *The Listener* (27 February 1935), *New Verse* (February 1935), *Criterion* (April 1935) and *The Times Literary Supplement* (14 March 1935). In the *European Quarterly* (February 1935) an anonymous reviewer, possibly the poet Edwin Muir, said this was

One of the most remarkable books of poetry which have appeared for several years.

For other young poets of Wales, of whom there were many, this was an exciting break-through, with Bert Trick stimulating a lively correspondence in the *South Wales Evening Post*, posing the question, 'Are these cultural circles so moribund that they cannot see a new star in the literary firmament?' (5 January 1935). He and Trevor Hughes started off another exchange in the *Swansea and West Wales Guardian* (beginning 8 February).

Glyn Jones had already written to Thomas, having seen his work in *Adelphi*. They had become good friends, finding that their family backgrounds ran in parallel, with their ancestors worshipping in neighbouring chapels. Now, with the publication of *18 Poems*, another aspiring Anglo Welsh poet arrived on his doorstep, Vernon Watkins, also an older man, working as a clerk for Lloyds Bank in Swansea although he, too, longed to break away and become a literary man.

Jones began writing as a young teacher. He was born at Merthyr Tydfil, although his grandfather came from Llanstephan. He and Thomas visited Laugharne at Whitsun, 1934, and at Thomas's suggestion Jones turned to short stories. His first book *The Blue Bed* was published in 1937, and has become one of Wales' best-known English language writers. His biographical essays *The Dragon Has Two Tongues* (1968) includes a section on Dylan Thomas. Born in Maesteg, Watkins also had Nonconformist roots in Carmarthenshire. Like Thomas, his parents were Welsh speaking. Educated at an English public school and Cambridge, Watkins was deeply religious. He and Thomas became particularly close, exchanging poems, discussing the finer points of grammar and language. Watkins' letters to Thomas did not survive, though he kept his *Letters to Vernon Watkins* (1957).

Through Jones and Watkins, Thomas became more aware of the Anglo Welsh writers, who mostly shared this same Nonconformist, rural West Wales background. They had much else in common – often Welsh-speaking parents, a childhood spent attending chapel and eisteddfodau, and a sympathy for the older values, even though they were writing mainly in English. There were many of them, notably Alun Lewis, one of the better poets of the Second World War; Brenda Chamberlain, who worked with Lewis and the artist John Petts in producing the Caseg broadsheets early in the War (which included Thomas's *After the Funeral*) and is remembered particularly for her poems *The Green Heart* and the autobiographical *Tide Race*; Huw Menai, a miner who produced nature poetry in the tradition of Wordsworth or Edward Thomas, and most particularly Idris Davies and R.S. Thomas.

Born in Rhymney and also the son of a miner, from a similar Noncomformist background, Idris Davies published four volumes of poetry during his lifetime – *Gwalia Deserta* (1938), *The Angry Summer* (1943), *Tonypandy* (1945) and *Selected Poems* (1953). Davies was a socialist poet with a true concern for the poor and genuine bite. His work was patchy, but the best stands up well and he was highly praised by T.S. Eliot. Davies and Thomas became personal friends, and when Thomas heard that Davies was dying of cancer he wrote, 'he's a fine chap and a real poet, God bless him.'

Nowadays, it is R.S. Thomas who is regarded as the leading poet of that generation. A Welsh clergyman until his retirement, R.S. Thomas has become a symbol of Welsh nationalism but his early poetry was written in English and he is at his best in his own dry environment, away from the banners and passions of Plaid Cymru.

The person who brought them all together in the Thirties and Forties, with some of the coherence of a genuine literary movement, was Keidrych Rhys, who founded the Druid Press in Carmarthen and launched the literary magazine *Wales* to which they all contributed. Rhys and his wife Lynette Roberts lived just across the river from Laugharne in Llanstephan and when they married in October, 1939, Dylan Thomas was Best Man, wearing a suit borrowed from Vernon Watkins. Lynette Roberts was also taken up by T.S. Eliot, with Faber publishing her *Poems* (1944) and *Gods with Stainless Ears* (1951). She maintained a lively correspondence with Robert Graves and helped him complete *The White Goddess*, but it was Keidrych Rhys who proved the moving force. He was a gifted editor, although he only produced one volume of poetry himself *The Van Pool* (1942). *Wales* achieved high standards, arguably better than those of *any* English literary magazine of the period, also publishing reviews, poems and short stories by writers such as Graves, John Cowper Powys, George Ewart Evans, D.S. Savage, Rhys Davies, Hugh MacDiarmid, Caradoc Evans, George Barker and Margiad Evans, although it was always produced on a shoestring and periodically ceased publication until a new source of finance could be found.

As the movement gathered strength and a sense of identity, its supporters began to claim that anyone with a Welsh connection – from the metaphysical poets of the seventeenth century to John Dyer, Edward Thomas, W.H. Davies, Rhys Davies, Jack Jones, Emlyn Williams and Richard Llewellyn – were all part of some continuing Anglo-Welsh tradition. Inevitably, the movement broadened out and weakened until there are now well over a hundred 'Anglo-Welsh Writers' with their own clubs, societies, magazines and writing schools, heavily dependent upon the Literature section of the Welsh Arts Council for grants, but this is not how it was 50 years ago when Dylan Thomas made that startling impact upon the *English* writing Establishment.

Until then the core of creative Anglo-Welsh writers, with their common background in rural West Wales, the language and literature of that area and its traditions of liberalism and nonconformity, had few outlets of their own. Some were published in the *Dublin Magazine*, notably R.S. Thomas (the English tend to forget that West Wales is closer to Ireland than it is to London and shares many common attitudes), and then, later, in the same London literary monthlies that had been featuring Thomas's poems and short stories. Soon afterwards, they launched another magazine, *The Welsh Review* (edited by Gwyn Jones), and with so much attention being given to the Writers of Wales began to dominate the Welsh BBC (one could write an interesting thesis on, *Which came first: Anglo-Welsh writing or the BBC?* for it is a classic chicken-and-egg story, with BBC Wales *now* one of the creative centres of Welsh life).

All this meant that Thomas was in the vanguard of a new literary movement that had real roots as strong as his own, and yet he, more than any of his contemporaries, built upon this foundation, making his background, its landscape and values, the cornerstone of his work.

By now his routine was firmly established. Most of each Swansea day was devoted to writing. He had acquired the habit of never settling down until the early afternoon. His evenings would be spent either talking left-wing politics and literature with friends like Bert Trick, Thomas Taig and Trevor Hughes, playing lighter games with Dan Jones, rehearsing with the Little Theatre, or drifting around the pubs, enjoying the conversation of older men. He described this pattern in another letter to Pamela Hansford Johnson:

(after rising late) . . . downstairs where, after another cigarette, I seat myself in front of the fire and commence to read, to read anything that is near, poetry or prose, translations out of the Greek or the *Film Pictorial*, a new novel from Smith's, a new book of criticism, or an old favourite like Grimm or George Herbert, anything in the world so long as it is printed. I read on until twelve or thereabouts, when perhaps I have read quarter of a novel, a couple of poems, a short story, an article on the keeping of bees in Upper Silesia, and a review by somebody I have never heard of on a play I never want to see. Then down the hill into the Uplands – a lowland collection of crossroads and shops, for one (or perhaps two) pints of beer in the Uplands Hotel. Then home for lunch. After lunch, I retire again to the fire where perhaps I shall read all the afternoon – and read a great deal of everything, or continue on a poem or short story I have left unfinished, or to start another or to start drafting another, or to add a note to a letter to you, or to type something already completed, or merely to write – to write anything, just to let the words and ideas, the half remembered, half forgotten images, tumble on the sheets of paper.[16]

It was becoming a far stricter regime than his light-hearted description suggests; Thomas was experimenting with conventional forms of poetry, occasionally trying free verse, but preferring the tougher requirements of metre and rhyme, which impose their own discipline. It was, he concluded, 'not a very British day. Too much thinkin', too much talkin', too much alcohol . . .'

His association with *Adelphi* was among the more important phases of Thomas's transition, bringing him to the attention of other writers. Richard Rees handed some of his work to Herbert Read, who in turn passed it on to T.S. Eliot, editor of *The Criterion*. Thomas's poem *From love's first fever* appeared in the October 1934 issue of *The Criterion*, followed by his short stories *The Visitors* (January 1935) and *The Orchards* (July 1936). Likewise, publication of his poem *Light breaks where no sun shines* in *The Listener* (14 March 1934) – which set off an angry correspondence, with readers accusing the poet of obscenity for using the phrase 'A candle in the thighs' – brought him to the attention of Stephen Spender and Geoffrey Grigson, editor of *New Verse*, another tiny monthly magazine that was to publish more of his poems. Grigson chose *Our eunuch dreams* (April 1934), *When once the twilight locks no longer* and *I see the boys of summer in their ruin* (June 1934) and *If I was tickled by the rub of love* (August 1934), also inviting Thomas to respond to a questionnaire (October 1934).

Whenever he had the opportunity, Thomas would meet editors like Eliot and Grigson, always trying to impress, anxious that they might publish more of his work. Sometimes his pushiness failed him. They seemed condescending, all too aware of his lack of a university education. Pamela Hansford Johnson would

never forget the day on which he first met T.S. Eliot. He didn't come back, and he didn't come back: it was late when he did. He was sober, but glowering, and for a long while would not speak. When he did, it was to say with awful bitterness – 'He treated me – he treated me – as if I were "from pit-boy to poet".'[17]

Such reactions may have been caused by shyness, for he combined confidence in his work, a belief that it should be more widely available and his occasional bombast with an awkward diffidence when coming face-to-face with better-known writers. This was observed by Grigson and also by Lawrence Durrell at a time when Thomas was making friends among other poets like Norman Cameron, Bernard Spencer, Louis MacNeice and Ruthven Todd. Grigson recalled:

Modernism's high command, whether it might be Wyndham Lewis hidden in Notting Hill Gate or T.S. Eliot cocooned in his publishing office in Russell Square, was not impressed; Eliot at least was offered and considered – and then refused – a collection of his poems . . . we caused less trepidation, kept him less on edge. Our appreciation, our laziness or easygoingness, our scepticism, were less forbidding. He could enjoy with us verbal jokes and myths and inventions which committed him to no decision, no ideal of mental or spiritual conduct. He could trust himself to clown, to swear, to talk of women, or sex; he could borrow our beds, our underclothes and our cash, be washed, be on occasion mended and dry-cleaned by our wives . . . . here was Dirty Dylan . . . Generally, he was the Toughish Boy elsewhere; he reappeared from zanies, from sluts (often combined), from drunkenness, he needed washing, so did his shirts, he needed a little regularity, a little sobriety; and accepted them all, for short whiles. In fears of disease, he had to be taken to doctors. I found him one day in the bath in my flat in Keats Grove pitying himself and mocking himself in verbal antics because a pink rash beautifully enflamed his back and front . . . the doctor assured him he had no need to worry.
I agree to Dylan's companionableness, to his clowning, fooling, mocking talent, to, best of all, a certain primal quality, rooted far behind our backs in suburban Swansea, in chock-a-block Welsh cemeteries, in the hilly viridian farms between Laugharne and Llanstephan or in the Gower; but he was also the snotty troll, *to himself enough*, when it suited him; he was also the changeling, who had been lifted from under the foxgloves and set in the proper and decent Calvinistic bed. He was also cartilaginous, out of humanity, the Disembodied Gland, which was my coinage; Ditch, which was Norman Cameron's; the Ugly Suckling, which was Bernard Spencer's, indicating a wilful and at times nasty babyishness. When he disappeared, it was a relief; when he reappeared, a pleasure.[18]

Grigson was another important patron. Besides featuring Thomas prominently in New Verse, he also found him work as a reviewer of detective fiction for *The Morning Post*, a daily newspaper that was later amalgamated with *The Daily Telegraph*. Thomas reviewed over 100 thrillers between January 1935 and September 1936, sometimes three or four at a time, sometimes less, work that earned him up to £5 a week, with extra money on the side from selling off his review copies to the secondhand book trade. In the summer of 1935 he and Grigson holidayed together on the West coast of Ireland, sharing a cottage overlooking the Atlantic at Glen Lough, County Donegal. This had previously been occupied by the American artist Rockwell Kent. Thomas was in his element:

Here are gannets and seals and puffins flying and puffing and playing a quarter of a mile outside my window where there are great rocks petrified like the old fates and destinies of Ireland & smooth, white pebbles under and around them like the souls of the dead Irish.[19]

However, Grigson's tolerance soon wore thin. Like most people who spent any amount of time with him, Grigson found Thomas's selfishness hard to take. The final straw was when Thomas stayed on in Ireland after Grigson had returned to London – and then vanished without paying his share of the rent. (As so often, Thomas had a less gracious explanation, describing Grigson as 'a mean little, cheap little, ostentatiously vulgar little, thumb-to-my-nose little runt', which was how he tended to mention former friends once they had fallen out.[20])

Lawrence Durrell first met Thomas soon after publication of *18 Poems*, and then later arranged for him to spend an evening with Henry Miller, who was staying in London with Anais Nin's husband, Hugo Guyler. They invited Thomas to dinner, but

on the evening in question he kept us waiting hours and we were on the point of giving him up for lost when the telephone rang. He said in hollow, muffled tones: 'Can't find the flat, so I'm not coming'. He wasn't tipsy. He just sounded terribly nervous and ill at ease. 'Where are you now? I said, 'Because I'll get a taxi and fetch you.' That startled him. 'As a matter of fact,' he said, 'I'm just too afraid to come. You'll have to excuse me.'[21]

After further exchanges they duly learned that he was calling from a telephone in the pub across the road, but Thomas still refused to join them, so Durrell ran to fetch him:

He was ruffled and tousled and looked as if he had been sleeping in a haystack. He had a huge muffler around his throat. He was also extremely jumpy and touchy and said he was too frightened to move from the pub and that I should stay there and have a drink with him. This I did . . . . Once we left the pub he completely changed, became absolutely himself, and took the whole thing with complete assurance and sang-froid. Within ten minutes the nervous man was teasing Miller and enjoying Hugo Guyler's good wine – and indeed offering to read us his latest poems, which he did there and then. Miller was delighted . . . . We talked and drank late into the night and altogether it was a splendid evening; and from then on we met fairly frequently, though he would never come direct to the house. He always rang from the pub and forced me to have a drink with him there before he would come into the house. I don't know why . . . he was robust and without any self-importance and rejoiced in a laugh. 'You know,' he once said, 'when I'm in company which contains admirers or fans or fellow-writers, I begin to feel I'm under false pretences. That is why I act the clown.' And he could be a splendid clown . . .

I went for one pub-crawl with him which was as full of comic and unreal incidents as an Irish novel . . . Once I visited thirteen drinking clubs in an afternoon with him in an attempt to trace a pair of shoes which he had absently taken off in one of them – he did not know which. The types of people we met, and the hallucinating conversations which ramified around these shoes would have made a whole novel. In one place three old men helped him crawl under a bar to see if they were there and one of them got stuck and couldn't be got out; in another, he nearly got tattooed by an elderly Indian . . . and finally, he told me, that when he got home he found the shoes standing beside his bed. He had simply forgotten to put them on . . . . under the clowning and the planned appearance of this wild and woolly public figure there was somebody quieter, somebody very much harassed by a gift . . .

— 5 —
'I'M A VERY HAPPY SORT OF BIRD, AND I DON'T CARE MUCH'

AME came so early to Dylan Thomas that it is easy to forget that he had learned to live with it, in his own way, long before legends of poverty and drunkenness overshadowed his memory. These only gathered momentum with publication of *Dylan Thomas in America*, two years after his death, and so too, did his reputation for being a womaniser.

For 20 years before those stories gained currency, Thomas was a highly successful, if profligate, writer and performer, accomplished in several different forms. The sales of *18 Poems* may not have been dramatic (books of poetry seldom find a mass market, although this one quickly went into two editions and was then brought out again by Fortune Press in at least another five editions during the early Forties), but its acclaim opened many doors for him. Within two years, his poems and short stories were being accepted by the main literary magazines of the day. His second volume, *Twenty-five Poems*, was published by J.M. Dent, who remained his British publishers for the rest of his life.

By the time he was 25, Thomas had published his third book, *Map of Love*, which included poems and short stories, and was working on his collection of autobiographical short stories, *Portrait of the Artist as a Young Dog*. His first volume of poetry, *The World That I Breathe*, had been published in the United States. He was being noticed by literary critics both there and in France, and had made his first appearances on BBC radio.

No other contemporary Welsh writer had made such an impact so early in his career, and in trying to assess Thomas's reputation at that time, 20 years before the first biographies were written, one should remember that this was a different age. Values had a constancy. Television was mentioned as a scientific discovery, but meant little to Everyman. Talking pictures had only recently been invented. Silent films were being shown still in remote, rural areas. In the towns, music hall remained the most lively form of entertainment. Newspapers were more stiff and formal, with far fewer illustrations, reflecting the customs of a more ordered society, structured in a hierarchical way. Working-class writers, as such, were almost unknown, for this was still a class-based society in which achievement was measured by conformity to its values.

Part of Thomas's appeal, both then and since, lay in his choosing to buck this system, and to follow a free lifestyle, hitherto the preserve of the rich. Seldom lacking in moral courage or confidence in his abilities, despite his shyness, Thomas had set out to storm the citadels of literary London with hardly a penny to his name and, once he had done that, he lived like a nomad.

To survive he lived by his wits, never hesitating to take advantage of anyone who would give him money or clothes, buy him food or drink, pay his bills or allow him to stay overnight at their London flats or country cottages. Ferris and Amis have dismissed this attitude as that of a sponger, but there was something deeper. Thomas had no material beliefs. He did not accept the concept of personal property; he had no desire for houses or motor cars, and held instead that his inner world of thoughts and words was of more importance than physical possessions. There was always a religious undercurrent to this inner world. Unlike his father Thomas never rejected that which he could not explain, although he also refused to accept beliefs that had no realistic foundation. It was the same with his socialism, which was never the politics of the practical man, with its committee procedures and frameworks in law, but that of the inner man who identified more with the metaphysical poets of the seventeenth century.[1]

In this father and son were drawing closer to the ideas of D.H. Lawrence, the novelist, poet and painter, and son of a Nottinghamshire miner, whose mother had encouraged him to become a teacher, as no doubt, D.J. had been encouraged. Lawrence also came from a Nonconformist chapel background, which would not have escaped the Thomases' attention, and had also cocked a snook at the pretensions of London society. Lawrence's novel *The Rainbow* (1915) had been banned by magistrates. His studies of sexual behaviour in that novel and *Women in Love* (1921) caused outrage. More recently, *Lady Chatterley's Lover* (1928) had been privately printed abroad to avoid prosecution. An exhibition of his paintings had been banned in 1929.

Much of Lawrence's work dealt with unconscious fantasy, but he, too, had absorbed ideas from classical literature and knew precisely where he was aiming. Keeping abreast of modern literature as he always did, D.J. would have read not only Lawrence's novels and poems, but also his essays, and discussed them with his son. Together they would probably have analysed the themes running through such seminal Lawrence writings as

Pornography and Obscenity (1929) or his numerous essays in the literary magazines of the time, (these were gathered together after his death as *Phoenix: The Posthumous Papers of D.H. Lawrence* (1936).)

The Lawrence message was clear. The artist had to stand by his principles, and those had little to do with society's customs. They were the artist's preserve, the backbone of the inner man – and *everything* took second place to them. Accept that, and the whole course of Thomas's subsequent life begins to make sense. Whether he was right or wrong, by whoever's standards, is neither here nor there; it was never anything that he felt he had to explain, being part of that inner self. Thomas believed there was 'only one position for an artist anywhere: and that is upright'.[2]

With that as his passport, Thomas started to travel. He stayed at Disley, Cheshire, with the historian A.J.P. Taylor whom he met through their friend Norman Cameron; he had that writing holiday in Ireland and others in Cornwall, where Lawrence had also escaped, frequently returning to Swansea and the cottages on the Llanstephan peninsula, where he had written in his teens. Like all tourists he returned home at the end of each journey, but never considered Swansea 'home' in the physical, bricks-and-mortar sense, because that meant little to him, either, although he enjoyed the warmth of coal fires and a soft mattress and frequently expressed nostalgia for past moments of happiness. This theme of nostalgia runs through his work, especially his short stories, and also through his letters to friends with whom he had shared an experience.

But he was always moving on, with that passport tucked away, no matter how reduced his resources, or where he might happen to lay his head. Once fame had found him, his pace was relentless because he knew (as only an artist knows) that the sum total of a man's life can be readily measured a century later, and everything else he does is incidental to that. His inner self was shaped early in life, and when he happened to meet a woman as selfish as he was (in the true sense of the word), he at once, within moments of meeting her, asked her to marry him, and slept with her that night.

Dylan Thomas had long boasted of his sexual conquests. That was how poets lived in his fantasy world (and he was always just as anxious to be A Poet as he was to write poetry); they were romantic heroes, formidable drinkers and powerful lovers, the envy of lesser mortals – but I know of no convincing evidence that Thomas was ever the man of his dreams. Ferris noted that frustration features constantly in Thomas's work and that nowhere is there a single reference to a happy and fulfilling act of love – and

Caitlin confirms that he was hopeless in bed and that she did not discover until after his death that it was possible for women to have a sexual climax.[3] No paternity suits were ever filed against him. He was never cited in any divorce cases. No one has claimed him as father, other than his three children born in wedlock. Nor has any woman stepped forward with tales of his prowess between the sheets.

If he was inclined to 'stupendous bluffing' in other areas of his life, as Pamela Hansford Johnson observed, is it not likely that he also exaggerated his appeal to women? After all, he loved to be the centre of attention in any bar, and he came from a social milieu where young men were prone to boasting about the quantities of beer that they could put away on Friday and Saturday nights and their success with women. I suspect that Thomas tried to 'keep up with the boys', but never did. Fred Janes and Mervyn Levy have told me that Dylan could never last the course as a drinker, either with them or Dan Jones, a fearsome drinker when 'the boys' got going. 'After a couple of pints, his eyes would glaze over and he'd be sliding under the table,' said Janes. 'He didn't have the capacity for heavy drinking, though he liked to pretend that he did, and would try to keep up . . . .' And so it was, I suspect, with his approach to women. Thomas was witty and charming, flirtatious and affectionate towards any attractive girl who joined his company in a bar, which was enough to make Caitlin fiercely jealous in later years because she always had to be the centre of attention, but there is no real evidence that he was ever an accomplished seducer or virile performer; at best, he was possibly the kind of man who engages in sexual intercourse if the opportunity presents itself, without giving.

However, he did have that strong vision of poets as heroic figures, carrying all before them, and to this crumpled young man who seldom washed and had no money, sex was probably just another part of his fantasies, suggesting a sense of adventure. 'Let's go roistering and rude bathing,' he would say to the girls at the Swansea Little Theatre,[4] but when they reached the beach at Langland Bay he wouldn't even take his socks off. His references to women are naïve, even as late as *Portrait of the Artist as a Young Dog* (1940), and he may well have been a virgin when he first started visiting Pamela Hansford Johnson. Of course, being A Poet, he would want to pretend otherwise, teasing her about her chastity (as he had so often teased the girls at the Little Theatre), telling slightly *risqué* jokes, and confessing, as their relationship drew to an end, 'I've always wondered why you won't come to bed with me.'[5] Earlier he had taunted her with an apparent admission that he had 'wasted some of my tremendous love for you on a lank redmouthed girl with a reputation like a hell',[6] which sounds more like melodramatic nonsense than the real thing – and, anyway, the girl denied it! Likewise, his letters and short stories suggest a knowledge of female sexuality that was no more than he could have learned from the writings of D.H. Lawrence or Henry Miller.

Pamela Hansford Johnson, who did not believe the wilder stories that were later told of him, wrote:

> one thing I cannot believe; and that is the figure of Dylan as a sort of congenital womaniser. He was not like that, basically. He admired Harpo Marx, thought himself not physically dissimilar – which was true – and liked to mimic him. I think he took the Harpo Marx side to America, and let it overcome till he was as powerless against it as he was against alcohol.
>
> He was thoughtless and unreliable: but he did have the wish to please. I think he would have found it hard to deny the longings of any ardent young girl, but I doubt whether his heart was ever much in it.[7]

The poet Paul Potts, who knew him well (and was helped financially by the Thomases who gave away money to those who needed it even when they were borrowing themselves) confirms this:

> Despite Mark Twain's remark, that a lie can travel around the world before the truth has time to get to the nearest corner, may I be allowed to record a fact, and this is the fact. That there are dozens of people, both men and women (all with a bit of common sense) who knew Dylan Thomas well, and who would agree with me when I say that he was no more a 'womaniser' than Adolf Hitler was a pacifist.[8]

On those early London forays, Dylan Thomas was the beer-drinking provincial poet trying so hard to make his mark with the city boys, still tiny and slim, wearing a sweater beneath his tweed jacket, woollen shirts, and a floppy scarf knotted loosely around his neck, which was how he thought A Poet should look. There had been women, he would claim airily in the public bars, inevitably finding a winning way of saying it, just as he would later boast in lectures, 'I should be ashamed, had not shame been lost to me in the back of a lorry in, I think, nineteen hundred and thirty.'[9]

However, the women he mostly stayed with appeared to have other attractions – they were either married or divorced, middle-aged and maternal, with homes of their own in the heart of the city (and often a country cottage, too), willing to put him up free of charge, wash his linen and keep him clean. These included Wyn Henderson and Veronica Sibthorp, who both owned cottages in Cornwall where he stayed; Emily Holmes Coleman, an American writer 15 years his senior who lived with her daughter; the poetess Anna Wickham, who hanged herself when cigarettes went up in price, and the composer Elisabeth Lutyens who is quoted as saying:

> When I lay a-bed of a morning, being by nature a noctambulant, Dylan would pop down, bright as a cricket at an ungoldly early hour, sit on my bed with a 'Give me a cigarette, love', and then proceed unfastidiously to lap up the dregs from the glasses of the night-before party and bounce off cheerful as a cherub.[10]

Lutyens, who later became a close friend of Caitlin's as well and stayed with the Thomases at The Boat House, witnessing their bursts of violence, never accepted the

> picture of Dylan as a maudlin, bloated drunk. Betty [Elisabeth Lutyens] always reacted angrily, maintaining that his undoing was his weak head and careless eating habits. But his firm belief that the world owed the artist a living went against her work ethic, which came from her father and verged on the Puritan. She belaboured him about it – and lent him money just the same.[11]

And it is hard to think of these other relationships as great love affairs. All seem unlikely heroines for a young poet, especially Wyn who was so fat that her friends called her Moby Dick; Thomas used to stay with her *and her mother*! The simpler explanation may be that they recognised his unusual talents – so he took advantage of them, just as he usually would anyone else, telling Caitlin later that these were all 'just bed and breakfast women'.

Thomas may still have been a virgin when he and Caitlin met at The Wheatsheaf on 12 April 1936, for his relationship with Pamela Hansford Johnson continued well into 1935. They were still corresponding occasionally the following year, and their friendship remained wholly platonic. There is nothing to suggest that Thomas was ever in love with anyone else, although he was still busily working on the image of himself as romantic hero. The suggestion that he may have caught venereal disease from a girl that he met at the International Surrealistic Exhibition comes later – the Exhibition was staged in July 1936 – and there is no real proof that he did.[12]

He may have been bluffing again.

At the time that he met Caitlin, Thomas was staying with Emily Holmes Coleman and her daughter. They had arranged to meet that night at The Wheatsheaf. When Emily arrived she found Dylan sitting on a stool with Caitlin's head in his lap, him telling her how much he loved her, how beautiful she was, and that he was determined to marry her; they had only met an hour or so earlier, or maybe minutes, for neither had much sense of time.[13]

Caitlin was fiery, strong and unpredicatable; almost as strong as he was, although she could pick him up in her arms, listen for hours to his 'endless jabber', and take him straight to bed. A trained dancer who had roughed it in Paris and worked in London theatres, she was lithe and womanly, with few inhibitions. Her father had abandoned the family home; a friend of her parents, Augustus John, had raped her, and she believed, 'all men are bastards'. Words had always been a powerful force in her father's life – Francis Macnamara was an Irish poet, part of the Gate Theatre crowd in Dublin, and a loud, booming declaimer – and now here she was in this London pub with a poet, obsessed by language, convinced of his genius, showering her with tenderness as though they had been living together for years.

Like Thomas, Caitlin came and went as she wished. The family home was at Ringwood, Hampshire, where her mother devoted much of her time to reading. Caitlin had two sisters, Nicolette and Brigid, and a brother, John. The Macnamaras had grown up with Augustus John's children, who lived nearby, diving in and out of each other's homes, riding horses, or tramping through the woods for family picnics. She was closest to Vivienne John who often used to book herself in for a night at the Eiffel Tower Hotel in Fitzrovia, charging this to her father's account. As Caitlin had allowed her abuse by Augustus John to develop into an affair, she was sure Augustus wouldn't mind if she did likewise that April night (although, in fact, he became intensely jealous on discovering that she had fallen in love with a younger man). Caitlin took Dylan back to the Eiffel Tower Hotel, and told the owner, a German named Stulik, that they wanted a room.

As they went to bed, Caitlin found Dylan eager, excited to have pulled off such a coup at the famous artist's expense, but unskilled. He was shy and careful not to let her see him naked, though she noticed that his clothes were stinking and he wore no underpants. He had no knowledge of foreplay or any techniques of arousal, leaving her to guide him, which she did inexpertly. Her own experiences had been disastrous. Apart from Augustus John (who often raped women who sat for him as models), she had an affair with a

Parisian artist that proved unrewarding. Now Dylan was to prove incompetent. Looking back on the relationship 50 years later, she described them clinging together in their borrowed bed. And yet, for years afterward Dylan would boast of this conquest, allowing others to believe him irresistible, which makes one think that he never really understood sex at all.

From that day on, possibly having slept with a woman for the first time, Dylan told everyone they met that this was the girl he was going to marry. For five days and nights, they went without food and lived on drink, hopping from pub to pub, meeting the artists, writers and painters who hovered around Chelsea and Fitzrovia, with Caitlin observing that they treated Dylan as a coming star.

By then, the poet's life was falling into a pattern. London was where he found fame and money (though never enough for his needs); it was where he went to sell himself, to keep in touch with those literary people who gave him *entrées*. Thomas believed in personal contact, that editors would be more likely to publish his work after meeting him themselves. No matter where he lived in the years that followed, he would catch a train to London if it meant that a magazine might publish his work, or a radio producer commission a script, even though he would often spend whatever there was in his pockets in the pub afterwards; it was something that had to be done, like going to market in Wales.

On that night in April 1936, he was spending just a few days in London before travelling back to Cornwall where he was staying in Wyn Henderson's cottage 'in a field with a garden full of ferrets and bees',[14] complaining that Wyn had 'unfortunately read too many books on psychology and talks about my ego over breakfast'. Caitlin was between sittings. Her portrait was being painted by Augustus John, and so, after their five nights at the Eiffel Tower Hotel, she returned to Ringwood and he went back to Penzance. Their letters to each other that summer do not survive,[15] but they met again on 15 July – in Laugharne. Augustus had driven her down there to stay with Richard Hughes and his wife at Castle House, and Caitlin probably wrote to Dylan telling him of their plans for he wrote to Hughes:

I'm going to Fishguard by car tomorrow, and passing awfully near Laugharne. I do hope you'll be there because we – that's painter Alfred Janes and me – would like very much to call on you. We shall, shall we, some time in the afternoon? Hope I shan't miss you as I did last time.[16]

and persuaded Janes to borrow his father's car for the day. They all went off to the Eisteddfod at Fishguard, and then ended the day with a pub crawl back. This ended with Augustus, jealous of the attentions that Dylan was paying to Caitlin, knocking him down in a Carmarthen car park and then driving her back to bed at the Hugheses.

Dates become difficult at this point, because of those lost letters and the fact that Caitlin never kept a diary. In the autumn of 1936, she holidayed at her family home at Ennistymon, County Clare, a Georgian mansion which had been turned into a country hotel, enabling her father to drink through what remained of the family fortune in some style.[17] When she and Thomas met again, they started living together, although they had nowhere to call their own, with her sometimes returning alone to Ringwood, and him going back to Swansea.

The second issue of *18 Poems* had been published earlier that year (February 1936). In September, Dent brought out *Twenty-five Poems*,[18] probably at the suggestion of Victor Neuburg. Thomas's poems and short stories were continuing to appear in the London literary monthlies, and this second book provoked an even more agreeable controversy than the one in *The Listener* 18 months before. This time, his virtues as a new poet were debated in the pages of *The Sunday Times*, a sure sign of success in the eyes of his Anglo-Welsh contemporaries who read:

After a prolonged stay in London, crowded more than usual with incident and notable chiefly for the long controversy regarding his latest book which spread, finally, to some of the most popular evening newspapers, Mr Dylan Thomas returned to Swansea. He is off again shortly, to the Universities of Oxford and Cambridge, where he has consented to address the English societies.[19]

Dame Edith Sitwell liked to hold court at the Sesame Club in Upper Grosvenor Street, in the heart of Mayfair. There she invited her young friends to tea, seated upstairs in a fine panelled drawing room, dressed in robes of flowing silk or velvet, set off by turbans or her hair swept back Plantagenet style.

The Sitwells held estates in Derbyshire, Yorkshire and Northumberland. There had been a baronetcy handed down since 1808, the sons went to Eton, and in Edith's generation both her brothers Osbert and Sacheverell turned to writing. They had become a formidable family, and Dame Edith enjoyed her status, publishing occasional slim volumes of verse, and writing magisterial reviews for the more important literary papers.

Thomas, who never let a useful friendship pass him by, may have written to her already; certainly, he had come to her attention for she had cited his poem *Our eunuch dreams*, after its appearance in *New Verse* (April 1934) as an example of lowering standards of contemporary writing in her book, *Aspects of Modern Poetry*, without even mentioning his name. This hurt, as is clear from a letter to Glyn Jones:

> So you've been reviewing Edith Sitwell's latest piece of virgin dung, have you? Isn't she a poisonous thing of a woman, lying, concealing, flipping, plagiarising, misquoting, and being as clever a crooked literary plagiarist as ever .... the majority of the book was cribbed from Herbert Read and Leavis, actually and criminally cribbed. She has misquoted Hopkins at least twenty times, reprinted many poems without the permission of publisher or poet. Yes, that was my poem all right . . .[20]

However, it seems likely that they had already corresponded; it was probably one of his falsely-modest, willing-to-please, apt-to-deceive letters that were employed as part of his armoury when trying to make new friends. Thomas had long concluded that literary London was all 'a racket', and if there were tricks that had to be played then tongue-tingling Thomas would tempt them all with his artful devices.

> Celebrities I meet often and too often, they being a lousy lot on the whole, or off it. Herbert Read, Grigson, Cameron, the Muirs and Heppenstall are the best. Racketeering abounds .... I've come into contact on a number of occasions with intellectual communism and communists . . . A.L. Morton . . . Cockburn . . . Esmond Romilly, editor of the schoolboys' communist monthly *Out of Bounds*, and with all the pseudo-revolutionaries such as John Lehmann, John Pudney etc. And I dislike them all . . . they are bogus from skull to navel . . . . I shall never, I hope, be mixed up in any political ramifications of literary, or pseudo literary London; honest writing does *not* mix with it; you can't be true to party and poetry; one must suffer, and, historically, poetry is the social and economic creed that endures.[21]

With the approach of the Spanish Civil War, which was high noon for the London literary left, Thomas was in town, fraternising politely, taking what he could, but viewing their antics with that cold eye with which he watched the world. He was more interested in Thomas, and in Thomas's place in the history of literature. Always the supreme egotist, and unashamed, he saw no place for *them* in that long line of poets stretching back through Shelley,

Byron and Keats to his Metaphysicals. He decried their boyish homosexuality and, as can be seen from that letter to Trick, thought their philosophy ran thin. He was, as ever, self-possessed. When Dame Edith Sitwell began to treat him as a new figure of importance, he responded as only he could. In his mind, she was right at last; he was only being given his due.

Her first letters were merely encouraging, and the more so because she admitted changing her mind on the value of his poetry. He was, at once, self-effacing and falsely apologetic, seeming to take her into his confidence (a favourite trick), and yet confessing

I'm a very happy sort of bird, and I don't care much.[22]

When she invited him to dine at the Sesame Club, he replied immediately, saying that he would be in London, visiting booksellers and publishers, asking

Are you sure you really don't mind taking all this trouble? I'm so very grateful to you. You must have listened to a great deal of the woes of young poets. And to take a regular job is the most sensible suggestion in the world . . . you shall have all my confidences when we meet.[23]

Thomas didn't turn up that first time. Having travelled all the way from Swansea intending to see her, he lost his nerve at the last minute, walking up and down Upper Grosvenor Street, too shy to go to the door. Later, he wrote again, apologising and seeking forgiveness and by the time they did meet had clearly made a favourable impression, for she began to commend his work, belatedly reviewing *18 Poems* in the *London Mercury* (February 1936), and then writing that review of *Twenty-five Poems* in *The Sunday Times* (15 November 1936), which did so much to establish his reputation. This was headed:

A NEW POET

and sub-headed

THE ACHIEVEMENT OF MR DYLAN THOMAS

and went on to comment

A year ago, the present reviewer became convinced that a new poet had

67

arisen who showed every promise of greatness. The work of this very young man (he is 22 years of age) is on a huge scale, both in theme and structurally – his themes are the mystery and holiness of all forms and aspects of life. He writes of the brotherhood of man with the mineral and vegetable world (as in the first poem of this book) – of

My man of leaves and the bronze root, mortal and unmortal

of the splendour and inexorability and fatefulness of spring –

Beginning with doom in the bulb, and the springing marvels

In all these poems, so strangely young in their strength and vitality, all things are identified with God, Who is present in 'the sensual root and sap', and where

the summer blood
knocked in the flesh that decked the vine

The form of many of these poems is superb. The eighth poem though not a sonnet either in rhyme, scheme or shape, yet, by its particular motion, gives the impression that here, alone among the poets of the younger generation, is one who could produce sonnets worthy of our great heritage.

and so the review continued, quoting phrases, lines and individual verses from *Twenty-five Poems*, commenting upon their use and meaning, noting that the poem *Altarwise by owl-light*, 'seems to me to be nothing short of magnificent', and concluding

I could not name one poet of this, the younger generation, who shows so great a promise, and even so great an achievement.[24]

To be praised so handsomely by such a famous critic in a leading national newspaper must have been exciting. That weekend Thomas was at home in Swansea, staying with his parents, meeting Fred Janes, visiting Vernon Watkins, whom he had been seeing occasionally since Watkins's first arrival in Cwmdonkin Drive. No letters or memories survive to tell us how they all reacted, but the father's pleasure can be imagined – and he must have been even more gratified by the vigorous correspondence that Dame Edith's review stimulated. Three letters were published in *The Sunday Times* on 29 November, and Dame Edith wrote back in his defence a week later when further letters were published from Pamela Hansford Johnson, Trevor Hughes and other readers. This correspondence continued for a further six weeks, with Dame Edith twice returning to the fray, and her protégé no doubt urging his friends to keep the debate going while he stayed on in Swansea; it was then that he *may* have been receiving treatment for a venereal infection, for he was avoiding drink for medical reasons, but if this was the case he would have taken great care to conceal it from his parents.

— 6 —

A MARRIAGE OF INNOCENTS

SOMEWHERE there was Caitlin, possibly still in Ringwood. All she can remember is that they were together whenever they could be, moving from friend to friend, with just their clothes, his working notebooks, and a few possessions, wholly in love and penniless. Their parents would give them small sums of money. Sometimes, a magazine would send a pound or two, although the fees paid by literary monthlies for poems or short stories could be counted in shillings.

Thomas left Swansea early in April 1937. Later that month they were in London, and on Wednesday 21 April, Thomas was in the BBC studios at Broadcasting House making his first broadcast 'down the line' for BBC Wales. It was titled *Life and the Modern Poet*. One letter survives from the weeks that followed, an anguished appeal to Caitlin:

The world is unbalanced unless, in the very centre of it, we little muts stand together all the time in a hairy, golden, more-or-less unintelligible haze of daftness . . . I love and love you. Only love, and true love. Caitlin Caitlin this is unbearable. Will you forgive me again – for being ill and too willy-minded & weak and full of useless (no God, not useless) love for you.[1]

They had nowhere to live and yet were, in some strange way, living together. By early June, they were in Cornwall, returning to the area where he had stayed the previous spring, this time borrowing a cottage in Mousehole owned by Jake Sibthorp, who had been married to Veronica Sibthorp and was part of that literary drinking crowd to which Thomas had attached himself over the previous three years. From there they moved to another cottage in Mousehole, adjoining the now renowned Lobster Pot restaurant, which was being developed by Wyn Henderson and her mother. Dylan and

Caitlin were planning to marry. Their parents had not been told. There had been no formal engagement. Caitlin was not bothered whether they married or not; it was just another piece of paper, she said, but Dylan continued to insist that he would, just as he had on the day they met. On reflection, she thought it rather a grand idea, believing in his genius as much as he did. Her faith was total.

And so he slipped down into Penzance without telling her, and bought two imitation silver wedding rings for six shillings each (30p in today's currency), and made all the arrangements. She went along with it, wearing a flimsy blue cotton dress, while he dressed as he always did, open-necked in a jacket and corduroys. The couple were married on 11 July 1937. It was a simple wedding in Penzance registry office, with both the Registrar, Samuel O. Watkins, and his deputy, George H. Hall, officiating, and two unknown witnesses. Caitlin says the Registrar sat there, stony-faced[2] for the wedding party was 'pretty well primed-up' and 'drink was predominant'. Most women can remember their wedding day, but not Caitlin; it is lost in a haze, in which details are fuzzy, but her recollection of her emotional feelings remains as sharply defined as ever.

Those weeks had been spent walking the cliffs and wandering the hedgerows. It was a warm June, and that year Wyn Henderson was down with her sons Nigel and Ian. Norman Cameron and his wife stayed there, too, and so did Rayner Heppenstall, the painter Max Chapman and other friends. Their little corner of literary London had moved to the sea, and this seemed as good a place as any to marry. So far as Caitlin recalls, they did not talk about it much. The wedding was just something that happened, when they had hardly a penny between them. A marriage licence cost £3 and the wedding was twice postponed because they drank the money that had been set aside; not heavy drinking, but the light, casual, happy, not-a-care-in-the-world everyday social drinking that remained a central part of their lives, whenever there was cash in the post or borrowed. It is known now (although Dylan did not tell Caitlin at the time) that his parents were distressed when he wrote to them a few days before the wedding, with D.J. asking Nancy's husband Haydn Taylor to intercede. His father also clearly wrote back to Dylan advising him against marriage before he had fully established himself as a writer, for another letter survives that he sent to Taylor:

I said all I had to say in my letter to him, & I put things as wisely & strongly as I could. What else to do I don't know; but perhaps you can think of some way to prevent what is a disaster. The idea, if it were not so serious, would be comic. The whole thing, to any normally-minded person, is grotesque and farcical . . . . I'm sure both Nancy and yourself must feel very upset over the insane idea of Dylan's marrying in his desperate financial straits. Marriage, too, as I pointed out to him, would still further damn his potential success as a writer and poet . . .[3]

Only small parts of Thomas's correspondence with his father survive, including the famous letter in which he announced his intentions:

This isn't thought of – I've told mother about it many times – speedily or sillily; we've been meaning to for a long time, & think we should carry it out at once.[4]

The others that passed between them have not survived; Dylan kept nothing, not even letters from his wife or parents, so that one has to rely upon others to realise how the family felt. D.J. accepted the *fait accompli* for Dylan wrote to his brother-in-law:

father's been desperately kind & sent me five pounds last week with sort of resigned wishes for my happiness.[5]

Caitlin's mother, Mrs Yvonne Macnamara, gave them money as well, and it is likely that Vernon Watkins, Edith Sitwell and Pamela Hansford Johnson also sent them cash rather than conventional gifts, for 'thank-you' letters survive.[6] After spending nearly three months in Cornwall, latterly in a Newlyn studio owned by Max Chapman, the couple went to stay with D.J. and Florence at their new home in Bishopston, Swansea, and then moved to Blashford, near Ringwood, where Mrs Macnamara put them up for six months, providing Dylan with a room where he could write for much of the day undisturbed.

Thomas was still receiving very little income for his work, although he remained as convinced as ever of its long-term importance. This showed an almost unnatural self-confidence. During those summer months of 1937, and the winter that followed, only occasional sums of money came in the morning post. Faber included his short story *The Orchards* in both their *Welsh Short Stories* and also their *Faber Book of Short Stories* (1937); he contributed occasionally to *Life and Letters Today*, *The New English Weekly* and *New Verse*, but with none of the driving urgency of the past three years, giving rise to a belief that his star had shone briefly, and that his life thereafter would become one constant rehearsal of youth.

It seems more likely that marriage unsettled him. Caitlin was, and is, a demanding woman, possessing fine natural accomplishments, but with little interest in mundane chores. Thomas was intensely proud of her, as well he might be, for she had striking beauty, with delicate bone structure and flowing hair; she was fiery and disturbing and drew admiring glances from other men. Those who met them together formed the impression that she may have been 'a lot to handle', without meaning that in just a sexual way. She enhanced this aura by dressing in brightly coloured cottons to complement her hair, and speaking with a soft lilting accent that certainly wasn't English (her father was Irish, her mother French, and Caitlin was born in Hammersmith). Having given up her career as a dancer to share his life, she wanted attention.

From the earliest days of their marriage, the pair were inseparable. Friends mentioned their name in one breath. They went everywhere together, playing like children, carousing like sailors, enjoying an intimacy that went far beyond a solely physical union. 'Twin souls' was how she described it to me, and this, one senses, was part of the magic, for Thomas would read to her in bed for hours on end, Shakespeare, Dickens or the Romantic poets; everything he wrote would be read to her first before being sent off to an editor or to Vernon Watkins. Caitlin plays down any influence that she might have had upon his work, but spending long periods in her company one is soon aware of a felicity with words, of nouns and verbs and remembered phrases tumbling over each other, which was something that I sought to capture in our book *Caitlin* – a combination of steely will, trust and a love of words. We spent hours on one page, just getting a word right, and then raced through others with hardly a doubt, and this, one suspects, may be something that Thomas enjoyed, the reason he called her his 'Cattleanchor', for her values remained constant, no matter what happened between them.

As she confirms,[7] theirs was never a profoundly sexual marriage, although they needed each other, had children, and both regarded sex as an important part of their lives. Their own relationship was never discussed. They just went to bed and that was it, although they would happily chatter away about the habits and inclinations of their friends, often suspecting homosexuality where none existed (as with Vernon Watkins), and never bothering to acquire those refined techniques that today's newly-weds learn through manuals. Instead, they were happily, unselfconsciously content.

That first winter at Blashford, they settled into the routine that was to form the pattern of their life together; it was roughly the same that Thomas had followed at Cwmdonkin Drive, always rising late and pottering about in the mornings, going for a drink at lunchtime if they could rustle up the cash, or wandering across the fields or through the bluebell woods near her mother's home, and then he would write during the afternoons. Caitlin says, 'Some days it wouldn't happen, the ideas wouldn't come . . . it's like, writing; never easy. It's taking something from within you, and there are some days when it just won't come – and then you have to go off and do something else.'

Many women would have worried where the next pound note was coming from, and there are times now when Caitlin says she should have done. At that time, she did not – and that was an enormous strength for the young poet who still believed that his inner life was more important than any other, and whose deepest tragedy may have lain in his failure to grasp the nature of her reliance upon him. It was a complex marriage, as many are, but sustained them in their carefree days, when all they sought was time together and time to write.

At Blashford, Thomas worked as slowly as ever, turning now to short stories and one of his most difficult poems, *Poem for Caitlin*, or *I make this in a warring absence*, which first appeared in *Twentieth Century Verse* (January–February 1938), or making vague plans for his third book. At one stage he was far advanced with a proposal for one titled *The Burning Baby* which was to be simultaneously published by George Reavey's Europa Press in Paris and London, with a signed limited edition. These plans came to naught (with some acrimony) and instead Thomas gathered together a collection of poems and short stories, *The Map of Love*, which was published by Dent in 1939.

Meanwhile, Thomas was beginning to enjoy a curious status, receiving a request from *New Verse* 'for a kind of obituary notice . . . or, perhaps, a tribute on his seventieth birthday' on W.H. Auden (who was actually thirty!); for a 'valuation', which was how the editor Julian Symons described it, of Wyndham Lewis for *Twentieth Century Verse*, and for a contribution to Lawrence Durrell's and Henry Miller's *The Booster*, to which he sent *I make this in a warring absence* and his *Prologue to an Adventure*, planned as the first chapter of his Pilgrim's Progress-in-reverse. (Although sent to *Booster*, these appeared in its successor *Delta*.

'Do you think this means, at last, that I'm a man of letters?' he asked the critic and novelist Desmond Hawkins,[8] only half-joking, for he was now being treated as just that by his Anglo-Welsh contemporaries with whom he was in frequent contact while they launched the first issues of *Wales*.

'I may get a job on the BBC; it all depends on the BBC,' he told Charlie Fisher, a journalist friend from Swansea[9] at the same time sounding wistfully homesick, as he always seemed to be, when far from Swansea or later, Laugharne.

Short stories were now beginning to occupy his afternoons. He continued to work on them for the next 18 months. There were reminiscences of his teens and childhood, affectionate studies of a grown-up world seen through young eyes and a child's place within his family. *A Visit to Grandpa's* was one of the first, followed by the others which were eventually to comprise his collection, *Portrait of the Artist as a Young Dog* (1940), namely *The Peaches, The Fight, Extraordinary Little Cough, Just Like Little Dogs, Where Tawe Flows, Who do you wish was with us?, Old Garbo* (which drew on his days in Swansea journalism), *One Warm Saturday* and *Patricia, Edith and Arnold.* Through them he was clearly yearning for another time, for the security of earlier younger days when he had no one to care for, but always someone to care for him; the only poem he finished at Blashford was *Poem for Caitlin,* which was in no sense the work of a happy man, suggesting rather that emotionally he was out of his depth. This is one of the few poems that he ever agreed to analyse: usually he believed poems stood for themselves, possessing layers of meaning for the reader that were not necessarily those intended by the poet. This one was different, being about his feelings for the woman he had married, and its explanation reveals anxiety, a hint of desolation, or even, maybe, a realisation that within marriage there were matters beyond the poet's control.[10]

By now, Thomas seems to have been troubled by many forms of doubt. At times, in his letters, he appears less certain of himself, worried by a sense of responsibility. Whenever he found himself overwhelmed, no matter how or by what, Thomas turned back to the remoter parts of Wales, where he always found reassurance. In London, or near to it, life always fell into a dismal pattern. Too many distractions, too many people to see, too many temptations, too many false expectations as those who had temporarily helped him became a disappointment (usually as a result of some act of selfishness on his part). Many friendships, notably those with Geoffrey Grigson and Richard Church, ended abruptly when he either failed to keep his word, or showed ingratitude. He was to comment bitterly on some of them, saying of Church, who had championed his cause with Dent, but became critical

Richard Church . . . . is, without due respect, a cliché-riddled humbug and pie-fingering hack, a man who has said to me, when I told him I was starving, that a genuine artist scorns monetary gain, and who later confessed, with a self-deprecatory shrug and a half-wishful smile that has brought tears to many a literary society, to a slight jealousy – 'we're not as young as we were, you know' – of the vitality of modern youth. He thinks like a Sunday paper.[11]

75

And of George Reavey, critic and poet, whose plans to publish *The Burning Baby* had been aborted, he wrote

that sandy, bandy, polite, lockjawed, French-lettered, i-dotted, Russian t'd, non-commital, B.A.'d, V.D.'d, mock-barmy, smarmy, chance-his-army tick of a piddling crook who lives in his own armpit.[12]

Everyone, everywhere, was marching out of step with the poet, and for that there was only one solution – back to Wales, and where better than Laugharne, where Richard Hughes was already ensconced, the pubs were neighbourly, family lived nearby, food was cheap, and he would be able to write, close by rivers and water birds. This was pure escapism, as it was to be, always, but what else was there for him to do when, as he admitted, he was trying

though always without success, to exist on my writing . . . I really am in a very bad, distressing position now, living on charity, unable to buy for myself even the smallest necessary luxuries, and having little peace of mind from those most small and nagging worries to work as well and carefully as I should like. I may have to stop writing altogether very soon – for writing is obviously full-time or not at all – and try to obtain some little, sure work.[13]

Somehow, with money begged or borrowed from Caitlin's mother or his parents, and with the promise of a small advance from the American publisher James Laughlin, who had started the company New Directions and wanted to publish Thomas's work in the United States, the couple shuffled along, not caring too much about the ethics of debt, and believing, anyway, that genius was a gift that the world should pay for. With such a philosophy, Laugharne was as good a place as anywhere to go, and more supportive than most.

Richard Hughes found them a small fisherman's cottage in Gosport Street. Like many houses in Laugharne, it had an unlikely name: Eros. Its tiny rooms were packed with velvety Victorian furniture, which they hated, but from its rear garden steps they could walk down to the estuary, watching broad-hipped cocklewomen leading their donkeys back from the sands at Ginst Point, panniers loaded with cockles. These tiny shellfish had long been Laugharne's staple industry. A few doors down from their cottage, opposite the Corporation Arms, the township's largest cockle factory steamed and sizzled as the cockles were boiled alive, with their shells then discarded by the ton in the outside yard.

This was and is a mainly working-class town, although its eighteenth-century houses in the main street give it delusions of grandeur and the fact that Laugharne is still largely self-governing under an ancient charter dating back to the beginning of the fourteenth century means that the townspeople themselves still decide how its mediaeval strip-fields are apportioned. Laugharne is still roughly the size and shape it was when the castle was built seven centuries ago, and remains a strange place, its customs and jealousies still intact. My family are happy to live here, knowing that we shall never be wholly accepted, any more than the Thomases were. For several generations, newcomers have moved into Laugharne, but there remains a native population that is distinctively tribal, although more prosperous than in years gone by, with jobs newly available in Carmarthen and four miles down the road in Pendine, where an experimental establishment employs many local people to test the nastier forms of modern weaponry. The real world is never far away in Laugharne, but remains intangible, with its young people preferring to stay rather than take up better paid jobs in the cities.

When the Thomases arrived on 1 May 1938, having spent Easter with his parents at Bishopston, the town had none of these modern sources of income. Few people owned cars, although some had bicycles, and the humble cockle ruled. By some natural fortune, cockles would arrive at the mouth of the River Taf, out on the skyline, and bury themselves just an inch or two below the surface of the sand. Those cocklewomen, now dead and gone, were legendary ladies with vast hips from bending and stretching with their rakes and cockle-sacks. They walked out along a pathway known as the cocklebank to gather their harvest as the tide went out, managing to work both tides on summer days when daylight hours were long. Anyone could go. The cockles were there for the taking, and sometimes the Thomases (or more often Caitlin while he was writing) would collect a bucketful, soak them in salt water and feed them with oats overnight (cockles clean themselves and fatten up), before boiling them and then eating them direct from their shells the following morning, with a splash of vinegar.

Laugharne was used to living like that, although some years (for reasons no one could ever explain) the cockles did not arrive, and then there would be hard times. Whatever happened, Laugharne survived, although so little money came into the town that its houses were seldom properly maintained. Roofs tended to leak. Dry rot was rampant. But nobody cared because Laugharne, as the Thomases soon discovered, had acquired a communal philosophy that nothing mattered and the world would still be the same in a hundred years' time. Meanwhile, one might as well drink, play cards or a game of darts. The place was feckless and irresponsible, and known as such for miles around. Men fought with knives and boathooks. The first policeman sent to the town vanished off the face of the earth. When a well was cleared, three skeletons were found at the bottom, and for several centuries travellers had been known to disappear when crossing the river. More recently, when two competing bus services were introduced into the area, the owner of one was found dead beside his vehicle. Laugharne savoured such memories, paying little more than lip service to its vicar or primary school headmaster who were both, naturally, well respected, so long as they kept themselves to themselves and made no attempt to change the place or the people.

Now, 50 years later, the older townspeople remember the Thomases well, as the first hippies to arrive in West Wales (which is the word they use), recalling them going down to the shops in their dressing-gowns, rolling their own cigarettes (Caitlin had a little trick of rolling hers with a deft flick of her fingers up her thigh, thus giving the locals a quick glimpse of her underwear; men talk of it still). Their clothes were poor, and they gained credit whenever they could on the promise of some cheque being due from a publisher. (Usually, a friend would arrive in the nick of time and clear their debts before the tradesmen turned nasty; Laugharne did not mind this overmuch because its milkmen, grocer, butcher and pubkeepers knew that if credit was not given when it was needed, customers might not return, and, anyway, life is short . . .)

The Thomases could not have found anywhere better, unless they had gone to the west coast of Ireland where similar attitudes prevail. Some days there were cockles, freshly boiled, fried with bacon, or cooked in a soup. Occasionally, rabbits, pheasants, wild duck or a salmon would mysteriously appear; no-one would ever ask from where. Other days there would be a flat fish, caught in the estuary with rod and line or a stabbing fork, and always a pot of bone broth, thick with vegetables, simmering away on the stove. Root crops were plentiful. Laugharne grew food of its own and there was always some to spare.

Even more to their point, Laugharne left them alone, minding its own eccentric affairs, taking the view that if writers want to sit in their cottages all day writing books, that's up to them – and if they don't, well, have another drink, tomorrow will soon be here. Once the Thomases were settled in Laugharne, they soon moved to a larger house named Sea View, near the Castle, and Dylan seemed to find his feet again. Richard Hughes was a help.

Having come to Laugharne and leased Castle House after his international success with *A High Wind in Jamaica*, Hughes had thrown himself into the life of the town, inviting local children to play with his own, holding frequent parties where writers and artists down from London would stretch out on deckchairs on the Castle lawns. One such event was described by Lance Sieveking, who worked for the BBC:

> There were several people sitting about, among whom were Frances Hughes, my wife and a rather mysterious lady who said she was a witch. Frances introduced me to the young man: 'Oh Dylan, this is Lance'. He grunted and frowned at the ground. I made one or two remarks to him, but he only replied with angry growls. Occasionally, he cast a baleful glare at the clean white flannel trousers I happened to be wearing, and then looked around as if in the hope of finding a pail of garbage or a pot of tar that he could throw over them. He was a stoutish young man, with round, slightly protruding eyes, and a mass of tangled brown curls. His nails were black and his bare feet dirty. He wore very old corduroy trousers, the flies of which gaped open. His dirty grey shirt was torn. He didn't look as if he had washed for a long time. I wondered why he was so grumpy.
>
> He turned to me at last and said, 'No.'
>
> A tremendous smell of beer reached me with the word. He got up and walked a few steps on to the grass . . . . when he returned, his face suddenly lit up in a smile so enchanting that his whole appearance was transformed. He sat down and began to talk to everyone in general, including me. It was obvious that they were all very fond of him, and I could understand why. His personality, once he had thrown off his grumpiness, shone with a sort of endearing bravado. He talked well, and his laugh was infectious. His voice had an astonishingly compelling quality and range.[14]

There were many other visitors, both to the Hugheses and the Thomases. Richard Hughes's wife Frances was related to the Stepneys, one of the few landed families in Carmarthenshire with a large estate near Llanelli, and that brought them into touch with the county families. Augustus John was an occasional guest, both at Castle House and Sea View, and there were often friends down from London or over from Swansea, including Henry Treece, Charlie Fisher, John Davenport, Vernon Watkins, Glyn Jones, Fred Janes and Bert Trick, although Thomas was now seeing less of those he had known in his teens, and more of the contemporary Anglo-Welsh writers, with Keidrych Rhys and Lynette Roberts living just across the river at Llanybri.

This was, Caitlin believes, their only really happy period together. They rented Sea View from the Williams family who, between them, owned much of the town, including Brown's Hotel, the bus company, the electricity generator and at one time (or so it was said) over 50 properties. Augustus John described Sea View as looking like a dolls' house, and so it does, still unchanged, four-storeyed and one room deep. The house was comfortably furnished. When Caitlin's aunt died, her mother arranged for all the furniture to be sent down to them. Vernon Watkins bought them a radio.

Quickly, the house was transformed and for nearly two years their life was neatly ordered, although their double bed (which was being bought on hire purchase) was repossessed by the finance company, and they had to sleep on the floor on a mattress. There was never enough money, but they always employed domestic help and Thomas was clearly progressing in his writing career. Augustus John and Rupert Shephard both painted his portrait. His books were going to be published in the United States by James Laughlin. There was occasional work from the BBC. He regularly reviewed books for *The New English Weekly*. His short stories appeared in *Life and Letters Today*, bringing in a little extra money in addition to the advance from J.M. Dent for *Portrait of the Artist as a Young Dog*, which they agreed to let him have in instalments to keep him going financially. *The Map of Love* was widely reviewed in the literary press, although it sold badly – the book was published on 24 August 1939, and was lost with the outbreak of war just ten days later.

Had it not been for the War, the Thomases would probably have stayed at Sea View, settled and secure, with poems and short stories to write, his career gently gathering momentum, and a baby to nurse. Their first child Llewelyn Edouard, his second name taken from the French side of Caitlin's family, had been born on 30 January 1939; they had gone back to her mother's home to await the birth, and then brought Llewelyn back to Laugharne when he was two months old. Augustus John, Richard Hughes and Vernon Watkins were his godparents. Such debts as they had were none too serious, and, by one device or another, the Thomases usually managed to wriggle through each crisis. Hughes, Watkins and Treece all helped financially and they both had families to fall back on in extremis.

Begging letters that survive from this period should not be taken too seriously, even the famous ones begging for five shillings or talking of pound notes singing in their envelopes, tradesmen threatening County Court action, or Thomas's endeavours to persuade all his friends to contribute five shillings a week to what he called The Thomas Flotation Fund, because the poet had now got into the habit of asking other people to solve his problems; it was a habit that he was never to lose, even when he had no real problems at all and money was rolling in. When Thomas had money, he either spent it – or hid it. He was always generous to drinkers in need, giving money away as readily as he borrowed it, irresponsible to the point of cruelty in his attitude to family finances, swearing that he was totally penniless even when there was money tucked away in his trousers. This was another unattractive side to his nature that made their life seem worse than it was, and the truth of it was (as Caitlin now realises) that their living expenses at Sea View were low, with just enough money coming in for them to live comfortably, if not well. The rent was only ten shillings (50p) a week. Other outgoings were minimal, and there was money coming in from Dent in Britain, from various magazines (albeit in small sums), from Laughlin in the United States, and from an American benefactress who sent them anonymously thirty dollars a month.[15] This was never a large income, but it was *enough* – and quite a lot more than his friends were earning. The average unskilled working man's wage at that time was only £4 a week, and in Laugharne it would have been less.[16]

For the Thomases, life was good – until the War brought their world tumbling down around their ears. The literary magazines closed as their readers went into uniform. Book sales plummeted with wartime restrictions on paper and general shortages. Their circle of benefactors diminished with Thomas's friends joining the Forces, while his drinking circle shrank as the men signed up, often appearing in Brown's Hotel, proudly wearing their uniforms and wondering aloud why the famous poet was not going off to defend his country.

This is another period of Thomas's life that is far from clear. His attempts to avoid conscription were much resented, but he was not a coward. He was tiny and, by this time, fat, having put on four stone in weight while Caitlin was pregnant, ballooning out to 12 stone 8 lbs., but he was also pugnacious and argumentative, frequently starting fights in pubs (and often ending up flat on his back). If anyone flirted with Caitlin (as some did), his fists flew, but those were normal, everyday aspects of Laugharne's social life. The outbreak of war was something different. A refusal to wear uniform and show willing to defend God, King and Country was to be unmanly. Few men wanted to go to War, with experiences of the 1914–18 conflict on the Western Front still sharply defined in collective memory, but faced with what was seen as a patriotic duty men volunteered without doubting, especially men from working-class communities like these.

Thomas's attitude to the War was curious. Caitlin says:

Dylan wasn't just a coward, although he could be weak at times. He had a total lack of hatred, and couldn't share the feelings that people had at that time. He didn't believe in all those false heroics, patriotism and all that nonsense. He thought there was nothing glorious about war, and he couldn't bring himself to write poems about its causes or its purpose. To him no one country was better than another: all men were equal, regardless of race or religion, and he recognised no boundaries between people. He bore no enmity against people because they were black or because they were German. The whole notion of war was ridiculous to him, and he told me that he would never ever, under any circumstances, kill a human being . . . .[17]

From these comments it is clear that his was not a simple case of cowardice, although he never wholly matured as a man, retaining childlike fears of mice and bats, and dreaming of vampires. Late at night he would run down roads in terror, fearing the furry creature flying overhead, his hands clasped around his ears, and he was constantly troubled by insomnia and fears of imaginary illnesses, although he rarely visited a doctor. 'He was much tougher than people think,' says Caitlin, but Thomas did have fears of death, especially towards the end of his life, and his reasons for not wanting to fight had these connotations, possibly deriving partly from his father, who was too old to fight in the First World War, and yet would have followed it closely, especially the reactions to that war of Robert Graves, Wilfred Owen, Isaac Rosenberg and Siegfried Sassoon.

A few days before the declaration of war, D.J. had sent his son a dictionary. It was, said Dylan, expressing thanks, 'a grand, magnificent dictionary', quite probably one of the rarer, more expensive dictionaries that would have been especially useful to a writer so careful and precise in his choice of language. Thomas went on to say:

These are awful days & we are very worried. It is terrible to have built, out of nothing, a complete happiness – from no money, no possessions, no material hopes – & a way of living, & then to see the immediate possibility of its being exploded & ruined through no fault of one's own. I expect you both are very anxious too. If I could pray, I'd pray for peace. I'm not a man of action & the brutal activities of war appal me – as they do every decent-thinking person. Even here the war atmosphere is thick and smelling: the kids dance in the streets, the mobilised soldiers sing *Tipperary* in the pub & wives and mothers weep around the stunted memorial in the Grist . . .[18]

To one friend, Thomas wrote 'this bloody war buggers the orderly mind'; to another he said, 'my one-&-only body I will not give', and to Desmond Hawkins he wrote:

What have we got to fight for or against? To prevent Fascism coming here? It's come. To stop shit by throwing it? To protect our incomes, bank balances, property, national reputations? I feel sick. All this flogged hate again . .[19]

To his friend Bert Trick, he wrote:

As one Daddy to another, what are you doing in the War? I'm very puzzled . . . My little body (though it's little no longer, I'm like a walrus) I don't intend to waste for the mysterious ends of others; and if there's any profiteering to be done, I, in my fashion, wish to be in on it.[20]

It would be wrong to describe Dylan Thomas as weak, because only someone of rare strength could have battled on as he did for public recognition, but he probably had little 'moral fibre' – one of the many ways in which he seemed to lack the normal maturity of a grown man. When he jokingly asked, 'What are you doing for your country? I'm letting mine rot,' there was nothing funny about his humour, for it suggests a lack of conscience. This is all the more appalling in an otherwise sensitive mind. Some of Thomas's supporters, including his widow, are puzzled by this and it is possible, if one is charitable enough, to accept that he possessed, despite his other forms of immaturity, a breadth of intellect so abnormal that he could not encompass thoughts that have a startling clarity for the rest of us. For what ordinary man could believe, or even say

You are right when you suggest that I think a squirrel's stumbling at least of equal importance as Hitler's invasions . . . .[21]

and yet there is no doubt that he meant it, and in such a belief lies both unreality and a truth, the first lying in the fact that we all have to react to the conditions of our time, and the second in the deeper reality that everything that happens during one lifetime matters little in the context of time itself. There is no doubt that this was how Dylan Thomas saw both the War and his writing.

— 7 —

LOVERS ADRIFT IN
WARTIME LONDON

D YLAN Thomas lost all sense of direction during the early years of
the War. With magazines closing, thinner newspapers and fewer
books being commissioned, his chances of earning a living
dwindled. Within a few months, the Thomases were deeply in debt. 'We'd
been living quite well until then,' says Caitlin, with a plaintive shrug,
realising 50 years later that this was the moment when they, like millions
more, had their lives disrupted, with the pieces never quite fitting back
together again.

Always a selfish man, Thomas found little inspiration in the language,
meaning or pity of war, and, instead, became a dissolute shadow of his
former self, neglecting his family and turning from a man who enjoyed his
drink into one who took refuge in it. From beginning to end, one fears that
his motives were ignoble. When the War came, he tried to avoid it. Faced
with the possibility of joining the Forces, he turned the other way,
eventually feigning sickness to avoid conscription. When air raids
threatened, he fled. When bombs fell, he cowered beneath the sheets (and
sometimes the kitchen table), covering his ears, sobbing, gibbering with
fear.

And yet, this was never cowardice in the sense that we know it, for he was
just as much afraid of killing as he was of death. His terrors lay within. It was
never a simple case of being given a rifle and disobeying a command for fear
of personal injury, although there was always that undertone. One cannot
wholly dismiss an impression of gutlessness, but has to consider also the
possibility that a childlike irresponsibility remained part of his character,
totally uncontrolled or controllable, while that inner creative self continually
absorbed new ideas without any sense of time.

The Thomases had been living beyond their means ever since they met.
That was to be the pattern of their lives. Much of their money went in drink,

although not necessarily in alcoholism; pubbing was as much a part of their lives as breakfast or going to bed. Caitlin swears that throughout their marriage, Dylan never once spent a single night at home. Neither did she. The Thomases had always had domestic help in Cwmdonkin Drive, and the Macnamaras came of the Anglo-Irish gentry, to whom household chores were anathema. Having married, Dylan easily adapted to this view of life. When their first child Llewelyn was born, Caitlin's mother provided a private nurse. On moving back to Laugharne, they employed a woman to look after the baby in the evenings while they went off to Brown's Hotel. Dylan would finish writing around 7 p.m. and go straight there; Caitlin would see that Llewelyn was fed (and in later years, her other children), and then join him in the bar, drinking spirits, and putting them back faster than he ever could.

Had their income continued to flow, there would have been few problems. Drink was cheap enough in those days. In any real emergency, there were family or friends to bail them out, but by the autumn of 1939, the war declared and Europe mobilising, it was already apparent that there wasn't enough money coming into Sea View to meet their everyday living expenses. They owed money to the butcher, grocer and milkman, were behind with their rent, and had run up a bill with Ivy and Ebie Williams at Brown's Hotel. The total debt was not enormous, but there was hardly any money coming in to begin paying some of it off. Thomas made this clear in a letter to his agent David Higham, urging him to ask his publishers Dent to commit themselves to some form of long-term financial support:

> I am very much in debt here, to landlord and tradesmen, for about £30 altogether, and unless I can begin, at least, to pay off the debts at once, I'll have to move . . . I'll have to shift house, which means shift from a house to no house, and get in such a mess of living again that it will be impossible to work on anything.[1]

Higham responded promptly, urging Dent to produce the necessary £30, which they did, also agreeing to make regular payments of £8 a month thereafter with a further £45 advanced before Christmas. However, with his other sources of income now drying up fast, these sums proved insufficient. Thomas urged his agent to get that monthly £8 as fast as he could, saying:

> As I don't intend fighting anyone my position is being made most uncomfortable; and a little money would, at least, ease it.[2]

which I take to be a reference to the hostility that he was facing in

Laugharne, where the young men were joining up to fight the Nazis and their families resented Thomas's unwillingness to follow suit.

Thomas was still working on his collection of short stories, *Portrait of the Artist as a Young Dog*, which he described as 'my adolescent autobiography'. For peace and quiet, he moved out of Sea View during the day, leaving Caitlin to look after Llewelyn, using the Laugharne Castle gazebo as his writing room. This was a small stone-built building, with windows on three sides, looking out over the tidal estuary. Richard Hughes had used the gazebo earlier that year to write his novel *In Hazard*, and now allowed Thomas to come and go as he pleased, unaware that Dylan was using this opportunity to plunder his wine cellar, deep in the Castle walls. With wine and peace, Thomas worked well, completing *Portrait of the Artist as a Young Dog* by the beginning of December, three weeks ahead of its due delivery date, thus enabling him to collect the next part of his advance before Christmas.

With that extra £45, his monthly £8, and still some money coming in from elsewhere (including his monthly dollars-cheque from Emma Swan), the Thomases should have been able to cope. Their rent was still only the equivalent of 50p a week, and with beer 3p a pint and cheap food readily available in Laugharne, there could even have been a little left over for a rainy day, if they chose to handle it well, which, of course, they never did. But they weren't in a state of crisis. The only troubling cloud on their horizon was the war itself, and Thomas's realisation that as a young man only 25 years old he would either have to fight or find a good excuse. 'I'm due to be conscripted in a few months' time, & by Christ I want to avoid it,' he told his literary agent.[3]

When he sought advice from Augustus John on how to avoid being called up, Thomas was urged to write to Sir Kenneth Clark at the Ministry of Information, asking for a job there, which he duly did.

> if I do have to register it will have to be as an objector. I don't want to do that, because, though I will not fight, I am perfectly willing to do some kind of work.[4]

Augustus John and Herbert Read both wrote to Clark on Thomas's behalf, but he clearly held out no hope of exemption for Thomas wrote again, thanking him for his letter, saying he had not realised 'getting a job was quite hopeless' and adding

> I'll join up, now, with my age-group, and trust to God and other people

86

that I may get a non-combatant's job within the Army. My great horror's killing.[5]

This last sentence may have touched Clark, for there was further correspondence between Thomas and Lady Clark, revealing that he also sought to join a unit of anti-aircraft gunners organised by the Member of Parliament, Victor Cazalet, on her recommendation. That may have been a ruse to avoid active military service since Cazalet's unit was classified as civil defence. Thomas also went into the possibilities of becoming a conscientious objector, and was told quite forcefully by the local branch of the Peace Pledge Union that it wouldn't look too good him joining them just as he was due to face conscription; so, instead, he took the coward's way out, tanking himself up with whisky, sherry, gin, port, beer and anything else that he could lay his hands on the night before he faced the tribunal that would decide whether or not he was medically fit to join the Forces. Next day he faced them quivering, sweating and covered in blotches. He was classified Grade 3 and given exemption on medical grounds.

Thomas boasted afterwards of his achievement. 'I've done it. I've done it. I've got away with it,' he said that night in Brown's Hotel, getting drunk again to celebrate. 'Many of his friends were envious,' says Caitlin, 'and kept asking him how he managed it, because they also wanted to avoid going into the Services. Whenever he described what he had done to himself it sounded pitifully painful, and for years afterwards that was one of his pub stories.'[6]

It was then April 1940 and with so many of his usual sources of income now curtailed, Thomas was anxious to find new ways of making money; he did not necessarily want to work for it. Instead, he asked various friends to help him financially. He was more or less begging – and it worked. Stephen Spender asked other leading writers and artists to help Thomas financially through an appeal launched in the magazine *Horizon*. Among those who did were Herbert Read, Henry Moore, Sir Kenneth and Lady Clark, T.S. Eliot and Francis Brett Young.

In a letter to Spender, Thomas strengthened his plea for help by saying that he had to

sneak my family away from our home in Carmarthenshire, because we could no longer obtain any credit and it was too awful to live there, among dunning and suspicion, from hand to mouth when I knew the hand would nearly always be empty. I've had to leave all our books and clothes, most of my papers, etc., and unless I pay our most important debts quickly, everything will be sold up: the beds & china & chairs & things that we've managed, with difficulty, to collect over three years ... my debts amount almost exactly to £70. If I could get £100, I could settle everything & make a new start there.[7]

In another letter to Gwyn Jones, Thomas said that he was 'in a very tough spot' but there may have been more to it than that. The Thomases lived on credit. This was not unusual in Laugharne where shopkeepers would allow customers goods 'on tick'. When money came in the Thomases settled up. They were no worse than others. If they did owe in total £70, this time, no one would have been expecting them to pay it off all at once. What was different about this occasion is that Thomas had just appeared before that military tribunal, which was held in Llandeilo. He had faked ill health and boasted of it when other young men in Laugharne were quietly going off to war. Few of them wanted to leave their wives and girlfriends. Their families were afraid they might never come back, and here was the young poet, with literary pretensions which they didn't understand, cheerily admitting that he had cheated to avoid being called up. My understanding is that he was 'taken outside and given a damned good hiding'.

When I suggested to Caitlin that this is what had happened, she first said she couldn't remember it and then didn't recall all the details. We talked about this for some minutes, and then she suddenly blurted, 'Well, he asked for it. That was a cowardly thing to do, wasn't it?' (which makes me think that the story about his 'hiding' is probably true).

Certainly, the Thomases left Laugharne almost immediately after the tribunal hearing, staying first with Dylan's parents at Bishopston, returning briefly to Laugharne during June, and then leaving for Marshfield, near Chippenham, Wiltshire, where John Davenport had invited them to join a house party of artists, writers and musicians, including Lennox Berkeley, Humphrey Searle, Arnold Cooke, Henry Boys and William Glock so that they could all stay well away from London during the Battle of Britain.

In all probability, the Thomases went off to Marshfield with every intention of returning to Laugharne as soon as the party was over. It was as good a retreat as any in July 1940, with the Germans now systematically bombing key industrial targets, including Swansea docks. It was generally understood, by the population as well as the military strategists, that their aim was to damage defences, demoralise the people, and prepare the ground for invasion. That was what had happened in Europe; Britain could be next, so why not go to the Davenports' fine Georgian home The Malting House, with its well stocked wine cellar, antique furniture, concert pianos (they owned not one, but two), and Picassos on the walls.

Here, miles from anywhere, disaster struck. Having been given that hiding in Laugharne, Thomas now felt threatened from within; this apparently confident, but inwardly childlike man suddenly realised that Caitlin *could* have been unfaithful. One weekend she returned to Laugharne, stopping over in Swansea to see his parents, and on speaking to his mother Thomas discovered that her dates did not tally. There was one missing night in her itinerary. She had spent that night in Cardiff, booking into a hotel, hoping to make love to William Glock, then a music critic, who was tall, blond and handsome; a fine-featured man who was altogether far more imposing than her tiny, fat and far-from-fastidious husband.[8]

Thomas soon realised what *might* have happened. Glock had been missing that night, too – and he and Caitlin had spent many hours together, with him playing the piano and her practising her dance steps, while Thomas and Davenport had been involved in a private fantasy of their own, writing a satirical detective story *The Death of the King's Canary*.[9]

At first Thomas could not believe it. His view of marriage was idealised. Sex was not something that he knew very much about, but he realised soon enough that she had made a fool of him, and that other people in The Malting House must have known of her intended liaison with Glock without telling him. He was deeply upset. Thomas struck his wife and also threw a knife at her (which missed). There were violent, tearful arguments, which ended with Caitlin protesting her innocence, him refusing to sleep with her – and her realisation that she was close to losing him. This mattered to them both, for they had a simple dependence upon each other, so they decided to leave Marshfield and, with Christmas coming (and Thomas perhaps fearful of another hiding in Laugharne, or, even worse, his neighbours there realising that there was something amiss in their marriage), they headed back to Swansea, staying with D.J. and Florence while they tried to sort themselves out. That can hardly have been a happy Christmas, for Florence was aware that Caitlin had been missing that one night. Now Thomas left his wife in Swansea while he went off to London, looking for work and somewhere for them to live, or so he said.

By now, they were frequently apart, sometimes for just a night or two, often longer. Thomas had no money to give Caitlin, so she and Llewelyn became wholly dependent upon his parents. Where he got to, nobody knows, but their trust had gone and Caitlin believes it likely that most nights he found another woman's bed to sleep in, without necessarily having prolonged affairs. Thomas often pursued women, with protestations of romantic love, without actually making love to them. Various wartime love letters to other women survive (including a bundle owned by the children of a Swansea woman who is said to have had an affair with him, that have never been published), but in each case there was no lasting relationship. Wynford Vaughan-Thomas, who was also in London during this period and met him intermittently, told me that he knew of two women who had gone to bed with Thomas. In both cases, nothing much happened before Dylan fell asleep.

Thomas was now travelling light, just as when he first arrived in London in 1934. Most of their possessions had been left in Laugharne. Caitlin had sold some to buy clothes for her affair with Glock, and has no idea what happened to the rest. His baggage consisted of not much more than his work-in-progress, and that was largely in the mind. *Portrait of the Artist as a Young Dog* had been published by Dent,[10] and he was already planning a longer story loosely based on his own arrival in London, *Adventures in the Skin Trade*,[11] which occupied him for several months until Dent, having seen the first 15,000 words, told his agent that the material was not good enough, and seemed to be 'quite without intellectual control . . . Thomas cannot build a literary career merely on the miniature furore created by his early work'. There were also one or two ideas for poems and short stories, but nothing firm. He was becoming slower and more careful in his writing, and easily distracted by drink away from Laugharne. When approached for contributions to *Penguin New Writing* and *Poetry London*, he replied that he had nothing new to offer, although he did finish the poems *Deaths and Entrances*[12] and *Into her lying down head*[13] in the months that followed, sending them off to other publications. Contrary to some suggestions, Thomas was not wholly inactive during this period. *On a Wedding Anniversary* appeared in *Poetry London* (15 January 1941); *Love in the Asylum* in a later issue (May–June 1941); *Ballad of the Long-legged Bait*[14] in *Horizon* (July 1941); *Among Those Killed in the Dawn Raid was a Man Aged a Hundred*, one of only two poems directly inspired by the war, in *Life and Letters Today* (August 1941); *The Hunchback in the park* and *On the Marriage of a Virgin* both appeared in *Life and Letters Today* (October 1941), and *Request to Leda*, which he had written at Marshfield during his collaboration with Davenport, was published in *Horizon* (July 1942).

These were all substantial poems, and although *The hunchback in the park* was the development of an idea first attempted eight years before[15] and *On the Marriage of a Virgin* also had an earlier relative, there was nothing strange in this. Thomas carried ideas for years. Similar images were used again and again. These poems, taken with the 15,000 words written of *Adventures in the Skin Trade*, make this a more productive period of his life than has been suggested in other biographies.

Much of *Adventures in the Skin Trade* was written during late 1940 and early 1941, beginning during his four or five months at Marshfield and continuing at Bishopston while he was staying there with his parents, then at Laugharne where he returned with Caitlin and Llewelyn in the spring of 1941. Then suddenly, for reasons that are far from clear (and may possibly have something to do with local hostility to his reappearance without a uniform), the Thomases left for London, with nowhere to stay, and no money in their pockets.

By this time the Thomases had hardly any regular income at all. They may have exhausted his parents' patience and Frances Hughes' kindness, and headed for London on the vague promise of work from the BBC or in films. Thomas believed, as he always did, that he would only clinch jobs like this through personal contact. There is little documentation for this, other than a letter to Vernon Watkins, dated 28 August 1941, giving their temporary address as the offices of *Horizon*:

> The place I'm staying in in London with Caitlin is closed after tomorrow or Friday and we haven't yet found anywhere new. We've been having an awful time, and I have felt like killing myself. We arrived with no money, after leaving Llewelyn in Ringwood, and have had none since. In Laugharne that was not so bad. In stinking friendless London it is unendurable. I am still looking for a film job, and have been offered several scripts to do 'in the near future', which might mean weeks.[16]

Writing scripts was a new departure, with an extra attraction. His poetry had always been composed in the belief that poems were best read aloud, and now he was being asked to produce material for use on radio, the medium for the spoken rather than the written word. This was to add another dimension to his career, although, initially, his commissions were of no great significance.

His first two scripts, *The Duque de Caxias* and *Cristobel Colon*, were written for the BBC Latin American Service at the request of Royston Morley, who had edited the pre-war literary magazine *Janus* and was now working for the BBC. Both scripts were written at Marshfield, and by the time Thomas left Laugharne for London he was clearly hoping for more BBC commissions. He also had some vague introductions to the film industry, which was developing a wartime life of its own at the behest of the Ministry of Information.

That this was of great importance to Thomas can be understood from a letter he wrote to Archie Harding of the BBC:

> Thank you very much for your long, and extremely helpful, letter about

the amount of backing the BBC could give me if they were questioned by the Ministry of Labour as to whether I was doing any work for you that could be called valuable. I understand, naturally, that you could not support me *in full*: but what you said in your letter, and what you said you could say to the Ministry of Labour if necessary, will, I hope, do the trick: – that is, keep me for a while longer out of the factories . . . .[17]

From this it is clear that Thomas saw the BBC as a means of avoiding the risk of being drummed into some other form of war work, such as munitions, once he had managed to evade military service. Such a dodge would have been far safer in wartime London, with thousands of other people engaged on war work, than in Laugharne where there were now few young men still wearing civilian clothes. In London, he would have been able to vanish into the crowd (which was, no doubt, his intention).

Finding employment directly, or indirectly, for the Ministry of Information was an even safer option, and here his key introduction was the American film director Ivan Moffatt, whom he had known slightly in Fitzrovia (Moffatt had the use of his father's flat in Fitzroy Square and was also a friend of Davenport's). By 1941, Moffatt was working for the film producer Donald Taylor, whose company Strand Films made documentaries for the Ministry of Information. Taylor needed scriptwriters. Thomas needed work. Moffatt introduced them.

Now, Dylan Thomas was safe from having to go to war, or even getting his hands dirty. His work for Strand Films provided him with a regular £8 a week, rising later to £10.[18] The job necessitated him travelling to different parts of the country when films were being made on location, and he was required to tailor scripts to production needs, but, in general, Taylor was happy to leave his writers to work in their own way, providing schedules were met. Likewise, he had no objection to their other freelance jobs providing they never let him down. This was ideal for Thomas, because it left him free to take up any offers from the BBC, and able to base himself wherever he wished but, as always, he landed in a muddle. Perhaps there were too many temptations; perhaps he had too much money. Whatever the explanation, he appears to have become disorientated.

For the next two years he and Caitlin were unsettled. Llewelyn was left with her mother, and they moved around London, with frequent trips to Wales, usually together but often apart, avoiding the worst of the bombing, with Thomas writing no poetry, but managing to maintain a constant output of film and radio work. There was always money coming in, but Caitlin saw little of it – and when they were apart he began to drink more heavily, frequently disappearing for days on end, without her having any idea where he had gone.

And yet, despite all this (and there are many wartime reminiscences of Thomas having difficulty holding his drink, engaged in scuffles, frequently sick), he managed to hold down his job with Strand and to carve out a new reputation for himself in radio.[19] Besides writing scripts, Thomas carved out a reputation for himself with the BBC as a performer in radio drama productions. He had more money in his pocket than at any previous time in his life, but his wife seldom knew. For a long time they had no home. She was rarely given enough money for food or clothes – and he had now acquired the skill of writing self-abasing letters whenever he wanted to 'borrow' from friends. He would steal from anyone they were staying with – clothes, family silver and even on one occasion a sewing machine – hoping to pawn the goods (in the belief that he could redeem the pledge before they found out).[20]

It is small wonder that Caitlin now describes him as 'a shit', but at the time she had little idea how much he was earning (because money was something they seldom discussed), genuinely believing that they were so poor that it would be better for them to leave Llewelyn with her mother at Ringwood and for her to stay with friends while he kept going off to London, always with the excuse of 'work'.

In the early war years she frequently stayed with Frances Hughes in Laugharne, and later with a friend, Vera Killick, at Talsarn, Cardiganshire, even after Dylan had found them a London flat – a studio apartment in Manresa Road, Chelsea, costing £1 a week – which they rented from the summer of 1942. Thomas would write loving letters to explain why he could not get down to see her, and she accepted whatever he said, particularly after the birth of their daughter Aeronwy, with whom she became wholly preoccupied.[21]

Strand Films provided Thomas with a regular income for nearly three years, and also gave him an entrée to another layer of London's literary social life. Film writers tended to gather in the pubs and restaurants around Wardour Street, Old Compton Street and St Martin's Lane, and were just as clannish as the boys up from Wales. At different times, Strand Films had premises in Upper St Martin's Lane, Golden Square and West Street, with the back bar of the Café Royal almost an extension of their office. Clubs like the Mandrake and the Gargoyle became everyday meeting places, and from there Thomas and Company would drift on down to the pubs (and often back again). The novelist Graham Greene also worked for Strand Films early in the war, and Thomas became especially close to Australian-born brothers Jack and Philip Lindsay, and, later, the novelist and short story writer Julian MacLaren-Ross. Caitlin tells me that his closest friend of all was Philip Lindsay, who had a staggering capacity for alcohol; he would return home from drinking bouts barely able to stand, and yet still sit down at his typewriter, hammering out whatever work had to be done to meet the next deadline. Through Jack, who went on to write 60 books, including poetry, autobiography and novels with classic Greek themes, Thomas found himself introduced to and moving freely among the left-wing writers, artists, politicians and diplomats. Constantine Fitzgibbon and John Davenport also mixed in these circles, which included the Russian spies Guy Burgess and Donald Maclean, whom Thomas knew well. There was much sexual ambivalence and heavy drinking. It is one of the least documented periods of Thomas's life. Strand Films' records were all destroyed and, anyway, this was wartime London when relationships were often casual and life expectancy short.

This film crowd might be hard drinkers but they were far more flexible writers, well read and experienced in different skills. Much work would be done over long expansive lunches, with ideas bouncing off the walls and no one worrying too much about expenses. This was a new world for him, for Thomas had always been fascinated by cinema and – until the end of his life – had the habit of slipping into matinées, whether visiting Carmarthen, Swansea or London, if only partially to sleep off the effects of mid-day drinking, or kill time until the pubs opened again. Thomas had to be on his mettle. Had he fallen down on the job, there would always be someone willing to take over his scripts. As it was, he threw himself into the work, initially keeping office hours other than on location.

When temporarily parted from Caitlin, even with a good excuse, he would write, 'I do not care a bugger about the Problems of Wartime Transport. All I know is that you are my wife, my lover, my joy, my Caitlin'[22] but that was just Thomas the Husband trying to reassure her that all was well. She realises now that throughout this period he was pursuing other women, even if the relationships meant little. When he returned from location filming she would notice from the texture of his skin and his body weight that he was drinking heavily, and spirits, not beer. Caitlin admits this did not worry her. The birth of Aeronwy had brought out some deep maternal instinct. She would spend her days cuddling and caressing her baby, endlessly combing her hair, not really bothered whether Dylan was there or not; a situation that he may have exploited.

It was the German flying bomb raids on London that brought the Thomases back together again; they sub-let their flat in Manresa Road, and moved down to Bosham in Sussex early in 1944 to avoid the first prolonged

The first poems I knew were nursery rhymes, and before I could read them for myself I had come to love just the words of them, the words alone. What the words were stood for, symbolised, or meant was of very secondary importance — what mattered was the very sound of them as I heard them for the first time on the lips of the remote and quite incomprehensible grown-ups who seemed, for some reason, to be living in my world. And these words were, to me, as the notes of bells, the sounds of musical instruments, the noises of wind, sea, and rain, the rattle of milkcarts, the clopping of hooves on cobbles, the fingering of branches on a window pane, might be to someone, deaf from birth, who has miraculously found his hearing.

Dylan Thomas

The sound of the words was what mattered: Dylan Thomas said this himself in these words dashed off for an admirer in a New York bar in May 1953.

The photograph of himself that Dylan Thomas sent to Pamela Hansford Johnson in 1933.

Caitlin's first lover – Augustus John.

Dylan and Caitlin shortly after their marriage, staying at her mother's house near Ringwood, Hampshire.

Descending into Laugharne. This is Gosport Street, approached from the West. The Thomases' first home was in the row of fishermen's cottages on the right. Their back gardens overlooked the Taf estuary.

Sea View, Laugharne: the Thomases' second home, described by Augustus John as 'looking like a dolls' house'. Dylan and Caitlin moved there in August 1938.

Brown's Hotel in King Street, Laugharne.

Dylan and Caitlin photographed in the bar of Brown's Hotel circa 1938.

Granny Thomas, Dylan's mother, at her home in King Street, Laugharne, shortly after his death. The house was called Pelican. Dylan had rented it for his parents when the family returned to Laugharne in 1949.

Dylan Thomas on the balcony of
The Boat House with John
Malcolm Brinnin.

The image that Brinnin did not
project: Dylan Thomas sitting
quietly after a reading at the
University of Vermont on 15
February 1952. Thomas is talking
to Professor Samuel N. Bogorad of
the University's Department of
English.

Perhaps the most famous Thomas image of all: a photograph taken at his first public reading of *Under Milk Wood* at the Kaufmann Auditorium, New York, on 14 May 1953.

Recording for the BBC. This was how Dylan Thomas made himself a household name in the immediate post-war years.

Wife, daughter and grandson: Caitlin and her daughter Aeronwy with son Huw in the back garden of the house in Delancey Street, Camden Town, on the day the commemorative plaque was unveiled. Behind them is the gypsy caravan in which Thomas worked – the same caravan that Margaret Taylor previously provided at South Leigh.

Standing at the bar of the White Horse Tavern in New York, which was Thomas's favourite
haunt during his US reading tours.

my house in Wales

A drawing by Dylan Thomas of his home The Boat House. This was
drawn for a friend on the bar at the White Horse Tavern, and signed
and dated, in May 1953. Thomas often drew rough sketches and occasionally experimented with painting in oils. He could also vamp tunes on
a piano.

Front view of The Boat House.

Rear view of The Boat House, as it was when the Thomases lived there, with a chicken run in the garden.

Looking through The Boat House window shortly after
Caitlin took the children to Italy, leaving the family furniture
behind.

The workshed on the cliff where Dylan Thomas wrote daily
during the last four years of his life. It was originally a garage,
built to accommodate Laugharne's first motor car. Every
morning Caitlin lit the coal stove so that the workshed would
be warm by the time he started writing around 2 p.m.

The poet is dead. The workshed is empty. Only his sticks remain.

air raids, and then four months later to Hedgerley Dean, near Slough, where they stayed with Donald Taylor, while he and Thomas worked together on a film treatment based on the Burke and Hare murders, *The Doctor and the Devils*.[23] Despite the heavy bombing, Taylor was confident that the War was entering its final phase. He was busily working up different film projects to go into production when, as he thought, the post-war cinema industry would be ready for new ideas, with new funding available. Taylor was an optimistic man, bustling and witty, and the pivotal figure in Thomas's life at the time. When the flying bombs started in June, Taylor agreed that the Thomases should move back to Wales, and keep well away from London until the skies were peaceful again; there were several projects for Dylan to work on, and he didn't mind where they went. Nothing could have suited them better; Dylan could now return home to West Wales with a regular guaranteed income.

At first they stayed with his parents, who had moved to Llangain where Florence had inherited one of the family cottages at Blaen Cwm from her sister Theodosia; they were there five or six weeks, hoping to rent another cottage in Laugharne, while Dylan completed a script for Donald Taylor, *The Unconquerable People*, describing the spirit of the Resistance movement in Europe. This was one of several projects they were working on together that were never made into films. From his letters, it is clear that Thomas was pinning his financial hopes on *The Doctor and the Devils*, but he was also composing a lyrical script for *Our Country*, a documentary which Taylor co-produced with Alexander Shaw for the Ministry of Information, describing the sentiments of a merchant seaman returning home from the war. That Thomas cared for the quality of these scripts is clear from his letters to Taylor, which are now in the Texas collection and can be read in *Collected Letters*. For some years thereafter, he cherished a hope of writing a script for a major film. The technique intrigued him. He was aware that

Written down, the verse (of a film script) looks a little chaotic – as it's bound to be . . . Heard spoken to a beautiful picture, the words gain a sense & authority which the printed word denies them.[24]

Having failed to find somewhere in Laugharne, they accepted a friend's offer to let them rent a bungalow at New Quay on the Cardiganshire coast. There began one of the most creative periods of Thomas's life. He was back where he wanted to be, in Wales and by the sea, with the cares of wartime London far away, his time his own, and no real financial worries. In the previous three years he had been so busy with film work that he had only managed to produce three poems *Ceremony After a Fire Raid*,[25] *Last night I dived my*

95

beggar arm[26] and *Your breath was shed*,[27] although Caitlin insists that he destroyed others thinking them not good enough. Now, back in Llangain and then New Quay, he worked on poems and scripts with renewed enthusiasm. The first poems that he wrote were *Poem in October*, which remains among his most popular, and the experimental *Vision and Prayer*.

In *Poem in October*, which begins

It was my thirtieth year to heaven

he developed an idea which he told Vernon Watkins[28] had been in his mind for three years. It was a 'Laugharne poem: the first place poem I've written,' and followed the contours of its landscape, with the poet returning to the township as day breaks, with its familiar patterns coming alive before his eyes. *Vision and Prayer* was more religious, with Thomas using diamond-shapes to define the linear appearance of each verse and so emphasising his theme, a device favoured by the metaphysical poets in the seventeenth century. It is possible that he also began work on *Fern Hill*, because there is a reference to a third poem in a letter to Watkins and *Fern Hill*[29] is similar in sentiment to the other two, although it was not completed until the following September when he had returned again to Blaen Cwm.

— 8 —
DEATHS AND ENTRANCES

THE Thomases moved to New Quay with their daughter on 4 September 1944. Their family life was still incomplete. Llewelyn had been left with Caitlin's mother for over three years. They had rarely seen him, and now settled into their new home Majoda, a timber-framed bungalow with walls of sheeted asbestos, standing high on the cliffs overlooking the sea, with stepped access down to a private beach. Nearby, Dylan rented a room above a pub so that he could work without being disturbed by Aeronwy.

He had much to do. Taylor had asked him to work on an adaptation of Maurice O'Sullivan's study of life in the Blasket Islands, *Twenty Years A'Growing*,[1] and while he was preparing this film script, Dent agreed that it was time for another volume of his poetry; his friend Oscar Williams[2] offered to place his work with the American literary magazines, and James Laughlin wrote from New York to say that he would be publishing Dylan Thomas's *Selected Writings*.[3]

Through his work for films Thomas had learned economy. His writing was now less complicated and more direct, with none of the fussiness and verbal extravagance that characterised his pre-war poems. 'Keep it simple,' Caitlin always said, and he knew that in cinema, with its close reliance of visual image upon spoken word, powerful effects could be achieved with simple language. It was to be a lesson well learned, and one that he was to apply both in scripts for Donald Taylor and also in experimenting with the use of sound in his work for radio. These thoughts all come together at New Quay. Thereafter his work was concentrated, forceful and always substantial.

This cohesion came with the war drawing to a close and new opportunities opening up as publishers and radio producers prepared for the new public mood. Faced with chances like these Thomas was as selfish as ever, working well when projects appealed to him and allowing others to fall by default. It was during this period that he failed to turn up at Vernon Watkins' wedding, even though he was in London at the time, only a few streets away, and due to be best man,[4] and also broke his contract to deliver the book *London Streets*.[5] This behaviour was never wholly unconscious. Thomas knew what he was doing, but seemed to care little for other people's feelings. It was the same as those thefts in wartime London. Thomas acted on the spur of the moment, with seldom a thought for the consequences; as ever, the untrained child. And yet, when the circumstances were right, other aspects of his complex personality prevailed.

Settled on the cliffs at New Quay, with only himself to think about (and occasional trips to London to see Donald Taylor, his agent or friends at the BBC), Thomas flopped back into his familiar routine, finding in The Black Lion a perfect haven for his evening drinking, or when friends came down from London. This had become another feature of the Thomases' life; wherever they settled, friends followed. All he had to do was work, which he did with but one distressing interruption. That was in March 1945.

Mary Keene, wife of one of Thomas's film industry friends Ralph Keene, was staying with them at Majoda. John Eldridge, who also worked for Strand Films, came down to join them with a production assistant and a secretary. They were all due to work together on a script. Another friend, a woman whom Thomas had known since childhood, was living next door with her young child. Her husband was a commando, who had recently returned from fighting with the Partisans behind the lines in Greece.

Back home in Wales, the officer was in some distress, which was exacerbated by a belief that his wife may have become too close to the Thomases; he suspected that she had been living with Dylan and Caitlin in a *ménage à trois*, a suggestion which Caitlin insists was ridiculous. Anyhow, that was what he had come to believe. There had been tensions between them, and one night at The Black Lion the secretary (who was an active Communist) said something that upset him. Realising that she was Jewish, he, in turn, made an anti-semitic remark – and a fight broke out. Thomas and friends threw the ex-commando out of the pub. He arrived back at the bungalow later that night with a sten gun, firing off 20 rounds into the building before finally producing a hand grenade with which he said he intended to blow them all up.

Eventually, they calmed him down, and he disappeared into the night. That might have been the end of the matter, but a neighbour heard the shots and called the police who charged the officer with attempted murder.[6] As the

Thomases had only gone to New Quay in the first place through their friendship with his wife, this incident effectively brought their stay to an end, although they remained at Majoda until the case came to trial. It was a slightly ridiculous end to this phase of his work.

Through those winter months, Thomas continued writing *Twenty Years A'Growing*, which he and Taylor both thought had all the ingredients for a successful film. It was a natural theme for Thomas's imagination, based on the book by Maurice O'Sullivan, describing as through a child's eyes his own upbringing on the Irish-speaking Blasket Islands off the coast of County Kerry. Much of Thomas's best short story writing was in similar vein, looking back on Swansea and family life in West Wales, and in *Twenty Years A'Growing*[7] he was adapting another man's perception of similar experiences, using devices of dialogue and poetry that he employed later in *Under Milk Wood*.

Twenty Years A'Growing was of similar length to *Under Milk Wood*, although this, too, remained unfinished because Taylor was unable to raise the finance for the film. The script occupied much of Thomas's time at New Quay, but he also managed to complete the radio script *Quite Early One Morning*,[8] which features sound techniques similar to *Under Milk Wood*; worked on at least three other film projects that were aborted, gathered together the material for *Selected Writings* and, produced seven more poems for the collection that became known as *Deaths and Entrances*.[9]

His new directness made *Deaths and Entrances* his strongest collection. The poems possessed force, simplicity and instant appeal. As each poem was written, he sent copies off to literary magazines in Britain and the United States, using Oscar Williams as his agent. This collection brought together in one volume the poems written in Laugharne and Swansea early in the war, the few that he had managed to write in London, and those composed at Llangain and New Quay. These were:

The Conversation of Prayer
A Refusal to Mourn the Death, by Fire, of a Child in London
Poem in October
This Side of the Truth
To Others than You
Love in the Asylum
Unluckily for a Death
The Hunchback in the Park
Into her lying down head
Papers and Sticks

Deaths and Entrances
A Winter's Tale
On a Wedding Anniversary
There was a Saviour
On the Marriage of a Virgin
In my Craft or Sullen Art
Ceremony After a Fire Raid
When I woke
Amongst those killed
In the Dawn Raid
Lie Still, Sleep Becalmed
Vision and Prayer
Ballad of the Long-legged Bait
Holy Spring
Fern Hill

Publication was delayed for many months, partly through his own indecision. Seeing his work in final book form was always traumatic for Thomas. The appearance of his words on printers' proofs invariably set him off again, changing punctuation, altering words, removing lines and, this time, making such a mess of his proofs that more had to be sent. There were no photocopiers in those days, and so he started all over again, completely rewriting one poem, deleting another, complaining about the type-setting of *Vision and Prayer* (his metaphysical poem set in diamonds), and asking that *Fern Hill* be included 'as it is an essential part of the feeling & meaning of the book as a whole'.[10] Thomas realised that the delays were his fault and that the publishers would be put to further expense in having so much of the printers' work reset; he said he was willing to pay for this himself, which is a clear indication of the importance he attached to *Deaths and Entrances*, knowing that it would be studied carefully by critics and fellow-poets to see whether his work had fulfilled its early promise.

As is often the way with authors, by the time *Deaths and Entrances* was published, his mind had moved on to something else; he was keen to move to the United States (a plan which did not come off for some years and only then on a visiting basis). With the court case resolved, the Thomases moved back to London, after spending a few more weeks at Llangain with his parents (which was when Thomas finished *Fern Hill*). The BBC was now taking much more interest in his work. He was writing regularly for its Overseas Service, and was occasionally asked to read the work of other poets, prepare talks and take part in drama programmes. Thomas seldom turned down this sort of work. It was well paid and, taken with his other income, brought his earnings to the level where he had the beginnings of a tax problem – although neither the Inland Revenue, the National Insurance, nor his wife had any idea how much money he was receiving. Thomas was still as secretive as ever about his finances, spending faster than he earned, constantly pleading poverty to his friends, and frequently borrowing from those with earnings less than his own.

Thomas's pleas have often been taken at face value. Even Caitlin believed that at the time, and there is no doubt that when the poet was depressed, as he frequently was, he could become consumed with self-pity, which was another childlike way of drawing attention to himself. His problems were more psychological than financial for, with the publication of *Deaths and Entrances*, he became one of Britain's more successful writers, his income arising not from that one tiny volume of poetry, important though it was, but from all the other commissions stimulated by its success. Acclaim is often a far greater burden for an author than failure. It imposes different demands. Risks can no longer be taken because there is an audience or a readership out there beyond his study wall that has its own expectations to be met, judging each new work by standards already set.

With his unerring instinct, Thomas clearly sensed that his status was changing. This is something that only those who have gone through a similar process, or witnessed its effect on others, can wholly understand, for it is far less common among writers than in other branches of the arts; in the Sixties it was something I observed at close hand when unknown musicians like The Beatles, The Who or The Rolling Stones had to cope not with sudden increases in income – because that comes later – but an immediate change in other people's attitudes towards them. It is that moment when the artist's work is more important than he is, when offers arrive almost daily, and he finds himself being asked to give interviews, sign autographs, make personal appearances, or express opinions on issues of the day.

That this happened to Thomas in the mid-forties is clear to me, although Fitzgibbon puts the date much later (and expresses it differently), and Ferris assumes that it was Thomas that was changing and not other people's attitude towards him.

The process had started much earlier with those minor controversies in *The Listener* and *The Sunday Times*, and the way he was regarded by other poets. It also seems probable that people he worked with in films treated him with a certain caution for his scripts had a rare lyrical quality. It is significant that when Thomas went to New Quay, people went to him. Clearly, he was seen as a man with rare gifts, and this may have affected his behaviour; that commando officer spotted it when he accused Thomas and friends of being 'a lot of egoists'. In a letter to Vernon Watkins, written from New Quay, Thomas admitted:

The ordinary moments of walking up village streets, opening doors or letters, speaking good-days to friends or strangers, looking out of windows, making telephone calls, are so inexplicably (to me) dangerous that I am trembling all over before I get out of bed in the mornings to meet them . . .[11]

Faced with what was, in its effect upon him, a crisis in his development of personality, Thomas became more secretive and inward-looking than ever, sharing his private thoughts with no one, fantasising, building elaborate deceptions, and one can only begin to sense this now, long after the events, by comparing all the different components of his life, and finding how much at variance they are with one another.

Deaths and Entrances was the turning-point, because even his most jealous contemporaries sensed a change in him, with the poets who had sought safe employment with the BBC now turning to him for ideas, and critics responding to the growing maturity of his work:

It is difficult to convey in a few words the quality of Mr Thomas's poetry, for it is in the truest sense of the word original . . . These verses are no careless expression of exuberance bursting the seams of imagination's garment: they are carefully wrought, in a rare combination of vigour and virtuosity.

Vita Sackville-West,
The Observer

Dylan Thomas is not only the best living Welsh poet, but is a great poet. He is sometimes difficult, but always rewarding, rich and arresting.

John Betjeman
The Daily Herald

In this new book of twenty-four poems, Mr Dylan Thomas shows himself to be the authentic, magical thing, a true poet – original and traditional, imperfect but outstanding, with the unmistakeable fire and power of genius. If anyone is looking for new contemporary poetry worthy of our great – and, I would add, world-supreme English tradition, here it is. For I do not find such wealth of poetry elsewhere among the poems of our deservedly known and genuinely gifted writers . . . here we are in an ocean of poetry and there is a spate of immense long rollers, huge-shouldered, transparent green with magic light and foaming into billows of the purest snow of creation with the energy of an earlier age . . . Mr Thomas is not an intellectual poet . . . he does not obtrude his intellectual processes upon us. That there are a powerful mind and a great driving force behind this remarkable poet is implied when I am ready to declare that not only is Mr Thomas a truly creative writer, but that this book alone, in my opinion, ranks him as a major poet.

W.J. Turner
The Spectator

This book represents a new maturity in Mr Dylan Thomas. His use of language and his imagery are as striking and felicitous as ever. He has added a mastery of intricate metrical forms. Half a dozen poems in this volume are, quite simply, entrancing.

Walter Allen
Time and Tide

Three at least of the poems in this volume – *A Winter's Tale, Poem In October* and *The Ballad of the Long-legged Bait* – must be placed among the outstanding poems written in our time; and there are half a dozen others on a hardly inferior level. If they are remarkable for nothing else, their grandeur would remove them from current trends.

G.W. Stonier
New Statesman

This acclaim came at a time when he was placed unusually as a poet. With that sonorous voice, he was a natural for radio at the very moment that radio was at the peak of its influence, with wireless sets in nearly every home. Family life was planned around the most popular programmes of the day. Parents and children sat around the dining room table with that week's *Radio Times*, building their leisure time around a choice of programmes that included variety shows, situation comedy, drama, every kind of music, even poetry. The mid-to-late Forties were the heyday of the spoken word.

For just a few years radio dominated Britain's life, making its personalities household names. More people listened to radio than bought any one national newspaper. Its stars were as real as those of films or television, their lives chronicled in the newspapers, their life stories published as comic strips in *Radio Fun* or serialised in the Sunday papers, their scandals a matter of public concern. The war had caused this, with families depending on radio for the latest news from the fronts. In moments of emergency, Churchill had broadcast to the people. It was an intimate medium. Those waiting by the fireside for news of loved ones could tell by inflexions of the announcer's voice whether this was good or bad. Then there were programmes like *ITMA*, *Variety Bandbox* or *Workers Playtime* that were intended to lift morale.

The emphasis changed during the post-war years, with more comedy like *The Goon Show*, which launched the careers of Peter Sellers, Spike Milligan and Harry Secombe; *Educating Archie*, through which Max Bygraves became a household name, and others like *Hancock's Half Hour* that attracted huge national audiences. There was relatively little pop music, but a wide range of light classical and middle-brow musical programmes; set-piece drama productions, lasting maybe an hour or 90 minutes; regular programmes like *The Brains Trust*, which featured celebrities discussing issues of the day: *Down Your Way*, which brought mobile broadcasting units to different towns and villages, or *In Town Tonight*, in which visitors to London were interviewed in the studio (in those early days of air passenger travel it was still a major event for an author or film star to arrive from New York).

This changed in June 1953, when there was a nationwide switch from radio to television with a boom in TV sales, anticipating live coverage of the Coronation, but when Dylan Thomas returned to London late in 1945, radio was the business to be in. The war in Europe was over. The war in the Far East was drawing to a close. The BBC was looking for new ideas and new people, with its Features Department, directed by Laurence Gilliam, anxious to be experimental and innovative, using the techniques of sound to new effect. Its staff included several poets of the Thirties whom Thomas had first met in the bars of Fitzrovia and Chelsea. Some were old drinking buddies like Rayner Heppenstall, Louis MacNeice and Roy Campbell. Other poets now working for the department included Terence Tiller, Patric Dickinson, D.G. Bridson and W.R. Rodgers. It was Campbell who remarked, accurately, that one advantage of being in the BBC was that you could give jobs to your friends. Thomas needed the money because Strand Films and its successor Gryphon were being wound up. He found himself in the right place at the right moment.

The first person to employ him regularly was George Orwell, who engaged Thomas to read for the BBC's Eastern Service. John Arlott, a published poet before the war, invited Thomas to appear on a weekly series,

Book of Verse, also for the Eastern Service. Arlott employed him 20 or 30 times a year on literary programmes of every type, and says that Thomas

was always open-minded to experiment: in his own word, 'easy'; while his immense depth of reading in poetry – which he never paraded – and his very real integrity made him the perfect touchstone for a producer . . . As a broadcast verse speaker, he was outstanding. His reading of his own poetry bridged the gap of comprehension for some and, even for those who knew his work intimately, it was never quite so exciting as when he spoke it. In fact, he wrote for the ear. After centuries of poetry on which the eye could – and frequently needed to – turn back, he returned to the oral tradition, in lines that moved perpetually on, a progression in shaped and measured form. Because, too, he was essentially a Welshman, his poetry although in itself a 'universal', was at its best in the regional voice . . . . . Each word he read was delivered shaped and carefully, lest its values should be lost in haste. He read with care for rhythm, and with a subtle gift for indicating a line-end when the meaning ran on unpunctuated without destroying the flow by a pause . . . He would sit through rehearsals smoking endlessly: he took production like a professional actor and, when he stepped up to the microphone to read, made a happily extravagant figure. Round, with the roundness of a Tintoretto urchin–cherub, and in a large, loose tweed jacket, he would stand, feet apart and head thrown back, a dead cigarette frequently adhering wispily to his lower lip, curls a little tousled and eyes half-closed, barely reading the poetry by eye, but rather understanding his way through it, one arm beating out a sympathetic double-rhythm as he read. His voice would be sometimes almost naïvely young and clearly tenor, while, at others, a dynamo throbbing seemed to drive him to an intense rolling depth.[12]

Patric Dickinson also employed him regularly on the Home Service, and Thomas soon found himself being invited to write, narrate or take part in major programmes produced both in London and in Wales. There were many of them.

These were well paid freelance jobs, for which he would receive variable fees, at least 12 or 15 guineas plus repeat fees, and occasionally much more, at a time when the average working wage in Britain for a skilled man was still only £6 10 shillings a week. For a reading of his poem *In Country Sleep* (1947), he was paid £25. When he was invited to adapt Wycherley's play *The Plain Dealer* (1949), the fee was £75. He was offered £300 to adapt *Peer Gynt* for television (these fees have been documented because he lost interest in them both and so the projects became matters of dispute). Because he let the BBC down on these two occasions, it has been suggested that he had a bad reputation. This is nonsense. He did have the annoying fault of accepting work when his heart was not really in it, just to get his hands on the initial advance, but this happened on a few, very well documented occasions. Much more frequent were his loudly heralded appearances on major programmes, which were given advance publicity in *Radio Times* and the daily newspapers, critically reviewed in the serious literary magazines, often bringing him in extra income when he had written them himself. Having retained copyright, he could sell other rights as well.

Dylan Thomas's major work for the BBC included:

Reminiscences of Childhood, a radio talk originally written for the Welsh Home Service in 1943 and repeated several times thereafter; published in *The Listener* (1943) with illustrations by John Petts, and subsequently included in the book *Quite Early One Morning* (1954);

Memories of Christmas, broadcast in 1945 and 1946 on the Welsh Home Service and the Third Programme, also published in *The Listener* (1945) and in many other magazines subsequently, and also in *Quite Early One Morning* (1954);

Holiday Memory, broadcast in October 1946 by the Welsh Home Service, published in *The Listener* and also subsequently repeated and published in *Quite Early One Morning* (1954);

How to Begin a Story and *The Crumbs of One Man's Year*, both broadcast in 1946 by the Home Service and reproduced in *The Listener*, and later published in *Quite Early One Morning* (1954);

The radio documentary *Return Journey*, which describes in verse his return to Swansea after the bombing, visiting people and places he had known, which was first broadcast in June 1947, and repeated six times in the next seven years, and is also in *Quite Early One Morning* (1954);

Quite Early One Morning itself, in which he experimented with dialogue and verse to capture the feel and sound of New Quay in much the same way that he later wrote *Under Milk Wood*; this was first broadcast in 1945, and has been repeated many times since.

There were dozens of other projects, such as his ten-part radio adaptation of Milton's *Comus* and *Paradise Lost*; his radio serialisation of W.H. Davies's *The Autobiography of a Super Tramp*, which I can remember listening to as a boy; his readings of his own short stories, taken from *Portrait of the Artist as a Young Dog*, and frequent recital of works by other twentieth-century writers such as Edith Sitwell, D.H. Lawrence, Robert Lowell, Walter de la Mare, Wilfred Owen, Edward Thomas, etc., besides taking part in other programmes as a critic of new books or reading classic literature like Blake, Sidney, Cervantes or Donne.

The full scale of his achievement as a radio performer remains undocumented, but its effect – with so many of the programmes repeated on different channels both in Britain and overseas – was that Thomas became a familiar voice in many homes, and in every sense a celebrity. His audience judged him by what they heard: the voice of a highly professional artist, and when they met him personally, sitting in a pub, they plied him with drinks and said, 'Give us a poem' or 'Tell us a story', never thinking that the private man might be someone different. Thomas would oblige with his old pub routine of mildly obscene limericks and shaggy dog stories, some of which were merely pathetic when told drunk:

There was a bloody sparrow
Flew up a bloody spout
Came a bloody thunderstorm
And blew the bugger out.[13]

Others had a comic punchline that was sometimes lost in alcohol. By the end of the evening, he would be slumped in a corner, drunk and dishevelled, often sick – and another group of fans would be able to go off and tell their friends that they had met Dylan Thomas; he was finding it hard to cope with fame.

Because of his failure to resist temptations, his inability to refuse a free drink, passing acquaintances thought him weak, but Thomas remained far more robust than he seemed, still rarely visiting a doctor. His illnesses were much more psychological, desperately nervous before each radio or stage appearance (though he usually pretended otherwise), insecure, uncertain of everything but his poetry, still craving affection (as he had done since childhood), using protestations of ill health, that were sometimes maudlin and at others comic, to arouse tenderness in women and commiseration in men. Much of this was a charade. Many of those begging letters claiming illness were false. After he had written them, he would go off to the pub with a grin, having staved off another crisis for a few days or weeks.

It is not an attractive picture that we have of this man, for all his great gifts, because his inner selfishness was so overwhelming and his belief in his own genius so obsessive that he would keep on performing, wherever he could, in studios or public bars, no matter what the cost to his family. He was now earning a considerable income, but his wife never knew it. They were still living off the charity of friends. In London, they stayed with her sister Nicolette, with the Fitzgibbons, or with Bill and Helen McAlpine, who became exceptionally close. For years, they lived off Margaret Taylor (see next chapter), then wife of the Oxford historian A.J.P. Taylor. She was convinced of Thomas's genius, and the Taylors allowed them to live in their summerhouse at Oxford until Margaret bought them The Manor House at South Leigh, near Witney, where they lived from August 1947 until May 1949, when they moved to The Boat House in Laugharne; she bought them that as well, then later found them a flat in Delancey Street, Camden Town, so that they could also have a London address.

Living in debt had become a habit, for Thomas knew that when a bill had to be paid, Margaret Taylor would arrive with her chequebook, and so would other friends like Marged Howard-Stepney, who even paid for one of Caitlin's abortions (though, characteristically, Thomas claimed to have paid for it himself). Undoubtedly, there were other patrons, too – because Thomas seldom told his wife where he had been begging or how much he had got. In 1951, he managed to raise a £300 grant from the Royal Literary Fund, writing yet another wheedling letter, pleading ill health and debt. Was their lifestyle sordid? Not really, because they managed to live in some comfort by the standards of the time. With his success in radio. Thomas started dressing well for his visits to London. First Llewelyn, and then, later, Aeronwy were sent to expensive private schools. The family employed domestic help, wherever they lived, and Thomas travelled nearly everywhere by taxi, frequently making journeys of 50 or 60 miles that would consume all the cash in his pocket. He enjoyed playing the part of the successful writer and radio performer, dining at Wheeler's or the Café Royal, visiting night clubs and theatres, and entertaining friends at his club (he first joined the National Liberal Club and then later the Savage). Thomas became one of those performers who must always have an audience, his life a wondrous fantasy in which the poet and lover conquered literary London, was acclaimed for his genius – and there was no one to prick the balloon, for he was humble as well, in other ways.

As each year passed, after the publication of *Deaths and Entrances*, his fame grew. The nature of his BBC work changed, with him becoming a star performer, commanding higher fees, appearing in programmes as well as writing them. As the film industry re-established itself after the war,

Thomas was recruited by Sidney Box to write scripts for Gainsborough Films, which gave him another regular income. There seems little doubt that throughout these last years of his life, Thomas was seldom earning less than £2,000–£3,000 a year gross, and possibly much more, at a time when the wages of a skilled man were no more than £7–8 a week, and yet he was constantly in difficulties, pursued by tradesmen's writs and bailiffs. At no time did the Thomases feel financially secure, and yet they should have been, for the income was there.

During those eight years Thomas completed a substantial body of work that was capable of being re-worked in different ways. There was always money coming in from somewhere. A radio talk might be repeated; the same talk might be published in magazine form; someone might want to use one of his poems in a radio programme or include it in an anthology; a book might be reprinted. Now, since his death, his work has been adapted for films and television; his poems have been put to music; his poems and stories have become paperback best sellers in many languages; his own recordings have been successful as LPs and cassettes, and no matter where his work appears, or in what form, the author's estate receives a percentage of the retail price.

This began to take shape during those radio years. Thomas was ill equipped to handle its consequences (which is scarcely surprising; no other British poet had broken through in quite the same way, and it wasn't until rock 'n' roll revolutionised the music industry in the Sixties that creative artists really began to harness all these different forms of income). Nevertheless, and this is equally strange, he seemed to embrace instinctively the more important opportunities that presented themselves, and was naturally cunning in his political manoeuvres within the BBC and at the street-trade end of contemporary literature. His acquaintances seldom realised how successful he was. Some, like Edith Sitwell, Norman Cameron and Ralph Keene, devoted much time to helping him.

It was Edith Sitwell who persuaded the Society of Authors to award him a travelling scholarship so that Thomas could take his family to Rapallo, Florence and Elba (1947); Norman Cameron who arranged for him to visit Czechoslovakia as a guest of the Czechoslovak Writers Union (1949), and Ralph Keene who made all the necessary introductions for Thomas to be commissioned to write a documentary film script on the oil industry, for which he visited Persia (1951).

Thomas would pretend that each new commission was a terrible burden on his health. He would compose complex tales of woe, trying to convince Caitlin or his parents that he did not want to do all these things, but was anxious to provide for his family and did not want to let people down after they had gone to so much trouble. Everything was an act, staged wherever he happened to be; he would say anything to anyone that might make life easier just for a moment. This man of wise perception possessed no conscience.

Many people were taken in, especially in the United States where he arrived to face a fresh audience, with all his different personae carefully cultivated, for Dylan Thomas seldom failed to be wholly professional in his work, no matter what the personal cost. It was in his personal relationships that he was a failure. His business correspondence was succinct and to the point. He rarely drank too much before a performance, although he would let himself go afterwards – and right to the very end applied himself diligently to his writing, no matter how debilitated he might feel after some punishing excursion. My perception, shaped by knowledge of his family, meeting many of his acquaintances and carefully retracing his life, is of a deeply troubled but childlike man, with few conventional moral feelings, little sense of responsibility for those who cared for him (although he was always loving towards his parents), increasingly withdrawn from social contact as he became more and more burdened by the consequences of fame.

Douglas Cleverdon, who worked with Thomas on several radio productions before overseeing *Under Milk Wood*, wrote:

I think it is worth putting on record that during BBC rehearsals his standards were thoroughly professional. He had a wonderful ear for rhythms and inflexions and accents, and could comprehend immediately the subtlest points of interpretation. He was, moreover, sober, hard-working and punctilious. So conscientious was he that I have known him leave a pub at lunch-time earlier than was necessary in order to return to the studio and con his script before the afternoon rehearsal. When rehearsals were over, of course, he relaxed . . .[14]

— 9 —
LIVING IN DEBT

FOR the last eight years of his life, Dylan Thomas depended largely upon one woman. His radio work, scripts, lectures and re-publication of his poems and stories brought him a steady income, but it was Margaret Taylor who provided the family with somewhere to live; not just once or twice, but continuously from Christmas 1945 until his death. Their relationship was an odd one, compounded by her marriage to A.J.P. Taylor. Caitlin was suspicious and sometimes jealous of her friendship with Dylan.

Thomas first met the Taylors during his earliest London forays, introduced by Norman Cameron, a poet and advertising executive, who befriended Thomas when he was penniless, letting him stay at his home in Chiswick; Thomas responded by making advances to his wife. Their feelings for Thomas were memorably expressed in Cameron's poem, *The Dirty Little Accuser*:

Who invited him in? What was he doing here,
That insolent little ruffian, that crapulous lout?
When he quitted a sofa, he left behind him a smear.
My wife says he even tried to paw her about

What was worse, if, as often happened, we caught him out
Stealing or pinching the maid's backside, he would leer,
With a cigarette on his lip and a shiny snout,
With a hint: 'You and I are all in the same galere'

Yesterday we ejected him, nearly by force,
To go on the parish, perhaps, or die of starvation;
As to that, we agreed, we felt no kind of remorse.

Yet there's this check on our righteous jubilation:
Now that the little accuser is gone, of course,
We shall never be able to answer his accusation.

Thomas spent a month with the Taylors in 1935, staying at the cottage in Disley, on the Derbyshire-Cheshire borders.

Alan Taylor and Margaret Adams met in Vienna. A former Communist and Oxford graduate, he had been at Oriel with Cameron. She was a lapsed Roman Catholic, born in India and educated at an English convent, who had gone out to Vienna to learn German and study the piano. They married in 1931, with Taylor saying his mother 'never forgave Margaret for not being a Leftwing intellectual'[1] Matrimony gave him

> nine years of great happiness and four children who were for long my mainstay in life. Thereafter it gave me a decade of intense, almost indescribable misery, which left me crippled and stunted emotionally, a person useless to God or man . . . fate certainly played me a lousy trick.

The trouble appears to have been that Margaret was a sort of literary groupie; a frustrated poet and writer who obsessively chased men who she thought possessed creative genius. The broadcaster Robert Kee was one, and Caitlin tells me there were several others. Taylor was at pains to stress that

> Robert, in my opinion, behaved faultlessly. He kept away from Margaret. He never complained to me. I sent him a note that I appreciated the situation and hoped it would not disturb our friendship. Otherwise we never mentioned the subject in all the years that it lasted. However I was soon better informed by others, though there was really nothing I needed to know. Robert had been at Stowe and took his troubles to Bill and Patience McElwee. They brought sympathy to me and also recounted the harassment Robert had to endure. Margaret often pursued him to his lodgings and once thrust herself physically upon him. He had to take refuge in the university library. Later, when he joined the R.A.F., she was away from home for days at a time. Once she haunted Robert's training camp and tried to make contact with him in the evenings. He had to warn the guard against her and dared not leave camp until he was sure that she had gone home. Margaret neglected the house. She neglected the children. She became a wraith, almost out of contact with real life.[2]

At what stage she turned her attentions to Thomas, or indicated her similar obsession, is unclear, but he knew that she thought him a genius. He would also have quickly realised her other attraction; Margaret was relatively rich with independent means. When the Thomases returned to London in September 1945 after their sojourn at New Quay and a few more weeks with D.J. and Florence at Llangain, they stayed briefly at 39 Markham Square, off the Kings Road, Chelsea, and then descended upon the Taylors at Oxford, having no doubt heard that as a Fellow of Magdalen, Alan had been provided with a College house, Holywell Ford, in the centre of Oxford; an ancient, almost mediaeval house on the banks of the river, surrounded by College grounds. The Taylors reared ducks and hens, grew their own vegetables, and delighted in the otters that fished in the pool below Holywell Ford, and learned to be wary of foxes.

Dylan and Caitlin gave them no warning that they were coming. No doubt this was intentional. Alan Taylor thought Dylan a sponger. Had enquiries been made first, he might have turned them away – and they might have anticipated that! As it was, they arrived on his doorstep with Aeronwy and a suitcase, Dylan with his arm in a sling, complaining that their London landlady had locked them out and that his arm had been broken while trying to clamber back into the flat to regain their possessions:

There they were, homeless. Margaret took pity on them; I acquiesced.[3]

Had he sent them packing, the Taylors' marriage might have survived. Instead, they moved into a wooden summerhouse on the banks of the Cherwell, supplied with gas and electricity but no running water, and stayed at least 15 months, with Dylan catching the train for Paddington whenever he had another radio broadcast to make for the BBC (and he made over 50 in the first year after the war ended). Invariably, he spent whatever he earned on drink, returning home penniless:

Then there would be a row with Caitlin. Dylan would cajole her in a wheedling Welsh voice, and Caitlin would succumb. Margaret became more involved. Here at last was the congenial company which university wives had not provided. Every night she went off drinking with Dylan and Caitlin at some local pub. She laid on literary and artistic dinner parties for them where I felt out of place. She pushed Dylan on the Oxford literary clubs. She even induced me to take Dylan into dinner at Magdalen High Table where he and President Tizard[4] sought to impress one another, a very curious conversation.[5]

For the Thomases this was heaven indeed; somewhere to live without having to pay for it. The only incidental price was that Thomas had to appear interested in Margaret's attempts to write poetry. Having never seen any of her poems, I have to rely upon Caitlin who says that Dylan thought them truly dreadful, which didn't stop him writing:

I was so glad to be allowed to see the poems and to keep them for such a long time . . . I kept them for so long, not because I had nothing to say about them but because I had so much.[6]

Thereafter, Thomas would always find time for Margaret Taylor – and she would invariably find whatever money was needed to bail them out of a crisis. 'She was very good to us,' says Caitlin, which sounds an understatement. Margaret Taylor's devotion cost her many thousands of pounds. For his part, Thomas knew that he now had a good source of support. Llewelyn was brought back from Caitlin's family to live with his parents for the first time since August 1941. 'Dylan tried to borrow money from me in which he did not succeed,' says Taylor, perhaps not realising then that there was no need for Thomas to persist with the husband when he had the wife to plunder. The Thomases had no shame. Freeloading never embarrassed them.

Writing to one friend, Thomas said:

Do you ever come up to Oxford? Do drop me a line if you do. We're here for quite a bit, I think.[7]

And to Vernon Watkins, he wrote:

I want to write a poem of my own again, but it's hard here with peace and no room, spring outside the window and the gascooker behind the back, sleep, food, loud wireless, broom and brush all in one kiosk, stunted bathing-hut or square milk-bottle.[8]

While Dan Jones, as always, was sent a daft, cheerful, affectionate and largely meaningless letter, saying:

I'm eely and oily
I'm hot buttered toast
I'm my cup of toe
I hate to earth: oh to hell with that incommensurable cowpad
Cleopatra smells of Marmite
Come again, King Cain, and have a cosh, I'm Abel[9]

The Thomases were happily ensconced in their riverside hut. Times were good, by their standards, for there was money flowing in from the BBC. A letter from Dylan to his agents in July 1946 shows that he was then awaiting 20 guineas plus rail fares for a talk on Wilfred Owen; 15 guineas for another radio broadcast, *Time for Verse*; 40 guineas for his appearance on *This Is London*; two further fees of seven guineas each plus expenses for *Book of Verse* readings for the BBC Eastern Service.

In August 1946, he was back in Laugharne house-hunting again, but still careful to maintain his landlady's goodwill, returning to Holywell Ford within a few weeks, anxiously keeping creditors at bay, and yet still writing briskly to his agents or other potential colleagues when the chance of a commercial project presented itself. He corresponded with the novelist Graham Greene, whom he had known early in the war and who was now a director of the publishers Eyre and Spottiswoode. Thomas hoped they might publish *The Doctor and the Devils*. The actor Michael Redgrave had shown interest in the script, and once Greene had read the manuscript Thomas wrote him a whingeing letter:

What I want, *frightfully urgently* – and this is the chief of the worries I want to worry you with – is some money for or from it or the chance of getting some, and ever so quickly . . . I've got a pile of doctors' bills for Caitlin and for my son Llewelyn who is never, I'm sorry, well; and a looming writ; and another one on the doorstep. I'm in a hell of a mess.[10]

It is by no means certain that he was in any real financial difficulty at all, for the following day he wrote a long letter to his parents, telling them how many Christmas presents had been given to Aeronwy, and how well they had all eaten over the holiday period, with the Taylors and other friends. On New Year's Eve, they had been to the Chelsea Arts Ball at the Albert Hall:

A tremendously bright affair. I went as a Chinaman, Caitlin as a grand Spanish lady. It really was very exciting: wonderful to look at: all the boxes round the great hall packed with pierrots, ballerinas, coster-mongers, Elizabethans, pirates, courtesans, tigers, Dutch dolls, empresses, clowns, & the huge floor rainbowed with dancers.[11]

The letter was packed with news. He was planning to go back to Swansea to research his radio documentary *Return Journey*, and would visit them in Llangain, and had been asked to write a libretto for William Walton set in the bombed East London Docks with sets by Michael Ayrton.[12] There were talks to be done for the BBC, and they were hoping to change their domestic arrangements to share a cottage in Oxford with Bill and Helen McAlpine, and also another on the banks of the River Thames near Richmond Bridge, which would become their London base. The Thomases periodically stayed there and also in East Twickenham, Chiswick and Hammersmith, with occasional visits to Wales, but the wooden summerhouse on the banks of the Cherwell remained their home, much to Alan Taylor's consternation. 'Neither of us ever liked Alan,' says Caitlin,[13] emphasising that it was always Margaret whom they regarded as a friend. 'I thought he was horrible: very opinionated and mean. There were times, too, when I loathed Margaret, but when I look back on it now, I realise that she was very generous and courageous to go against Alan's preachings. She thought Dylan was a genius, but I didn't want to hear her saying that; I wanted to be the only one . . .'

Night after night the Thomases would be drifting from pub to pub, with Margaret buying the drinks and Alan at home with the children. In the mornings, after Alan had gone off to his work at the university Margaret would be hot-foot down to the summer house, busily planning their day while the Thomases were still semi-sleeping, half-way out of their latest hangover. 'We used to have all our meals with them. She was a keen cook, but the meals were awful. She hadn't got the gift at all,' says Caitlin. 'Maggs wasn't a stupid woman by any means, but she wasn't a creative artist, either . . . I think he (Alan) hated the sight of us, right from the start, because we were taking money from Margaret. We saw no sign of affection between them at all; he was not an affectionate man . . . I think Alan was jealous of Dylan, but I don't think Margaret ever slept with Dylan. I was always asking myself that (and him), but whenever I brought it up he would shudder. Some time later, I did find a letter that she'd written to Dylan in which she said "to sleep with you would be like sleeping with a god." *That* told me they hadn't got very far with it!'

From Alan Taylor's account and Caitlin's recollections, it seems likely that Margaret's obsession never developed into a sexual relationship. Indeed, there is little convincing evidence that Thomas ever had such a relationship with anyone other than his wife, though he could be so outrageous when talking to women that onlookers thought otherwise. Instead, the devoted Margaret saw it as part of her mission in life to help the Thomases broaden their horizons, travel and live in comfort while Dylan concentrated upon his writing. She urged them to visit Europe, and in April 1947 Dylan and Caitlin went off to Italy, accompanied by Caitlin's sister

Brigid and her son Tobias. Their four-month holiday was partially funded by the £150 travelling scholarship from the Society of Authors. Margaret told them that while they were away, she would find them somewhere better to live.

This was Thomas's first journey abroad. He did not like it. They first visited Rapallo and then stayed in a villa in the hills above Florence before moving on to the island of Elba, with Dylan often insisting that he should stay indoors, ears glued to the radio for news of cricket, while the women and children went off to the beach. 'He didn't look at many of the sights, I'm afraid; he wasn't really aware of Florence at all; he hadn't got much sense of visual beauty, and was never very interested in sight-seeing,' says Caitlin.

Nevertheless, they met many Italian writers, painters and musicians, largely through the influence of Ronald Bottrall, a poet whom Dylan had known in London before the War and who was now director of the British Institute in Florence. As always, Thomas found somewhere away from the house and the children, a farm cottage, where he could work during the afternoons. He spent three months slowly constructing *In Country Heaven*, a long and intricate poem in which he meditates upon his sleeping daughter, wondering what may befall her in future years.

While they stayed on at their villa, with a private swimming pool and an Italian woman to cook their meals and do their cleaning, Margaret Taylor threw herself into house-hunting with all her usual zeal, sending them regular progress reports with her parcels of books, Sunday newspapers and magazines (plus extra money when they needed it). She wrote in May to say that she had found The Manor House at South Leigh, near Witney and 25 minutes by train from Oxford, and would be able to rent it to them for £1 a week. Thomas wrote back thanking her for

the house, the home, the haven, the pound-a-week Manor. Thank you with all of my heart, from the depth of my teapot, from the marrow of my slippers warm before the fire.[14]

He urged her to go ahead with the purchase without ever seeing it, although The Manor House was nowhere near as grand as it sounded. It was actually a three-bedroomed cottage with two downstairs rooms, a kitchen and wash-house in which Margaret installed a bath. She also arranged for water and electricity to be connected, for them to apply for a telephone, and for their furniture to be brought up from Bishopston and from Holywell Ford (having not had a permanent home for four years, the Thomases had left some of their possessions with his parents and the rest in Oxford after retrieving it from their former studio flat in Manresa Road, which had been sublet). Margaret also found Llewelyn a place as a boarder at Magdalen College School where her son Sebastian was already a chorister.

Although it is his wife who is usually credited with being their benefactress at South Leigh (and it was certainly she who made all the plans and kept in touch with the Thomases), Alan Taylor tells it differently in his memoirs:

The situation with Dylan deteriorated steadily and became unendurable in the autumn of 1947. He had always lived by sponging. Now reports reached me that he was boasting around the Oxford pubs that he had got the wife of a rich don hooked on him – a boast followed no doubt by an evil giggle. Margaret had inherited some money when her mother died in 1941. She spent some of the money on pictures – a Sickert, a Boudin, a Degas, a Renoir, a Utrillo. They now began to disappear along with crystal decanters and the piano. I might not have minded so much if it had not been for Dylan's boasting. It was intolerable that I should be supposed to be contributing to his support.

I then did a very foolish thing. Dylan was groaning that he would like a house of his own near Oxford. I, too, had come into some money when my mother died and I told Margaret that I would finance a house for Dylan on condition she gave him nothing more. Margaret accepted my offer with many professions of gratitude – how generous I was, how she would observe my condition and how appreciative Dylan would be. As a matter of fact Dylan took the house for granted and, I think, assumed that he had swindled it out of Margaret – at any rate it is credited to her in all the books about him. Margaret found a derelict cottage grandiloquently called South Leigh Manor, a pretty rough place with no electricity, no gas and only one cold water tap. Even so it cost me quite a lot to make it habitable. My foolish action of course brought me no reward. Margaret was soon giving Dylan more money than ever. Also, with South Leigh remote from Oxford, she developed the habit of keeping house for Dylan and Caitlin while they went to the pub. Often, coming back from London, I found Holywell Ford deserted except for the children and our resident domestic.[15]

To make matters worse, the Thomases had no sooner settled at South Leigh than Dylan began to get homesick again for Laugharne, a feeling that he expressed in a radio talk *Living in Wales*[16] in which he recalled travelling by train from Oxford to London, perched on a stool in the buffet car looking at his fellow-passengers, 'egghead dons, smelling of water biscuits . . . cowlike girls in, may be, hessian . . . and furtive small damp physicists' when

then and there, as I watched them all, desire raised its little fist. I did not want to be in England, now that they were there. I did not want to be in England, whether they were there or not. I wanted to be in Wales.

By then, the Thomases' marriage was in trouble again. Caitlin left him at least twice, returning to stay with her mother, and says she would have made the separation permanent had she the resources to live independently with the children. She still did not know how much he earned, for he was sly and she had that aristocratic notion that it was 'vulgar' to talk about money. Substantial sums were being paid to him. Donald Taylor had sold the film rights to *The Doctor and the Devils* to Gainsborough Films, with Thomas receiving £365 in monthly instalments. He had also been commissioned to write three other scripts for Gainsborough, for each of which he was due to receive £1,000 in staged payments. There was other re-writing work for British National Pictures, a steady flow of scripts and readings for the BBC, and occasional income from the United States, where Oscar Williams was placing serial rights to his poems and stories. No one really knew how much he was earning, for Thomas had still never paid a penny in income tax. He kept no accounts and cheerfully cashed any cheque he received with anyone who would give him money for it. Even his agents had little idea of the total money passing through his hands for he would willingly bypass them if it meant saving ten per cent.

Nevertheless, he was always broke; begged and borrowed from whoever would listen, and frequently left a trail of worthless cheques behind him (which was not a criminal offence in those days, although it did little to help his reputation). Somehow, he usually raised enough to go drinking and Caitlin would be furious when he returned from London after discussing some new project without a penny in his pocket, having spent whatever was left on travelling home by taxi.

There were many tensions between them. These were exacerbated soon after their move to South Leigh. Margaret Taylor bought him a gypsy caravan so that he could write in peace away from the house. It also meant that whenever she arrived from Oxford, which was often daily, Margaret shut herself away in the caravan with Dylan, discussing her latest poems, while Caitlin fumed in the kitchen at The Manor House. One day Caitlin became so upset by this that she attacked the caravan with them inside it, and turned it over.

Margaret was as obsessive as ever, and on one occasion told Thomas that she would have her bags ready and packed at Paddington Station so that they could elope; Dylan didn't turn up and Caitlin still doesn't know whether she did.

'We'll be better if we can get back to Laugharne,' insisted Dylan, who now had his parents to worry about as well. His mother had fallen and broken a leg, and his father was now too elderly to be left alone. Laugharne became the dream solution to all their worries. Six months after moving into The Manor House Dylan and Caitlin returned there to see what property was available. Initially, they were hoping to take a lease on Castle House now that Richard Hughes had moved away. Margaret Taylor went down to discuss the possibilities and reported back favourably, prompting an ecstatic response from Dylan that she had

set us dreamily grinning, hopelessly shaking our heads, then beaming and gabbling together again as we think of the great house at the end of the cherrytreed best street in the world, bang next to the Utrillo tower, with its wild gardens and owly ruins, the grey estuary, forever linked to me with poems done and to be[17]

These negotiations came to nothing, and a few weeks later the Thomases learned that The Boat House was available. This suited them even better. It was a building that Dylan had known since childhood, standing just by the ferry which he had used as a boy. For Alan Taylor this was another shocking twist in his marital affairs:

Margaret casually proposed to break her promise not to give Dylan any more money. For of course Dylan, having made one killing, was now eager to make another. He was hardly established at South Leigh before he became again discontented. What he really wanted, it seemed, was to live in The Boat House at Laugharne, a house he had coveted in his youth. Margaret agreed to buy it for him. I protested and as usual acquiesced. Though I did not give her any more of my own money, I arranged for her to sell some of her capital. So she sold South Leigh Manor, added a further £2,000 and established Dylan in The Boat House.[18]

Taylor wrote to Dylan complaining that this constant drain upon the Taylors' resources was destroying their marriage, and says that Thomas 'did not reply except in the sense of squeezing more money out of Margaret'.

Caitlin has told me that Dylan most certainly did reply; he sent Taylor a postcard telling him to FUCK OFF.

A few months later the Taylors moved to London, Margaret and their children into one house and Alan into a flat elsewhere, unaware that she had also found the Thomases a flat in Delancey Street, Camden Town, so that they could have a London base as well as their home in Laugharne – or that she had bought another house in Laugharne herself, adjoining the Grist Square, so that wherever they happened to lay their heads she would never be far away. 'I suppose she thought Dylan more important than me, but I never asked and she never explained,' wrote Taylor. Not long afterwards the Taylors were divorced.

Had Margaret Taylor been the only woman with an obsession for Dylan Thomas, one might ascribe her fantasies to love or even some psychotic condition, given her previous pursuit of Robert Kee and other poets and creative artists, but there seems to have been far more to it than that; something in Thomas's character that made him appealing to women and also, apparently, to homosexuals.

Throughout their marriage, Caitlin was aware of this attraction *to* homosexuals. He never, so far as she knew, responded to them. In other company, sure of his audience, Thomas would tell crude stories against 'queers' and 'pansies', as he called them, and Pamela Hansford Johnson recalled one that he used to tell about himself going into a public lavatory where a workman said with a leer, 'Wouldn't think I was a pansy, would you, mate?' to which Thomas allegedly replied, 'And you wouldn't think I wasn't, would you?' (This joke was obviously part of his pub repertoire, developed in Swansea days, for it was repeated to me many years later by Wynford Vaughan-Thomas.)

Caitlin says that when they were in bed, 'it was like embracing a child rather than a man; he felt so young and tender, so soft and sweet. He wasn't aggressive in a masculine sense; he wasn't strong enough. He was able to make love; he functioned, but I can't remember much about it because it didn't make much impression on me; somehow, the actual fucking didn't touch me. His sweetness and kindness and loveableness was child-like and that was how I loved him . . . I never felt that he was a full-grown man . . . though Dylan was precocious in many ways, he had not had much sexual experience; he appeared timid and inhibited, depending on how many drinks he'd had (I don't think we ever made love without having a lot to drink first), and he had an almost juvenile approach to sex . . . there are many things about Dylan that are hard to explain. It is strange that a full-grown man should have wanted baby comforts and should have been so lacking in sexual drive.'[19]

She was also aware of suggestions that Dylan might have had homosexual relationships with Max Chapman and Oswell Blakeston, but thinks it unlikely, though 'it did faintly worry me because he was effeminate, in some ways, but I don't think Dylan was ever a practising homosexual; when he talked about homosexuality, he always said how much the physical side of it revolted him, and I think he probably talked about that too much. If he had had homosexual relationships, they would have been occasional or under protest; they certainly hadn't become a habit. I don't think he was ever buggered . . .'[20]

Whatever it was, there was something in Thomas's personality that had this attraction to women as well; a passive, feminine, childlike quality sensed through his bearing, voice and power to communicate. This was a rare gift in a poet, although it is often found in other branches of the entertainment industry.

Margaret Taylor was not the first to find this attraction, but she was willing to help the Thomases financially and this drew her even closer to them. She became almost part of the family, taking her children down to her cottage in Laugharne so that she could spend her evenings with Dylan and Caitlin, and arranging her life so that when they were staying in Delancey Street she was living nearby. And her obsession happened to coincide with Thomas's emergence as a national celebrity in the wake of *Deaths and Entrances* and his most successful years in radio.

Other women also found themselves drawn to him, notably Marged Howard-Stepney who would have given the Thomases as much as Margaret Taylor had she been able to. Marged was descended from a landed family who had held vast estates in Carmarthenshire since the sixteenth century, and was related to Richard Hughes by marriage. She had been married twice according to Caitlin and was 'stinking rich' but luckily for her family much of the money was tied up in trust. She had access to sufficient funds to drink gin like water, carrying a case of it with her wherever she went, but her trustees ensured that Marged never spent it all, and a travelling companion (whom the Thomases called her 'keeper') looked after her needs and watched her expenditure.

Thomas used to describe Marged as the best friend he ever had and she gave him money freely, only to die unexpectedly from a drugs overdose, with Dylan revealing that she promised me a real lot of money for oh so little in return .... and left no will, and her son, the heir, could hardly be expected to fulfil *that* kind of unwritten agreement.[21]

The implication in remarks like that, and later still in *Dylan Thomas in America*, is that these relationships had some sexual undertone, but it is seldom more than a hint, and it is possible that he was trying to live up to his heroic image of himself as the romantic poet that he had sought to project since his teens, exploiting Margaret and Marged just as keenly as he had once used Veronica Sibthorp, Wyn Henderson, Emily Holmes Coleman and Elisabeth Lutyens, when all they may have really wanted was to be close to genius, to hero-worship – and all he wanted was free bed and board. Whatever the true explanation (and I suspect that Thomas was not half the man he wanted to be), Dylan Thomas had certainly learned that women would respond to his wheedling – and seldom missed a trick, whatever the price someone like A.J.P. Taylor might have to pay.

The Thomases moved in to The Boat House at the beginning of May 1949. They were now back where he had longed to be since childhood, overlooking the tidal waters of the River Taf, hearing them lap against the walls at high tide and watching them recede to reveal a vast expanse of sandy river bed. This was his

> seashaken house
> On a breakneck of rocks
> Tangled with chirrup and fruit[22]

and

> his house on stilts high among beaks
> And palavers of birds

where

> the rhymer in the long tongued room,
> who tolls his birthday bell,
> Toils towards the ambush of his wounds[23]

The Boat House was everything he had ever wanted, quiet and remote, close to the water's edge, tucked in to the red sandstone cliffs, and yet only a few minutes from Brown's Hotel. The vistas changed with every tide and the weather. At low tides in summer, the river bed would be golden sands, stretching five or six miles to the low-lying hills above Ferryside; in winter, wind and rain beat heavily over the incoming tides, its reflective waters turning steely grey.

From the front, with its white-washed walls and traditional grey slate roof, The Boat House looks like a traditional Welsh cottage, but its elevations are deceptive. Adjoining a descending cliff face, it is two-storeyed at the front, with an inner staircase down to a lower floor that is only accessible at the rear, with a kitchen and dining-room just above water-level, overlooking what was then a rough-growing garden area at the back that was covered in water at the seasonal high tides; the sea came in through holes that had been left in the garden wall. Externally, a wooden balcony with a hand rail stretched around the sides facing the estuary, entered at ground-floor level at the front. No one is quite sure when The Boat House was built, for it was leased by Laugharne Corporation in 1834 and then converted into two cottages in the 1850s, each of them three-storeyed with adjoining front doors and a common rear entrance. In 1889, the building became one cottage again and thereafter changed hands only twice before Margaret Taylor bought it for the Thomases. She paid £2,500, and, just as she had done at South Leigh, arranged for mains water and electricity to be installed, which didn't stop Dylan complaining that when he used the outside lavatory 'the rats titter while we shit'. Whatever its minor inconveniences, he was profoundly grateful to be able to move into it with Caitlin nearly seven months pregnant, and thanked Margaret Taylor profusely:

I can never thank you enough for making this fresh beginning possible by all the trust you have put in me, by all the gifts you have made me by all your labour & anxiety in face of callous & ungrateful behaviour. I know that the only way to express my deep deep gratitude is to be happy & to write. Here I am happy and writing. All I shall write in this water and tree room on the cliff, every word, will be my thanks to you . . . you have given me a life. And now I am going to live it.[24]

HOLLYWOOD BECKONS

A few days after Dylan Thomas moved into The Boat House, he received an unexpected letter in the morning mail. It was from John Malcolm Brinnin, whom he had never met although they had both contributed to British and American poetry magazines over the previous 15 years. Sometimes their work had been used in the same issues of *New Verse* and *Adelphi*, and Brinnin had long admired Thomas from afar, buying his books and envying Thomas's intricate mastery of language.

Brinnin was then 33 year old, two years younger than Thomas, and had recently been appointed Director of the Poetry Center at the Young Men's and Young Women's Hebrew Association in New York. Almost the first thing he did was to write inviting Thomas to give a reading at the Center, offering a fee of 500 US dollars. Thomas was delighted. For the past four years he had been asking Oscar Williams to help him find a way of travelling to the United States, where he believed he might earn far more than in Britain, either as a broadcaster or in a university post.

The letter had been delayed because Thomas had forgotten to leave a forwarding address with the post office in South Leigh, and arrived just as he was settling into his work room on The Cliff (a wooden garage resting on stilts that a previous owner had built for Laugharne's first motor car), wondering

> now that I am back in Wales, am I the same person, sadly staring over the flat, sad, estuary sands, watching the herons walk like women poets, hearing the gab of the gulls, alone and lost in a soft kangaroo pocket of the sad, salt West . . . I know that I am home again because I feel just as I felt when I was not at home, only more so . . .[1]

Dylan had returned hoping to earn enough during six months of each year writing film scripts to devote the rest of his time to poetry. It was now three years since *Deaths and Entrances*, and Dent had been asking him for the past 18 months to collate his *Collected Poems*. They also wanted to publish his film treatment, *The Doctor and The Devils*, and were now showing interest in the semi-autobiographical novel *Adventures In The Skin Trade* which had been shelved soon after he left Sea View nine years earlier. 'I hope to get a real lot of work done here, & have already started. I must get a book ready this year,' he told his agent.

The only poem he had finished since the publication of *Deaths and Entrances* had been the one written in Italy, *In Country Sleep*, originally planned as part of a sequence of poems with the title *In Country Heaven*. Thomas had been so busy working in films and radio that he hadn't had time to devote to poetry, knowing that his standing was such that each new poem had to be shaped to perfection before he dare allow it to be published.

And then there was *Under Milk Wood*, which had also been on his mind for the last decade, discussed intermittently with various friends in Laugharne early in the war and then later over long lunches at the Café Royal. Ideas like these would be tossed around for years before Thomas finally decided which way he wanted to present them.

Caitlin has confirmed, in direct contradiction of his biographers, that apart from minor ailments, Thomas was physically fit and intellectually fertile with no sign of any diminution in his powers, and now that he was back once more where he wanted to be, he returned to his poetry, spending

a long time thinking about a new poem before starting to write, turning over ideas and deciding what he wanted the poem to say. The structure of the poem and its meaning were clear in his mind before he began, even though it then might take him months and months of work to find the words and the images, the rhymes and the rhythms that he later built around his structure.[2]

That was his mood in May 1949, as he started work on his first poem in two years, *Over Sir John's Hill*, constructed around the view from his workshed window, and received that encouraging letter from Brinnin. The move from South Leigh had been an upheaval, for he had also brought his parents down to Laugharne, renting for them the ground floor flat at Pelican, just across the street from Brown's Hotel, but now he was easing himself back into his old working routine, eager to look ahead:

I should like to come to New York to give my reading early in 1950, probably in January or February. I should be only too glad to accept your sponsorship and to read in other places, including California.

Now about the financial side of it: I quite understand that you, as a non-profit making organisation, must work on a modest budget, and, apart from transatlantic expenses, I should be prepared to accept, for my reading at your headquarters in New York, any fee that you yourselves think adequate. I must, however, point out that I have no private money, that I will arrive in New York with almost none and therefore must, by other arrangements made by you, make money immediately . . .[3]

Having set that in train, Thomas resumed the life that he had been forced to abandon eight years earlier. His routine hardly changed for here people, landscape and water birds; tides, cockles and pub games have an unbroken continuity, each day flowing into the next. Many of those he had known before the War were still here, the ferryman carrying visitors across the estuary, Ivy and Ebie Williams running Brown's Hotel, the Gleeds with bones for broth in the butcher's shop, and the Davies family behind the counter in the general store. Every night farmers, plumbers, drivers, plasterers, bricklayers, carpenters, postmen, tradesmen and men who did no work at all drank and gossiped in Brown's, making fun of each other's weaknesses with an easygoing harmless malice. This, they tell me, is how Laugharne was before Dylan arrived, his surname seldom being used since there are two other Thomas families in the town who are no relation at all.

It is an easygoing town where minor crimes and misdemeanours are a source of fun. One Brown's customer caught poaching in the Taf has his framed summons proudly displayed on the wall – with a photograph of him holding a far finer catch, a 20–25lb. salmon at least. Another is remembered for the day he took his pig to the slaughterhouse, and was seen standing at the bus stop on the Grist Square. When the bus arrived, Donald said: 'Two to St Clears. A return for me – and a single for him!' A third was fined for putting his fist through another pub's window. 'How do you feel now?' asked the magistrate, imposing a fine of £75. 'Depressed,' said Howie – which indeed he was, until he won £150 that night at bingo.

Laugharne is like that, happy-go-lucky, at ease with itself, and Dylan felt totally at home, even though his mother soon developed the habit of standing at her window in Pelican, just out of sight behind the lace curtains, to see if he fell over as he walked down the steps of Brown's Hotel. One night he did and a stranger stepped forward to help him. 'Fuck off,' said Thomas, for that was how he was, a totally unpretentious man who had found his own way of living.

Often he would tip-toe half a mile home in his stockinged feet, dangling his shoes by their laces, when he stayed drinking until 3 a.m., anxious not to alert the neighbours who sometimes peeped through their bedroom windows to see him urinating against the town's prized cherry trees.

The discovery of Beaker graves on nearby hills suggests that people have lived here for 6,000 years, with little change in the surrounding landscape since the hedgerows became defined. It is a natural place for settlement, protected by hills and rivers with fertile soil and its own fresh water supply from wells and the River Corran. Many houses are seventeenth and eighteenth century, with traces of older dwellings and the original town walls in their foundations. The adult population is around 400, but families stay for generations and when a son goes off to university or to serve in the army he often returns with a wife. Like all such communities, the world over, the town turns out in black to bury its dead.

Here Thomas had a sense of being close to those elemental forces that inspired his better work, a feeling expressed in a letter to Margaret Taylor as she first began her search for their home:

poems are waiting like people one has always loved but never met, and O to sit there, lost, found, alone in the universe, at home, at last . . .[4]

At South Leigh, Thomas's work had either been for the BBC or film companies. He was constantly writing. Directors and producers whom he had met through his wartime work for Strand had now moved on to post-war film production with Gainsborough, British National Pictures, Ealing Studios and Gryphon (which was also formed by Donald Taylor). Thomas kept in touch with them all; in their clubs, pubs and restaurants, testing ideas and seldom short of work.

As always in this industry, there was great enthusiasm for films that never got made, either because the producer could not raise the finance or someone else came up with a better idea. The wastage rate was high, but this did not mean that Thomas was idle. Taylor still had hopes for *Twenty Years A'Growing*, and they also worked together on another project, titled at different times *Suffer Little Children* and *Betty London*. Some of this script was used for the Diana Dors film *Good Time Girl*. He also worked on dramatised film biographies of Robert Burns and Dr Crippen, and three other films for Sidney Box, who was then with Gainsborough. These were *Me and My Bike*, intended as a film operetta; *Rebecca's Daughters*, which dealt with a popular revolt against toll gate charges in Carmarthenshire in the nineteenth century, and *The Beach of Falesa*, an adaptation of the story by Robert Louis Stevenson.[5] Thomas also worked with the director Dan Birt on two films for British National Pictures, *Three Weird Sisters* (which was made in 1948) and *No Room at the Inn*, for which he completed a screenplay with Dan Birt the same year.

Although Thomas frequently complained of money problems, often borrowed from friends, and left a trail of dishonoured cheques, he was as cold-eyed as ever when he thought his work was undervalued. When the Welsh actor Clifford Evans wanted him to adapt a short story the project foundered only because Ealing Studios would not pay him what he thought he was worth:

> Ealing was offering me £250 for a full treatment, this to be done under a month . . . . I wrote back to the agent, saying that he & I had agreed that I should work on this film for Ealing only if Ealing paid me what Sidney Box was prepared to pay me: i.e. £1000 for a shooting-script.[6]

Where money matters were concerned, he had become highly devious, taking care to cover his tracks, paying no bills unless forced to, keeping Caitlin as short as ever, and yet usually having enough in his pocket to meet any personal needs. When John Davenport wrote asking for a loan, Thomas cheerily declined with an explanation of all his own woes, saying that he lived on credit, had nothing to sell, his wits were wandering, body wobbling, and Aeronwy was too young to be put on the streets – but he was coming to London 'to wheedle' so why didn't they meet for a few drinks and 'whimper together' (which strongly suggests that debt was something he had learned to live with – and exploit).[7]

His life had become more than an act. Dylan Thomas was now a walking one-man melodrama, living in a world of fantasy, in which the highly successful scriptwriter and radio star was as dazzling as ever, with a repertoire of songs, poems and crazy stories and a thousand social tricks that had made him the mainstay of many a bar.

In London, he could get away with it (although there were times when he drank too much and became simply boring); in South Leigh and Laugharne, he was more restrained (for these were people with whom he lived every day), but John Malcolm Brinnin, awaiting the arrival of a distinguished man of letters, was totally unprepared for the wisecracking tornado that ripped through his life early in 1950.

Brinnin was fey and genteel, slim and prematurely balding, with pursed lips. Caitlin says that his mannerisms were feminine. Brinnin worried about his clothes and personal appearance, carried a case of pills and potions with him wherever he went, and loved the company of rich or famous homosexual writers.[8]

Brinnin and Thomas corresponded intermittently during 1949 as the date for the first American tour drew near, and then on 21 February 1950 the big moment of John Malcolm Brinnin's life arrived.

Dylan Thomas had been drinking with Caitlin, Margaret Taylor, Harry and Cordelia Locke, and Douglas Cleverdon before the airport coach left Victoria. At Heathrow, he primed himself with drink before boarding the plane for the 17-hour journey that lay ahead; air travel took longer in those days with stops for refuelling and to pick up other passengers at Dublin, 'somewhere in Canada' and Boston, which meant that Thomas was 'cooped up in the stratosphere with twenty of the nastiest people in the sky . . . gnomes, spies and Presbyterians,[9] which was his way of saying that he had been drinking alone throughout much of the journey, finding that 'the terrible height makes one's ears hurt like hell, one's lips chap, one's belly turn'. He said that he had been nearly suffocated by the heat on the plane, and had then found himself shivering in temperatures just above zero in Canada and New York.

Brinnin, who evidently found it hard to imagine anyone else's feelings, observed that Thomas 'seemed unable to shake off some massive discomfort . . .'[10] A more understanding host would have made sure that Thomas had some rest before trying to adjust to the different climate, but Brinnin was anxious to show him New York.

As Brinnin drove Thomas into Manhattan, they passed through a dimly lit tunnel. 'I can never help shuddering a little when I have to go through one of these passages,' said Brinnin. 'Do you suppose it has something to do with the memories of birth trauma?'. There was a snort from Thomas, and as they emerged into Manhattan, with its towering skyscrapers reaching for the clouds, the poet remarked: 'EeeeeeEEEEEE . . . . it does remind me of Mummy!'

Brinnin drove him straight to the Beekman Tower Hotel, gave him time to shave and change into a shiny blue serge suit, and then took him off to his first American bar, with Thomas 'gawping at the soaring Babylon'. And so began a frantic round of drinking and socialising with writers and editors, poets and literary pimps, which Brinnin describes with such a wealth of extraneous detail that it is soon apparent, if one compares his version of events with Thomas's (which can be found in Thomas's letters home to his parents and Caitlin), that Thomas was taking it all in his stride – but that

Brinnin was overwhelmed. Brinnin thought that his guest was outrageous, while Thomas thought that everyone he met was 'furiously polite and respectable', described Greenwich Village as 'a feeble Soho with stronger drinks', and noted that he was always being introduced to 'dons, critics, writers, poets, all of the older and more respectable kind'.[11]

Both men were doing their best – but Brinnin had imported more than he had bargained for, and Thomas hadn't yet noticed that the New York literati were much different to the hard-drinking, tough-livered film people and BBC poets with whom he was used to drinking in London pubs; these American literary gentlemen were frequently dismayed by the poet's humour, his ribald jokes, his deterioration when drunk and, in particular, his vivid and constant use of four-letter words, especially in front of their wives.

And yet it is quite clear from Thomas's letters, which Brinnin would never have seen, that the visiting poet was observing them all acutely, noting

There seems, at first, to be no reality at all in the life here: it is all an enormous façade of speed and efficiency & power behind which millions of little individuals are wrestling, in vain, with their own anxieties.[12]

I have been driven for what seems like, and probably are, thousands of miles, along neoned, jerrybuilt, motel-ed, turbined, ice-cream-salooned, gigantically hoarded roads of the lower region of the damned, from town to town, college to college, university to university, hotel to hotel, and all I want, before Christ, before you, is to hold you in my arms in our house in Laugharne.... The distance from New York – where I shall be tomorrow – to Los Angeles is further than the distance from London to New York. Oh Cat, my beautiful, my love, what am I doing here? I am no globe-trotter, no cosmopolitan. I have no desire to hurl across the American nightmare like one of their damned motorcars.[13]

But oh San Francisco! It is and has everything. Here in Canada, five hours away by plane, you wouldn't think that such a place as San Francisco could exist. The wonderful sunlight there, the hills, the great bridges, the Pacific at your shoes. Beautiful Chinatown. Every race in the world. The sardine fleets sailing out. The little cable-cars whizzing down the city hills. The lobsters, clams & crabs . . . Seafood is cheap. Chinese food is cheaper, & lovely Californian wine is good . . . it dances in the sun for nine months of the year; & the Pacific Ocean never runs dry.[14]

Last week I went to Big Sur, a mountainous region by the sea, and stayed the night with Henry Miller . . . He lives about 6,000 ft up in the hills, over the blinding blue Pacific, in a hut of his ownmaking. He has married a pretty young Polish girl, & they have two small children. He is gentle and mellow and gay.[15]

Everything is not terrible here. I have met many kind, intelligent, humorous people, & a few, a very few, who hate the American scene, the driving lust for success, the adulation of power, as much as I do.[16]

These letters (and there were many more) convey an impression of a man far from home, intensely lonely, but observing all he saw with open eyes, whether it was from up the Empire State Building (which terrified him), or the 'phallic towers' in the cities, or what seemed strange to him that 'everybody uses the telephone all the time'. He was desperately anxious to return to Wales, aware always that Caitlin was without enough money to pay bills, or feed their children; there is a sense of responsibility in these letters that was often not apparent at other times:

I am the man you used to say you loved. I used to sleep in your arms – do you remember?[17]

Sometimes I think I shall go mad, & this time properly, thinking of you all day & night as I fly over the continent . . . after readings, I fall into bed, into sweaty half-awoken nightmares. I couldn't write but I do hope you got the £17 cheque from San Francisco & the one last week from Boston. And I hope they helped a little.[18]

Dylan Thomas spent three months in the United States, visiting over 40 universities, schools and colleges, seeing old friends like the novelist Malcolm Lowry and making new ones like the poet Theodore Roethke, presenting as he travelled a one-man stage show that included his own poems and others by Yeats, Lawrence, Hopkins, Milton, Auden, Donne, Edward Thomas, Henry Reed and Vernon Watkins. As on radio, he paused for effect, varied his pitch and tone, and for these American stages also made limited use of hands and movement, introducing some performances with a short lecture, and then interspersing his chosen poems with jokes, and on some – like Henry Reed's *Chard Witlow* and *Naming of Parts* – using accents to create light and shade. These were skills that the poet embraced to sell his wares with chameleon grace . . . and then, just as he had always done after a BBC radio broadcast, he would relax, drink whatever was going (which usually meant too much bourbon whisky), sing songs to anyone who would listen, let bawdy jokes trip off his tongue, roll off to whatever bedroom was available, and wake up with a hangover the following day. He travelled alone, often arriving in cities with just an address to go to and no idea where he would stay the night.

Brinnin viewed his guest with troubled emotions, both horror and affection, for these after-the-show bursts of ribaldry were *not* what he had expected. When The Beatles came less than 15 years later there were managers, attendants, police and security guards to protect them in their private moments, but Dylan Thomas was all on his own, breaking new ground, presenting a show for the ear of classic English poetry with those large audiences of often a thousand-and-more at a time, many of them girls, marvelling at his skill, hanging on to every word, and there was no one to shield him. When Caitlin accompanied Dylan on his second tour, between 20 January and 16 May 1952, she was appalled by what she saw – by his constant need to respond to their affection, his willingness to drink whatever was put in his hand, and the passive acceptance with which he greeted any woman's advances; she thought it foolish to pay such a price for fame and attention. When Brinnin arrived in Europe after that second tour, making plans for a third, he called on his friend Truman Capote, and discussed his relationship with Thomas as they sat overlooking the Mediterranean. Capote had never met Thomas. They came from different worlds, and yet both were obsessively mother-conscious, the one born in New Orleans and abandoned, the other still clinging to childhood.

'Why spend half your life taking care of someone whose mind is on nothing but a pint of beer and a piece of tail? Why should you join a poor man's pub crawl to the grave?' asked Capote.

The suave, sophisticated but none too wise American stage manager replied: 'Dylan's not poor. He makes more money than I do, a lot more.'

'All the more reason to quit playing wet nurse to an overgrown baby who'll destroy every last thing he can get his hands on, including himself,' said Capote.[19]

But was it as simple as that, or had Thomas made the fatal mistake of misjudging his audience? They responded well to that resonant voice toned and turned with an actor's skill, but were they ready for the private Thomas who had starred in a thousand bars with his mixture of bawdy jokes, music hall songs, party games and *risqué* advances to any girl with half a twinkle in her eye? That – and the fact that the poor man never could hold his drink as well as he liked to suggest, and all too often ended an evening by peeing on someone's carpet.

Brinnin hardly touched the heart of this tragedy in *Dylan Thomas in America*, which dealt with it largely on a superficial level (telling us how embarrassed Mr Brinnin was by the behaviour of his guest); a far more amusing illustration of Thomas's inability to play the part expected of him comes from the film star Shelley Winters, who was every bit as broad-minded and met Thomas on his first night in Hollywood in March 1950. They were introduced over dinner with Christopher Isherwood and Ivan Moffatt, whom Thomas had known in London before the War. She had no idea who Thomas was. Moffatt made a joke of this, saying that Thomas 'draws accurate and biting images of people and events'. Miss Winters assumed this meant that Thomas was a cartoonist, and asked why he had come to Hollywood.

'To touch the titties of a beautiful blonde starlet and to meet Charlie Chaplin,' whispered Thomas, gazing into her eyes. She looked at Isherwood and Moffatt. They said nothing.

'Okay,' said Miss Winters. 'I can grant both your wishes, and

When we had finished the dessert and brandy, I announced, 'You may touch each of my breasts with one finger, and the day after tomorrow will be Sunday, and Charlie Chaplin has open house, as Christopher and Ivan will know. I will take you there.

Ivan bought us a bottle of champagne and poured it. Then, with great ceremony, Mr Thomas sterilised his index finger in the champagne and delicately brushed each breast with the finger, leaving a streak in my pancake body makeup. A look of supreme ecstasy came over this Welsh elf's face. 'Oh, God, Nirvana,' he uttered. 'I do not believe it's necessary for me to meet Charlie Chaplin now . . . .'[20]

It is clear from this anecdote that the actress could cope with the poet and would have held her own in any Soho bar, but Brinnin, whose whole thesis was that

The sexual life of Dylan Thomas was already as much a source of legend as was his fabulous capacity for alcohol [21]

tells the story differently:

While Dylan had not previously heard of her, she surprised him by remarks that showed she knew not only of him, but that she was acquainted with his work. Nevertheless, Dylan refused to address her by her given name – because, he told her, that would be odd and upsetting. Shortly after they had met, they sat down for drinks somewhere and, according to Dylan, talked mostly of baseball, of which he knew nothing. Eventually the conversation changed, becoming centred in Dylan's appreciate enumeration of Miss Winter's more obvious physical attractions, which he had wanted to measure for himself. But he was rebuffed, he said, in a language which was as direct as a stevedore's and notably more colourful.[22]

This difference in describing one minor incident illustrates what is so worrying about *Dylan Thomas in America*. Brinnin was not present when Thomas met Shelley Winters; Brinnin had, by his own account, given Thomas 'a fistful of plane and train tickets and written directions' and then didn't meet him again until six weeks later. So who does one believe? Miss Winters, who was there? Or Brinnin, who was not?

The same doubt arises from their different accounts of Thomas's meeting Charlie Chaplin. This time, Thomas surpassed himself. Shelley Winters invited him and another guest, journalist Sidney Skolsky, to join them for dinner with her flat-mate Marilyn Monroe, and she describes in detail what happened thereafter:

Marilyn and I spent the entire day cleaning the apartment, and we prepared dinner. The arrangement was that I did the real cooking and she did the dishes and the cleaning up. Not only could Marilyn not cook, if you handed her a leg of lamb she just stared at it. Once I asked her to wash the salad while I went to the store. When I came back an hour later, she was still scrubbing each leaf. Her idea of making a salad was to scrub each lettuce leaf with a Brillo pad.[23]

On this occasion, Marilyn went to a nearby waste site and picked wild flowers which she used to decorate their apartment, arranged Japanese lanterns along the awning of the balcony and lit candles, while Shelley prepared the roast:

Mr Thomas drank practically all his dinner. Marilyn had made a pitcher of gin martinis, and since we didn't have a pitcher, she made it in a milk bottle. She and I had two juice glasses of martini each, Sidney had none and Mr Thomas drank the rest. To slow him down, Sidney suggested a straw. A bottle of red and a bottle of white wine at his elbow disappeared next, followed by six bottles of beer he had bought in a supermarket.

As the evening progressed, Dylan, by now clearly in his element, began singing:

> Come all ye fair and tender maids
> Who flourish in your prime, prime,
> Beware, beware, keep your garden fair,
> Let no man steal your time, time
> Let no man steal your time
>
> 'Cause when your time is past and gone,
> He'll care no more for you, you
> And many a day that your garden is waste,
> 'Twill spread all over with rue, rue
> 'Twill spread all over with rue
>
> A woman is a branch, a tree,
> A man a clinging vine, vine,
> And from her branches carelessly
> He takes what he can find, find
> He takes what he can find

Shelley Winters says that she heard Richard Burton sing this traditional folk song on another occasion, but this time she and Marilyn were deeply moved by the way that Thomas sang it; they sat there nearly in tears while Skolsky busily took notes for his column in the *Citizen-News*. By the time they were due to leave for Chaplin's house, Thomas was cheerfully drunk although when he climbed into their open-top car he was disconcerted to find it left-hand drive.

'Where's the bloody steering wheel?' he yelled.

'It's over here on the left, where I'm sitting.'

'Every fucking thing's backwards in this country,' he said, pretending he would drive although, in fact, Thomas had never driven a car in his life. On the way to Chaplin's house, they picked up six more bottles of beer at another supermarket and he sat drinking from those (and also from a bottle of gin produced from an inner pocket), taking over the steering wheel as they arrived, with the result that the car ended up in Chaplin's tennis court, tangled in the net.

I had made him leave his bottles of gin and beer outside in the bushes. But he was such a mess he looked like a stoned leprechaun. He wore strange brogues with flapping tongues that seemed to flap in unison with his belt and tie and his real tongue. I was ashamed to introduce him to anyone except Oona (Chaplin's wife), and she quickly got him into an armchair with a cup of black coffee.

That evening Chaplin's guests included Greta Garbo, Lotte Lenya, Thomas Mann, Marlene Dietrich and Katharine Hepburn, but Thomas didn't want to speak to anyone but Chaplin, who was sitting at his piano playing the theme from *Limelight*. Looking across the room, Shelley Winters saw that Thomas had now got his hands on a supply of brandy. She thought that the only way she could immobilise him was by sitting on his lap. As she did so, Thomas muttered: 'Isn't that bloody genius ever going to talk to me? That's why I came to California. He's ignoring me like he's the governor and I'm the colonial . . .'

A few moments later, Chaplin's son started to sing his father's song. Dylan promptly rose to his feet, causing Shelley Winters to fall off his lap on to the floor, and he

suddenly seemed cold sober and took Charlie junior's hands and danced around the room with him, humming the tune in his melodious voice . . . . Charlie senior crashed his hands on the keyboard, got up and knocked Charlie junior's hands away from Dylan. Unable to distinguish who was doing what, Charlie senior hissed at Dylan, 'Even great poetry cannot excuse such rude, drunken behaviour.' . . . Dylan turned on his heel and, in a very dignified manner, walked out into the solarium . . . As the guests left hurriedly, we heard a sound like running water. Dylan was peeing on a large plant on Charlie's porch.

Shelley Winters is a natural storyteller, and in her hands these scenes have moments of pure comedy; Brinnin has neither such gifts nor an attention to detail, and he reduces the scene to this:

Shaken by his contretemps with Miss Winters, who herself had been made morose by the behaviour of this tipsy poet from Wales, Dylan was at first not wholly in command of himself. But, before long, exhilarated to hear Chaplin laughing at *his* jokes, Dylan had bounced back.[24]

And so it goes on, through scene after scene, page after page. Where there is direct personal evidence available, either from Dylan's letters to his wife and parents or from personal recollections of people who were present when Brinnin was not, one is left thinking not that Brinnin is untruthful, but came from a more selfconscious literary culture and he just couldn't grasp the spontaneous and unpredictable nature of Thomas's personality. Brinnin wasn't alone; other semi-distinguished American literati responded to Thomas's behaviour either with a self-righteous sneer – or by encouraging it (and sometimes both).

A student present at Thomas's reading at the University of Michigan that same month recalled

One of my professors announced in class that a most colourful and brilliant Welsh poet was coming on campus as part of an American tour. He gave a few anecdotes, related mostly to drinking, and convinced me (and most of the class) that seeing Dylan Thomas would be an experience we'd remember for the rest of our lives.

I went. The place was packed. The poet didn't seem drunk, but it was an experience I'll remember for the rest of my life . . . Dylan Thomas made poetry come alive. Listening to his beautiful voice, I was touched deep in my heart by poetry, not in my head . . . I guess what I remember mostly is the glee in my English professor's eyes when he told about taking Thomas to a tavern, along with other members of the faculty, and getting him mildly drunk. Not as drunk as they would have liked, since Thomas had a reputation for being most interesting when he was drunk – but drunk enough to have something to brag about.[25]

This is another factor missing from Brinnin's account; balancing the behaviour of those who were welcoming Thomas to their colleges or homes with those of the poet himself, for it is clear that many of them pushed drinks down his throat as fast as they refilled his glass – and he was too weak-willed (or polite?) to say, 'No'. His body could not handle it all, and yet he was trying to hold his own – and would recover quickly with friends like Oscar Williams, who accepted him as he was. This was observed by a total stranger, Helen Lillie of Washington, who was taken to the White Horse Tavern one night by a friend, Talcott Williams.

When we came in, there was the most hungover man I ever saw, sitting at a table staring at an untouched mug of beer. Tal said casually to me, 'This is Dylan' and sat us down beside him. It took me a complete round of drinks before I realised that this silent, sick, unhappy soul was the celebrated poet. Meanwhile, we'd been joined by a tidy gentleman with a bow tie, Oscar Williams, whom Dylan had come to meet. The conversation grew animated, somehow we started on the subject of true crimes, and just as suddenly Dylan came to life and started talking about the Christie murders, telling us how he had gone to the 'murder house' with the police who had broken down walls and discovered various female bodies . . . as he talked, he grew animated, also drank down his beer, got some colour in his cheeks, and looked much better. Oscar Williams, who struck me as a nice thoughtful man, quietly signalled to the waiter who thereupon put a sandwich down in front of Dylan, and he ate it, more or less without thinking.

We sat there for hours, talking about crimes and criminals and listening to Dylan . . . he had such a wonderful voice and such a magnetic presence that what he said wasn't as memorable as the way he said it, and the change from complete apathy to vibrant life (after he'd had his hair of the dog) was dramatic.[26]

Another reminiscence far closer to the real man comes from Samuel N. Bogorad, later Professor of English at the University of Vermont, who spent a day with Thomas during his third tour:

Mostly it's the warmth of Dylan Thomas that I remember, an essential warmth, a warmth emanating from his genuine humanity, a warmth always there even when his humanity expressed itself momentarily in petulance or annoyance or contempt. From the moment in the forenoon when we almost missed him at the airport (because he'd slept through the landing and the stewardess got him off just before the plane left for Montreal) until the late-early moment of the next morning, it was his vital heat that impressed me and now sticks in my memory.

I remember his normally puffy face even more puffy with sleep, his normally unruly hair more than usually dishevelled, his ill-fitting, baggy suit perhaps more than usually out of press. I remember his uproariously funny account of a concert he'd attended in New York a day or two earlier, during which some chap literally crawled into a piano to pluck the strings. I remember his lapse into sullen silence when he was obviously uncomfortable at the stiffness of our trying too hard to be friendly. I remember how appalled he was to discover he would have fourteen hundred people in his audience in the Chapel . . . I remember how un-eager he was to meet some students informally in the Student Lounge that afternoon – but he did meet them there and was plainly ill at ease. And why not? It couldn't have been much fun to answer (or parry) some of the questions: 'Mr Thomas, what do you think about Stephen Spender?' 'Do you approve of free verse, Mr Thomas?' 'Is T.S. Eliot still a force in modern poetry?' I remember how warmly he responded when someone mentioned Charles Laughton's reading Dickens and the Bible, and did Mr Thomas ever read from the Bible in his lectures? He found this enormously amusing, and he formulated an on-the-spot program which he was sure would be very successful: Charles Laughton reading the Bible, John Carradine (who was then also on a reading tour) playing the part of Jesus Christ, and Dylan Thomas impersonating the Devil. One or two of the students were shocked at the irreverence, and Thomas enjoyed their discomfiture.

I remember his sudden thought, at nearly 5.30 pm, that he had to buy a white shirt for his evening appearance; how we rushed downtown to a haberdashery a minute before closing; how in his increasing nervousness at the approach of the evening lecture he fumblingly took the pins out of the new shirt, pricking himself, and counterpointing the whole procedure with hot, full-bodied curses . . . I remember his agonized stage-fright in the minutes before he went onto the platform . . . There was no trace of stage-fright as the deep-toned resonance of that magic voice warmed every corner of the auditorium . . .

I remember the informal gathering after the reading, in the living room of a faculty member. With the apprehension of the public appearance behind him, Thomas was astonishingly relaxed – as he had not been at any moment that day. In some ways, it was here, in these pleasant surroundings, that Thomas was at his best, his most human, his warmest . . .[27]

This sense of excitement and personal warmth is missing from Brinnin's account, and it meant so much for those who were there in the colleges and universities of America, listening to Dylan Thomas bringing poetry alive. One American poet who heard him, Mac Hammond, told me that the performance

was electricifying, so electrifying that I sat up the whole night reading the whole of Auden's *Collected Poems*, having heard Thomas read the one that started,
As I walked out one Evening[28]

but what they couldn't accept, easily, was that Thomas was still himself, with no artificial airs and graces – and was determined to remain that way.

Mac Hammond saw Thomas again at a private party, and showed him a current book of literary criticism in which Thomas was ranked with the surrealists; Thomas took it from him and wrote – DYLAN (NO SURREALIST HE) SIGNS HIS FUCKING NAME, and then dated it – which was not the way visiting celebrities usually handled such queries.

A student, Roselle Lewis, who later became an English teacher, was present when Thomas gave a two-hour reading in Los Angeles, and confirms that when there was work to be done and an audience to please, Thomas tried hard to entertain them with a quirky mixture of literary insight and personal humour, which she was able to capture because someone had the prescience to record him – and she discovered the tape again, 30 years later:

> The tape unrolls: 'Oh, blimey! Let's do without these damn gadgets. One of my dreads (a Kafka dream) is that I'm talking into a microphone that doesn't work.' His dark, sonorous voice steadily on course, he vowed not to lecture. He knew nothing at all about poetry, but promised to read a few poets he liked – Yeats, Hardy, Auden – chosen because they were 'direct and clear'. Then he would 'descend' into his own poems, which even his mother would not call lucid.
>
> But first, would he respond to questions such as the link between poet and society in our prehydrogenous age? In droll parody of student queries, he stated the impossiblity of knowing the relationship between W.C. Fields and Virginia Woolf or Rilke and the Gold Standard.[29]

and then he read poems by James Stephens and warned his audience not to be put off Thomas Hardy 'by the sheer bulk and the small print' and that W.H. Davies was 'not a tame Georgian poet' or a 'naturalist staring at cows', bringing in work by W.R. Rodgers and Alun Lewis, before suddenly varying the tempo to make them laugh again by reading an extract from Andrew Lang's *Passing the Graveyard*:

> That like a woman who has wed
> You undressed first and went to bed

before introducing them to John Betjeman and two poems by W.H. Auden, *As I Walked Out One Evening* and *Master and Boatswain Song*, a selection from Yeats, and his own work.

Thomas would tailor each talk to his audience, dropping poems or adding them, depending upon the mood he sensed, and dealing with any interruptions with a humility that surprised them. As he was reading one of his own poems at Harvard – it was either *Do not go gentle into that good night* or *The force that through the green fuse drives the flower* – someone in the audience shouted, 'That took three minutes 45 seconds.'

'Read it as fast as I could,' said Thomas, to great applause.

It was in moments like that that Thomas captured the hearts of students across America; and yet that same evening, as he relaxed after the reading at a party organised by the Harvard alumni, he approached one full-breasted student, swaying as he chanted rhythmically,

I would like to take you back with me to Wales, that I might suckle at your paps.[30]

and at a reception in Santa Barbara, after reading at both the University and the County Art Museum, he horrified a faculty group 'by not quite making it to the bathroom'.[31]

Brinnin was seldom present on these occasions, was far too shockable to see them in a deeper context, and was, in any case, much too anxious to record his own role in arranging for Dylan Thomas to tour America to be able to observe, as did the poet David Lougee, that Thomas

was very tired. He was just lionized from the moment he got here, what with all the cocktail parties, and he wasn't used to whisky. Actually, he preferred beer. But he wasn't a drunk. People don't understand that he was just whimsical. It's interesting that, even with some of the people he knew and respected, he could be colourful and theatrical, and lie at the same time . . . (Caitlin) was picking up stories that he was spending money drinking and sleeping around, and he wasn't. He had one girlfriend she was worried about, but he was in no condition for that. He liked being around women, but he adored Caitlin. I never saw him drunk, never saw him slipping. He was very well aware of the people, and he listened intently . . . People say that he was self-destructive, and I just don't believe that. It's easy to say a person is self-destructive. Doctors love to say that. Although some people do gravitate towards the wrong choices, I don't think that was true of Dylan. It was a lot of hard work for him, and he was very dedicated. He had dedication, but also gaiety . . .[32]

OVER THE HILLS AND
UNDER THE WOOD

IN the last four years of his life, Dylan Thomas had few real problems, financial or otherwise, except for those familiar to any freelance writer. Physically, he was fitter than he liked to pretend. His body had thickened out ten years earlier during Caitlin's first pregnancy and now he was overweight for his height, still as 'chesty' as in childhood, smoking constantly and coughing dramatically, whether he needed to or not, but there wasn't much actually *wrong* with him. His doctor has told me that he rarely saw him. The only medical attention that he received regularly was bone-resetting. Thomas was born with what his mother called 'chicken-bones' and was forever breaking them.

Caitlin insists that, generally speaking, Dylan's health was good, now that he was living where he wanted to be, with a daily routine that he enjoyed.

Those American tours made money. His publishers wanted more work than he had time to complete. His friends at the BBC could always be relied upon for commissions to write scripts, perform readings, or act in radio drama productions. *Under Milk Wood* was nearing completion, and he was now writing poetry again, aware that 'as you get older, poems become harder, not because the gift is gone, but because your standards are higher.'[1]

His total earnings have never been disclosed, not that these would necessarily give much indication of the money actually passing through his hands since there would have been, in his case (with so many genuine expenses) a large difference between gross income and net. This would have been confused even more by his frequently receiving fees direct, rather than through his agent; by money received from the US when Oscar Williams placed his writings or 'work-sheets', and his level of borrowing.

That he had more access to money is clear, for he wore better clothes and shoes, visiting expensive dentists, taking more care of his appearance generally, and playing the generous host either at his London club or in the

Soho drinking dens, the Mandrake and Gargoyle, where he was fêted as a writer who had broken through in America (although he still had the trick, as Shelley Winters observed, of sitting tightly, looking intently at his plate when a waiter approached a dinner table with the bill). Caitlin did not know it, but there was usually money in his pocket; he enjoyed expensive restaurants, going to the theatre and night clubs or drinking with friends while she was 'stuck in Laugharne' – which meant that he was always borrowing more.

Those tax problems, which recur in some detail in *Collected Letters* and the Ferris and Fitzgibbon lives, lay well within his earning capacity; Caitlin has told me that he often lay awake at night, unable to sleep, claiming that it was the tax that was worrying him, but she realises now that he had many other matters on his mind that he preferred not to discuss with her (one of the problems with drinking so much at the end of the day was that he usually went into a deep sleep soon after climbing into bed and then awoke in the early hours, restless, sleepless and only partially refreshed).

His deepest anxieties were probably psychological for, as Dr B.W. Murphy[2] observed:

he can best be considered as suffering from a character neurosis, with increasing depression, dangerous alcoholic acting out, tormenting worry, progressive creative inhibition, indicating a state of neurotic helplessness ... Few have manifested neurosis in a fashion more baroque than Dylan Thomas, in the self-defeating conduct of his life with all its painful complications, the self-produced financial miseries, and inability to meet the inescapable requirements of reality involved in being an adult male, husband and father ...

Dr Murphy argues convincingly that scrutiny of *any* aspect of Thomas's life suggests neurotic processes:

but the money troubles he perpetually brought about do so very clearly. Vernon Watkins reported Dylan possessed an uncanny ability to divest himself quickly of large sums of money; where the money went usually remained a mystery[3]

There is no logical explanation for Thomas's financial difficulties, for he was earning high fees for his work, both in Britain and the United States, with tiny outgoings – Margaret Taylor charged him a nominal rent for The Boat House; property bills were usually paid for him, and his main personal expenses were school fees (Llewelyn was already at boarding school; Aeronwy went later), the annual subscription to his London club and the everyday costs of food, drink and clothes. His only possessions were a secondhand bicycle, a few clothes, and the odd sticks of furniture that he and Caitlin had brought to The Boat House.

No matter how much he earned, Thomas would still have thought himself poor for he had an innocence of mind; this is clear from the observations of E.F. Bozman, his editor at Dent, who worked with Thomas closely, if intermittently, for over 15 years:

Courteous in manner, soft-spoken and persuasive in conversation, apparently business-like, without any sign of self-importance and grateful for and mildly surprised at anything that was done for him commercially, he could nevertheless be counted on to miss every opportunity that came his way for making a practical success of his authorship and to set at naught every effort that was made to persuade him to help himself. It was as if the everyday successes of the writer only touched the surface of him – as if there was something else in his mind that mattered far more than the ordinary human satisfactions. He would flip through a bundle of 'rave' reviews, treating them like the products of a children's competition – let the critics have their little games, his manner indicated, it's nothing to do with me. Even his own poetry, of which he was very fond indeed he had no desire to understand. In fact he used to say that he couldn't be expected to do so. Hadn't he written it? Surely that was enough to ask of anyone?[4]

Part of the problem may have been that Thomas was disorganised. Having never employed a secretary or even a filing system, he had no record of what he had written and failed to retain copies of magazines that printed his work. Even now, 40 years after his death, unknown poems occasionally surface. I have found anonymous contributions to pre-war issues of *Adelphi* that were probably his, because of the subject-matter and use of language, and a signed poem in *Lilliput* that seems to have been forgotten. For years he might have been able to muddle through, dropping most incoming mail in the nearest waste bin, no matter who it was from (so Caitlin tells me) and having few details of his published work to give his first bibliographer J. Alexander Rolph. Some of his earliest poems are known because of the four notebooks sold to Texas, but six other notebooks vanished and no one knows what happened to those.

For years he had been able to fudge the boundaries of normal social behaviour. Friends made allowances for him, because of his charm and rare gifts. No one called the police when he stole their shoes or shirts, and if he went too far, they tolerated it – until success in America brought him up with a jolt. 'He must have found it very hard to adjust after that,' Caitlin told me. Most of the time he managed it. Only one reading engagement was missed during those four American tours, and he was rarely more than a few minutes late. He would be at the airport or railway station on time to get to the next city, no matter how bad his hangover, and he would be standing there in the wings, ready to walk out on stage for that evening's performance, but at what price? And how long could he continue without proper organisational support to underpin his career when every tuppeny-halfpenny academic had secretaries and assistants at their beck and call, all imposing upon his time, expecting him to perform for *them*. Bill Read observed

I think you can't emphasise too much the point you make that Dylan was a frightened youth who found it difficult to accept his great gifts and feel equal to his celebrated peers. A great deal of this came from lack of formal education; he just never learned how to handle intellectuals . . . . They knew that they were his inferiors but *he* didn't.[5]

Within his home, there were problems of another kind. Young love had matured into vinegary tension between husband and wife. His first American tour made Thomas aware of a wider audience. He had been pampered and pursued by what Caitlin describes as 'blue stockinged women'. Some were just students, but they sat at his feet adoringly, enraptured by his voice and presence, his gift with words and sounds, responding to his affectionate wordplay. As always, a few thought themselves in love with him.

How far this went is far from clear, for several women said they loved Dylan Thomas, but there is little evidence that he *loved* them. When he returned from his first tour, highly excited by the reception he had been given, letters started arriving from them, but Dylan made little secret of this. He showed Caitlin the letters and told her that this was how women behaved in America. He even persuaded her to accompany him on his second tour to see for herself how audiences reacted.

He may have had an affair with one woman on that first tour, but, if so, they spent little time together; a few nights at the most. Whether or not it was consummated together is far from clear, although Brinnin, who calls her Sarah (which was not her real name) implies that they did, saying that she was 'highly educated, had taught for several years at one of the leading women's colleges, and was knowledgeably devoted to Dylan's work from the time of its earliest publication'. Brinnin continues:

These qualities, combined with her dark handsomeness and social poise, made her precisely the sort of woman from whom one would expect Dylan only to flee. How deeply he felt about her I did not then know, since neither he nor Sarah confided in me except to let me know that they were lovers[6]

Later in his book, Brinnin says that when he met Thomas in London in September 1950, Sarah joined them. She had arrived from New York by sea to begin a holiday in Europe. Brinnin claims:

At one point, when Sarah had gone to fetch us drinks from the bar, he turned to me 'John, what am I going to do'. His face, suddenly sober, showed bewilderment and his eyes were set upon something far away. 'About what?' 'I'm in love with Sarah, and I'm in love with my wife. I don't know what to do.' It was a question no one could have answered save himself, and I did not attempt to. But this was a new confidence, and my first experience of Dylan wrestling with a problem rather than seeking out means to circumvent it.

We disembarked at Waterloo Bridge (they had been on a boat trip to Greenwich) and walked through Trafalgar Square back up to St Martins Lane where in the midst of passing traffic we stopped to say good-bye. Like the illicit lovers of a thousand English novels, they were going off to Brighton for a day or two; I was flying to Paris in the morning . . . .[7]

Like many of Brinnin's stories, this one is uncorroborated; he knew who Sarah was (as do all Thomas's biographers), but did not name her or produce any letters from Thomas that would have proved his point. Neither did he explain that 'Sarah' was a senior executive with a leading American magazine to which Thomas wanted to contribute.

Brinnin suggests that Sarah invited Thomas to travel with her to France, but he did not do so (and neither, apparently, did he answer her subsequent letters). Instead, he went back home to his wife. A few days later, Caitlin found a letter from Sarah. Thomas had casually thrown his jacket over the back of a chair, and there it was, protruding from a pocket; he had made no attempt to conceal it. She read the letter and confronted him. 'It's nothing, it's nothing,' he insisted, swearing there were lots of women like that in America, that she mustn't let it worry her, that Sarah worked for this magazine for which he wished to write. 'Like a fool I believed him,' says Caitlin, only to have her worst fears dramatically strengthened when

Margaret Taylor suddenly arrived from London to say that Sarah had arrived from New York and been seen in London with him; even worse, he had taken her around the pubs and clubs where Caitlin was well known. Understandably, Caitlin felt humiliated and a sad letter survives from Thomas to Helen McAlpine:

> I came back to find Caitlin terribly distressed, but managed to tell her that all that grey fiend had pumped into her was lies and poison. And so it was. And Cat believed me. And now we are happy, as always, together again, and that other thing is over for ever. So please, Helen: remember, for Cat's sake if not for mine; all, all, all that grey scum said was LIES.[8]

Which all tends to suggest that Sarah and Brinnin had got the affair out of proportion, with Thomas backing out rather than become 'like the illicit lovers of a thousand English novels'. Whatever the truth of Brinnin's revelation (and it is possible that Thomas was doing no more than seek to impress an influential magazine executive who might publish his work), Margaret Taylor's confirmation that Dylan and Sarah had been seen in London seriously damaged the Thomases' marriage. Their relationship never fully recovered from Caitlin's sense of betrayal.

For the remaining part of their life together, Caitlin was suspicious and her husband, wary. Their old easy familiar trust had gone. Rows became more frequent and increasingly violent. Returning home from nights at Brown's Hotel, well tanked up with spirits, she would rage and scream, tearing at his body and hair with her fists, trying to pin him to the floor so that she could straddle his chest and beat him around the ears. Whenever he went off to London for a few days, to appear on yet another BBC radio programme or to discuss more projects with his agent, Caitlin would berate him.

And yet, even when these tensions were at their worst, Thomas still kept working; he would retreat each day to his shed, and write ('not always, because writing's not like that; some days it just doesn't come'). Bozman insists:

> Undoubtedly the publishing event that meant most to him was the issue of his *Collected Poems*. But in putting them together, and revising them, he lost all interest periodically, even going so far as to lose the actual material on several occasions, and when the book proved to be an outstanding success, he was neither elated nor surprised.[9]

Publication of *Collected Poems* gave Thomas the chance to take stock, to decide which poems mattered most to him, to choose a sequence, and to present them carefully, writing a complex *Author's Prologue*, describing his purpose within the disciplines of an internal acrostic that was 102 lines in length, with the first line rhyming with the last, the second with the penultimate, the third with the 100th, and so on. He was prepared to go to such lengths because, he explained in a separate preface

I read somewhere of a shepherd who, when asked why he made, from within fairy rings, ritual observances to the moon to protect his flocks, replied: 'I'd be a damn fool if I didn't!' These poems, with all their crudities, doubts and confusions, are written for the love of Man and in praise of God, and I'd be a damn fool if they weren't.

Dent published his *Collected Poems* on 10 November 1952, issuing 4,760 copies of the first trade edition and also a special limited edition of 65 copies, each signed by Thomas, printed on moulded paper and bound in dark blue crushed morocco leather. These were sold then at five guineas, compared with a price for the trade issue of 12s. 6d. Anyone lucky enough to have bought one could trade it in now for a car.

The volume includes all but one of the poems that Thomas worked on in the last phase of his writing career. *Over Sir John's Hill*[10] was set in the landscape that lay before him in his worcshed, looking across the estuary of the River Corran joins the Taf; *In The White Giant's Thigh* begins with a description of the waters beneath him

> Through throats where many rivers meet,
> the curlews cry[11]

bringing together older memories and past fascinations that weave their way through all his work. *Do Not Go Gentle Into That Good Night*[12] describes better than any other form of words his feelings as his father prepared for death. *Lament*,[13] a highly accomplished poem written especially for stage performance, expresses an awareness that, sexually, he was no longer the man he once thought he was. *Poem On His Birthday*[14] again uses the images conceived through his worcshed window:

> In the mustardseed sun
> By full tilt river and switchback sea
> Where the cormorants scud
> In his house on stilts high among beaks
> And palavers of birds

Nothing has changed much in Laugharne since he wrote those poems and his unfinished *Elegy*,[15] which begins

> Too proud to die, broken and blind he died
> The darkest way, and did not turn away,
> A cold kind man brave in his narrow pride

and describes his father approaching death without any belief in God, sure that this was the end. None of these poems came easily. In the last years, more than in the first, every poem was an event of deep significance in Thomas's life; there is not a spare word, superfluous comma or casual thought in any of them.

His *Collected Poems* were hailed as a major literary achievement, building on the reputation that Thomas had established first with *18 Poems* and *Twenty-five Poems* before the War, and then with *Deaths and Entrances* when the War ended. Now, he was recognised as one of Britain's great poets, with *Collected Poems* awarded the William Foyle Poetry Prize in 1952 and the Etna-Taormina International Prize in Poetry in 1953.

Critically, their publication set the seal upon his reputation. *The Times Literary Supplement* devoted a page to its anonymous review, referring also to his autobiographical short stories:

> It is noticeable how well the form of autobiography suits Mr Thomas. He himself is the centre of everything he writes, and his sense of the dramatic is perpetually evoked by the incidents of his own life . . . Several of his finest poems draw on his memories of the exaltations and terrors of being a boy. The glories of childhood are the theme of the incomparable *Fern Hill* . . . And richly as he can draw on his childhood for memories, his poetry is evidence that he is as receptive to experience now as he was then. *Poem in October*, which is probably his highest achievement, is a celebration of his thirtieth birthday. Few poems have such a power of evocation . . . Yet to describe Mr Thomas as essentially an autobiographical poet is no more completely adequate than to describe him as essentially a romantic poet . . . if Shelley was right in claiming that poetry 'creates anew the universe, after it has been annihilated in our minds by the recurrence of impressions blunted by reiteration', then Mr Thomas is a poet of poets. For him, the summer's end, 'geese nearly in heaven', the shouting of boys in the park and the hawk that rides in the air above Sir John's Hill are alike new and vivid expressions of God's will . . .

In *The Listener*, Raymond Preston observed

Mr Thomas has discovered that if you let grow what the mind throws up, then you may have something worth declaiming at a microphone. Tempted to vaporous mumbo jumbo, he nevertheless obeys the command of the psalmist, to sing to the Lord a new song. At his best – when every word in a line stands firm as a rock, yet every line still moves within his own form – he is a psalmist of our own, thanking heaven for children and the fruit of the womb, and with an eye for the hopping of the high hills.

In a BBC radio broadcast, Graham Hough commented

The appearance of the *Collected Poems* of Dylan Thomas is by any standards an important literary event . . . of the younger generation of established poets, Dylan Thomas seems to me far the best – the most exciting, the most original, with the fullest and grandest command of language.

In *The Sunday Times*, Cyril Connolly, who had published many of Thomas's wartime poems in *Horizon*, wrote

At his best he is unique, for he distils an exquisite mysterious moving quality which defies analysis as supreme lyrical poetry always has and – let us hope – always will.

In *The National and English Review*, Eric Gillett's verdict was

Most impressive, Mr Thomas is not afraid of traditional forms and he is willing to experiment at times . . . His imagery is clear cut and striking, and his inspiration is authentic.

In *The Observer*, Philip Toynbee acclaimed Thomas as

the greatest living poet in the English language . . . His language is seldom colloquial, nearly always in the grandest of grand manners, yet he is an adept at transforming an old and dead familiarity.

Typically, when told that he had been described as 'the greatest living poet in the English language', Thomas suggested that Toynbee must have been thinking of someone else, but the observation would have brought great joy to his father, now in constant suffering. Dylan was having to cope with fame just as his father's life was ending. Theirs had always been a special intimacy with D.J. introducing his son to the contemplative joys of literature; the 'inner life' that belonged to them alone. Caitlin accepted this as something that Dylan did not expect her to share, but others never grasped its significance for D.J. discouraged Dylan's friends from visiting Cwmdonkin Drive in childhood and saw little of them during the years that followed when he and Florence moved first to Bishopston, then to Llangain, South Leigh and back down to West Wales, and their last home in Laugharne. With each move, D.J. whittled down his library, giving away his books, complaining as he did so that his life was diminishing, even though he still retained a substantial collection of books.

Once D.J. and Florence had settled in Pelican, Dylan would call each morning, discuss his current work, show him anything recently finished, borrow a reference book if he needed one, share *The Times* crossword (which they liked to finish in a few minutes as a sort of parlour game), and then go their separate ways. They seldom drank together. That was one of the simple rules by which they had always lived. Dylan would cross the road to Brown's Hotel to see Ivy and Ebie Williams at lunch-time, and D.J. would walk down the hill to The Cross House, still dressed as formally as ever, with suit, collar and tie, and hat, to see Phil Richards who became a particular friend.

There was an apparent formality between father and son, a lack of physical affection, but this was deceiving, for their friendship was deeper than ever, with D.J. often helping to find the right word or metaphor. Dylan would seek his advice just as in boyhood, not so much in a familial way, but as craftsmen will when bound together by skills and disciplines known only to them.

'I don't understand that at all,' D.J. was sometimes heard to say handing back the sheet of paper on which his son was currently working. Dylan would then stand there in the kitchen at Pelican, reading his latest verses aloud, stressing the vowels and dipthongs within his chosen metres while D.J. listened intently.

'I see. Get it now,' he'd say with a half-smile, never wasting a word.

Theirs was a relationship upon which neither mother nor wife sought to intrude, for Dylan had made it clear to Caitlin that he did not want theirs to be an intellectual bond. She was wise enough not to seek one, but noticed that he would often return from Pelican with two or three borrowed books, knowing that D.J. would be anxious to get them back for Dylan was careless wanting books solely for what they contained and not for their binding or presentation. Unless he was urged to return them promptly, she knew they might easily end up as beer mats or wedged under a table leg.

Towards the end, Dylan still saw his father daily and was much distressed by the way he seemed to physically shrink within himself while his pride and intellect remained intact. D.J. was around six stone in weight by the time he died. Dylan observed his life ebbing away. They shared thoughts and language much as they had always done, although now with that intimate poignancy which underlines *Do Not Go Gentle Into That Good Night* and his unfinished *Elegy*. D.J. died on December 16th, 1952, at the age of seventy six, with his senses wandering in his final hours. 'Poor old boy, he was in awful pain at the end and nearly blind,' Thomas wrote to Fred Janes.[16] 'The day before he died, he wanted to get out of bed & go into the kitchen where his mother was making onion soup for him. Then, a few hours afterwards, he suddenly remembered everything & where he was, & he said, 'It's full circle now.' D.J. died with his son holding his hand.

Many years earlier D.J., Florence and his brother Arthur had agreed that when their time came they all three wished to be cremated. This was respected. D.J. was cremated three days later at the Glyntaff Crematorium, Pontypridd. It was one of the most distressing experiences of the poet's life. Someone said that his father's head exploded in the oven (which is not an uncommon phenomenon, although seldom talked about), and a few moments later the wind started blowing the oven's smoke in the wrong direction. Thomas felt that he was breathing his father's remains and was violently sick. When they returned home that evening, Dylan asked his wife to ensure that 'nothing like that ever happens to me.' She agreed, not thinking for a moment that such a decision was only eleven months away.

Collected Poems confirmed Thomas's growing international reputation. The hardback sales in Britain exceeded 30,000 in the first two years, and even more were sold in the United Sates where he went to promote the book in April–May 1953, just as today's rock stars travel the world selling their latest LP. This third US tour was also an opportunity to present *Under Milk Wood* on stage for the first time. The unfinished play was given its world première at the Fogg Museum, Harvard University, on 3 May 1953.

Thomas had been working on the play, on and off, for 13 years, although long periods had passed without him devoting any time to it at all. Originally, Thomas had planned to call it *The Town That Was Mad*, his idea being that the small Welsh town, based on Laugharne, was so eccentric that a Government inspector was sent down to seal it off with barbed wire and conduct an inquiry to find out what was wrong with them all. In the end, he would discover that they had found happiness and it was the rest of the world that was mad, after all. Gradually, Thomas's concept changed until it became 'a play for voices', describing the life of the town, Llareggub, through one day, beginning at dawn and ending with a night scene in the town pub which he never managed to complete.

For a long time, *Llareggub* was the working title; it was a place-name that Thomas first used in a short story before the War, referring to 'the sow-faced woman Llareggub' in *The Burning Baby* (1934) and then using it again as a place name in *The Orchards*, the story which T.S. Eliot published in *Criterion* (1936). It was a word that seemed so definitively Welsh, and so much less spelt back to front.

Under Milk Wood occupied much of his last four years, though he would often pick it up, lay it down, and switch to something else. In 1950, when it was still *The Town That Was Mad*, he agreed to write it for the BBC, and was under some pressure from Douglas Cleverdon to deliver the final manuscript. The following year he raised some extra cash from it, offering the half-finished work to Princess Caetani[17] for her magazine *Botteghe Oscure*, explaining that it was

> a play, an impression for voices, an entertainment out of the darkness, of the town I love in, and . . . [he said he was trying] to write it simply and warmly and comically with lots of movement and varieties of moods, so that, at many levels, through sight and speech, description and dialogue, evocation and parody, you come to know the town as an inhabitant of it . . . the piece will develop . . . through all the activities of the morning town – seen through a number of eyes, heard from a number of voices – through the long lazy lyrical afternoon, through the multifariously busy little town evening of meals & drinks and loves & quarrels and dreams and wishes, into the night and the slowing-down lull again and the repetition of the first word: Silence.[18]

Thomas told Princess Caetani of the different people who lived in the town; of their loves, dreams and pleasures, and the contrary forces that ran between them:

> the cobbler who thinks the town is the wickedest place to live in the world, but who can never leave it while there is hope of reforming it . . . and the

old woman who every morning shouts her age to the heavens; she believes the town is the chosen land, & the little river Dewi the River of Jordan; she is not at all mad; she merely believes in heaven and earth. And so with all of them, all the eccentrics whose eccentricities, in these first pages, are but briefly & impressionistically noted: all, by their own rights, are ordinary & good; & the 1st Voice, & the poet preacher, never judge nor condemn but explain and make strangely simple and simply strange.

While working on *Under Milk Wood*, Thomas was also hoping to be commissioned to write a film script based on Homer's *Odyssey*;[19] was writing another play, mostly in verse, although how far he got with this project is still not known,[20] toyed with a fourth idea, *Two Streets*, about a boy and a girl being born the same day in separate streets with the same midwife, and finding their lives come slowly together,[21] promised his publishers that he would collect together another volume of short stories, planned to finish *Adventures in the Skin Trade*, continued to write for radio, was commissioned to write his first story for television (simply called *A Story* at the time, although it has since become known as *The Outing*). He was driving himself too hard in too many directions to find the repose needed for writing poetry, although each one that he wrote in those final years was a major poem.

He had now become an international celebrity; in the last four and a half year of his life, since returning to Laugharne, he spent 40 weeks touring the United States, six weeks in Persia working on a documentary film on the oil industry, made frequent visits to London to discuss the projects mentioned in the previous paragraph, and to take part in 30 BBC radio productions. None of this meant much in Laugharne, where he was happier playing darts, cards or shove-halfpenny in Brown's Hotel, mulling over local gossip, standing at the bar, drinking slowly, always listening for words and phrases. When he heard one, Thomas would take a pencil stub and a scrap of paper, a cigarette packet or a used envelope, and jot it down there and then, popping it back in his pocket without a word. Older Laugharne people, now in their 70s, remember this clearly. It was something he did night after night, without saying why. They thought it odd, quirky, perhaps the sort of thing writers had to do when ideas came, lest they forgot them, not realising that he was noting the way they spoke, gathering material for *Under Milk Wood*, knowing that each of his characters would have to speak with different intonation to give his play movement, tension and rhythm.

Thomas was a craftsman through and through, but none of them knew that *they* were his raw material. When *Under Milk Wood* was first broadcast after his death, some were upset. They thought he had been laughing at them, for there were real people in the town upon whom he had modelled Captain Cat, Polly Garter, Mog Edwards, Myfanwy Price, the Rev Eli Jenkins, Nogood Boyo, Dancing Williams, Cherry Owen, Sinbad and the rest, and he had caught the innocent but ribald way in which they talked about each other.

Now their children say, especially to visiting Americans writing theses, 'Ah yes, now Captain Cat – that was Johnny Thomas, lived down Holloway Road. We called him Johnny Holloway. Johnny had been away to sea, travelled the world and never stopped telling stories. Dylan spent hours talking to him . . . and Milk Wood; that would be the wood up The Laques, looking down on the town and owned by Dickie Lewis. He was Dylan's milkman; Dickie Milk's Wood . . . . Butcher Beynon; that was Eynon the Butcher who also owned The Butcher's Arms in St Clears. Dylan used to drop off the bus to call in there on his way back from Carmarthen . . . and there was a Rosie Probert, lost her baby in the river down Horsepool Road . . .'

Laugharne is like this now, and was before Thomas came; a thriving, extended family, which shares life's sorrows, accepting each other's shortcomings with humour. There are so many Dais or Davids that each has a different name – there is Dai the Milk, who delivers it; Dai Bananas, who is daft, and Dai Survivor, who hid in the ladies' toilet the night the police raided one of the pubs for drinking after hours . . . and then there are the two Bobs, father and son. One lost three fingers in an accident. He's Seven Bob. His son is Ten Bob . . . and Kenny Cabbage who has never lived down asking for seconds at school one lunch-time thirty odd years ago.

These were the attitudes and underlying humour that Thomas captured in *Under Milk Wood*, even though Caitlin always told him he was being 'far too whimsical', realising perhaps that he saw himself as part of it all, First Voice.

Despite the range of his work in those last years, or maybe because of it, Thomas continued to tread that dangerous path between fantasy and reality, sharing his anxieties with anyone who would listen (and there was always someone who would whenever he walked into a pub). On visits to London, the States or Swansea, his faults drew wide attention. *Time* magazine reported

When he settles down to guzzle beer, which is most of the time, his incredible yarns tumble over each other in a wild Welsh dithyramb in which truth and fact become hopelessly smothered in boozy invention.

He borrows with no thought of returning what is lent, seldom shows up on time, is a trial to his friends, and a worry to his family.*

Back home in his workshed, Thomas would switch from project to project, sometimes finding it hard to find the enthusiasm for those that had become most pressing (and especially those like his commission to adapt *Peer Gynt* for the BBC in which he had lost interest); this is a familiar problem to anyone who has worked in the modern entertainment industry, which relies so much upon creative ability to produce a song – or a poem – to specific deadlines so that it can then be mass produced in many different ways.

Thomas had begun his career with a fascination for words; their use, texture and flexibility, as much as their meaning. Now, he had moved on to radio, films and live performance, making his first two television appearances in 1953, using the skills of a new technology to convey his meaning, for he knew, instinctively, that words could be used with different effect when complemented by visual images or magnified by the microphone. Today, there is an international industry geared to develop, market and protect those blessed with this creative skill. The rock industry has an international turnover of £12bn per year, and it depends upon the ability of just a few major artists of world renown to blend words, images and sounds to catch their audience by the ear. Those who have this ability are cossetted and guided, made financially secure, and provided with those managerial supports and domestic comforts that they need to take the strain from their lives. Dylan Thomas made his break-through largely unaided; Brinnin's support was minimal and, in my view, misapplied. His agents were trying to put his financial affairs upon a proper footing with the help of an accountant, but the creative artist who has this ability to touch the heart often needs much greater help than this. People flock to him and he needs protection from them so that he can concentrate upon his work, for his fame is such – and Thomas had crossed this threshold with his radio and TV appearances, concerts and first recordings – that he can no longer go to theatres or

*Thomas thought this libellous, and went to the Swansea solicitor Stuart Thomas asking him to issue a writ. *Time* responded by hiring a private detective to follow him during his fourth visit to the United States. This is why so much detail is known about his last days. Caitlin says they had never needed to go to a solicitor before and that Dylan went to Stuart Thomas simply because they had both been to Swansea Grammar School. The only minor error in that *Time* paragraph was the reference to him *seldom* showing up on time – but it was far from minor for him. Thomas very rarely missed a performance and was usually punctual for professional engagements, as opposed to private appointments, and needed to protect his reputation in that respect. The writ lapsed with his death.

cinemas, shopping, or even walk down a street without being accosted by fans who mean well, but just don't understand.

Dylan Thomas was on his own. The first rock star.

But he didn't know how to handle it, and neither did anyone else, for no one realised then that television and recording processes would have as great an impact on the communication of words as Caxton's invention of the printing press or the first newspapers, and that artists like Dylan Thomas would be exposed in all their frailty.

Mostly, he met the consequences of fame with grace and humour. He missed only that one reading in the United States, and also an after-dinner speech in Swansea; occasionally, *very occasionally*, he drank before a performance, and then his voice would be thicker in resonance and somewhat blurred, but these lapses were so rare that there may have been another explanation.

His burden, as Caitlin describes it, was considerable. The normal everyday responsibilities of wife and children, mother and father, home and bills, had always seemed too much for him. When faced with a distressed wife, he would often retreat to bed. Any matters of parental discipline were left to her (and Caitlin was strict). His attitude to family finances did not improve these last years. She was still left short of money, no matter how much he earned or begged, and was never given any kind of allowance. Throughout their marriage, Caitlin never once handled a personal chequebook or had a tiny sum of money in reserve that she could go to when needed. When they travelled en famille, she would sit in one railway compartment with the children and he would be alone in another reading, or in the buffet car, drinking. Children were another ordeal. Although Thomas carried their photographs in his wallet, returned with gifts or sweets, and made Christmas the highlight of their year, [his daughter tells me] he still retained a distance.

A sense of loneliness pervades these last years. Thomas was sharing his inner world with no one. Caitlin was drawing away from him, and he knew that he had only himself to blame for that; with his father's death, the poet became stranded and isolated in his fame, and all the more so because he had been trying to achieve it for much of his life. He was famous throughout the English-speaking world, but his props had gone. D.J. was dead. Caitlin no longer trusted him. His early friendships had fallen away, as they often do when fame takes a man away from his contemporaries. All normal privacy had gone.

A RED ROBE, A CROWN
OF THORNS AND THE FINAL
CASTING OF DICE

D YLAN Thomas left Laugharne for the last time on 9 October 1953,
planning to spend a few days in London with Caitlin before flying
to New York. Although he hated aeroplane travel, Thomas now
steeled himself to it, anxious to save time. He was to die exactly one month
later.

How he spent that last month is far from clear. The recollections of those
who saw him do not agree, and there were unknown, underlying factors of
which they were unaware. It has been suggested that Thomas only agreed to
this fourth American visit to raise money to pay the Inland Revenue,
household bills and school fees, but this seems unlikely for he was now a
performer whose services were in demand – and his tax payments were being
deducted from his earnings by David Higham.

Another favourite theory, which I do not accept, is that Thomas was
unable to write; that he feared his creative powers were coming to an end,
and seized upon this opportunity of another US tour as a 'means of escape'
from his everyday realities. Anyone can refute this argument by comparing
Thomas's known literary output with the performing schedule that he
imposed upon himself, between other commitments.

The wonder is that he did so much, working away at his desk, collating
Collected Poems, writing his *Author's Prologue*, finishing *Under Milk Wood*,
beginning to gather together his material for *Quite Early One Morning* (his
collected radio scripts), completing his last major poems, and working up the
future projects mentioned in the last chapter – all at a time of much stress in
his everyday life. Those constant rows with Caitlin had a serious cause; he
was now a celebrity, a performer whose work kept him away from home.
Whether she was angry, jealous of his stardom or simply feeling ignored is

beside the point; much more disturbing for his peace of mind was that she now taunted him with losing his way, neglecting his 'real work', poetry, and giving in to temptations of 'idleness, flattery and fornication'. She did not understand the nature of his new status, either.

The truth of her allegations is also immaterial, for what they suggest is something else – a marriage falling apart, torn asunder, and her feeling of betrayal just as Dylan Thomas was gaining international acceptance as a writer of rare felicity. Vernon Watkins seems to have sensed their tragedy, for Gwen Watkins observes that he

> could have gone down to Laugharne as he used to, but for some reason he did not do so. I think perhaps he was made uneasy by the continual rows between Dylan and Caitlin. He could no longer pretend that the quarrels were not serious. Caitlin seemed by now permanently embittered by her life; and although she made me uneasy and often indignant because of her behaviour in public, I was firmly on her side and against Dylan's treatment of her. Her life seemed to me intolerable.[1]

Their despair was known to only a few intimates like Bill and Helen McAlpine, and Harry and Cordelia Locke, who respected the Thomases' confidence, with the result that Fitzgibbon and Ferris touch upon the troubles that beset the Thomases towards the end of his life without forming convincing judgements. Brinnin may have had an inkling, since he visited the Thomases in Laugharne in September 1953. Caitlin later wrote to him privately saying she feared the marriage was over. She does not know whether Brinnin kept the letter.[2] In any case, immediately after Dylan's death, his mother took it upon herself to find and destroy any letters that reflected badly upon her son's reputation. Knowing these factors, and that nearly all Thomas's personal papers were burnt after he died, one can look upon the last period of his life with more understanding.

During that third visit to the United States, which lasted six weeks between 21 April and 2 June 1953, Thomas presented a further 20 readings of his and other poets' work, including three performances of *Under Milk Wood*. One of these was taped for Caedmon who released many of his recordings after his death. He also visited Igor Stravinsky to discuss his proposal that they should work together on an opera, with Thomas writing the libretto; this was to be his next major project after revising *Under Milk Wood* in readiness for its British radio production by Douglas Cleverdon.

Their idea was to describe a second Garden of Eden, after the present world had been destroyed in a holocaust, with an international language derived from the Tree of Knowledge. Stravinsky was hoping that Boston University would fund their collaboration, providing a sufficient advance for Dylan to take Caitlin to the United States (she would have stayed with a friend, Ruth de Witt Diamant in San Francisco, while Thomas lived with Stravinsky in Hollywood). The possibilities were exciting, the more so because Stravinsky had already worked with W.H. Auden on *The Rake's Progress*, proving that this kind of joint project could work well:

All this news was exhilarating, all the plans were wonderful – just what Dylan needed to lift spirits that had become heavy under the press of too many engagements and under the prospect of a return to Wales where all the old financial problems would move in as inevitably as the tides in the estuary[3]

observed Brinnin, who saw Thomas the day he first met the composer.

However, although Stravinsky was anxious to press ahead and had extended his home to accommodate his guest, the Boston funding did not materialise – and Thomas knew that he would have to pay his own expenses, from his readings income, at least initially. This troubled him, for he would have to leave Caitlin behind, not knowing when or if she would be able to join him.

That September Brinnin spent a holiday in Italy. He returned to the United States via Britain, driving down to Laugharne with Bill Read and the photographer Rollie McKenna, who had been commissioned to produce an illustrated feature on the Thomases to accompany one-shot serialisation of *Under Milk Wood* in the US magazine *Mademoiselle*. Brinnin arrived to find them ill at ease, with Dylan anxious to join Stravinsky as planned, and Caitlin opposed to his plans; Dylan also knew that if he could get to New York there was every chance that he would be able to finalise a contract with an American lecture agency that would give him a guaranteed income of $1,000 a week, and was still hoping that Michael Powell would come up with the funding for his *Ulysses* project.

Brinnin claims

Listening to Dylan's somewhat anguished account of so many uncertainties, I had one strong and simple reaction; he should stay in Laugharne and get on with his work. When he asked me what I thought he should do, I first of all tried to have him put aside the notion of another American reading tour of the sort he had completed only three months before. This, I felt, would be something to do again, certainly, but at least not for four or five years hence . . . I sensed, now that he was back in Wales, beleaguered by financial worries and creative aridity that almost any means of escape seemed attractive. I told him I felt he should try to stay in Laugharne, by whatever devices, and find his way back to a working routine . . .[4]

That afternoon, Florence accompanied her son and their American visitors on a tour of the Llanstephan peninsula, pointing out the chapels, cottages and farmsteads that had been home to her family for generations. Rollie McKenna photographed them, and these were the illustrations used for *Mademoiselle* and, later, Bill Read's book *The Days of Dylan Thomas* (1964) and Rollie McKenna's own *Portrait of Dylan* (1982). Brinnin noticed that Dylan drank nothing all day, 'except for a single glass of beer at Brown's Hotel in the morning'.

The following day, after more photos and a farewell lunch, Brinnin, Read and McKenna returned to London, aware that Dylan did not want to cause a further dispute with Caitlin by confirming his plans but sure that

Dylan's mind was really quite made up, I felt, and he would come to America against all hazards, but this decision would not be announced until he had conferred with Caitlin and found some means of overcoming her intransigence. I felt in any case that the difficulty in coming to a decision was due to some basic disagreement between them for which present issues offered but a new focus.[5]

A few days later Thomas wrote to Stravinsky, confirming that he was indeed going to join him in Hollywood, adding

the lecture-agent there in New York (i.e. Brinnin), who makes my coming across possible, has been terribly slow in arranging things . . . . I shall be in New York on the 16th of October; and I'll have to stay there, giving some poetry-readings and taking part in a couple of performances of a small play of mine, until the end of October. I should like then, if I may, to come straight to California to be with you . . .[6]

Reading his letters side by side with the accounts of Brinnin, Fitzgibbon and Ferris, and knowing what was amiss between husband and wife, one begins to sense a determination on Thomas's part to press ahead and make the most of the opportunities now opening up for him . . . that September he learned that Michael Powell had been unable to raise the money for his *Ulysses* film, yet, but Thomas knew that if he could only get to Hollywood he would begin what could prove to be the major project of his life with Stravinsky. That offer of $1,000 a week for future lecture tours would make him financially secure at last, and give him a better platform for his work than Brinnin could ever provide. He also knew that his publishers were prepared to publish his collected radio scripts, his collected stories and his novel, *Adventures in the Skin Trade*, which he now planned to finish, Thomas possessed a kind of inner steel which would enable him to make hard choices if necessary. He had always had this core of steel, though he successfully concealed it.

Dylan told Caitlin that he would be going to New York as planned, would undertake another series of readings to fund his visit to California and then send for her as soon as he had the money. She was livid. How could she believe him when he had let her down, or betrayed her, so often before?

On 8 October Fred Janes drove over to see Dylan, taking with him the Welsh artist Ceri Richards who wanted to discuss staging a joint exhibition at the Glynn Vivian Art Gallery in Swansea, featuring Richards' paintings, with Thomas reading his poems. Thomas agreed, and Janes has told me that he seemed fit. Nothing happened that day to make him even consider the possibility that Dylan might be unwell, although Caitlin was quarrelsome and clearly angry that she was being left behind.

That evening the Thomases went to the cinema in Carmarthen. Ferris reports that

> According to Florence Thomas, Dylan fainted during the film. The family doctor, who was at the cinema that evening, disputes this. He and his wife were sitting in front of the Thomases. Before the film began, Caitlin approached him and said she was worried about Dylan. He was having severe headaches; and in the morning they were going away. The doctor said he would pick them up in his car after the film and take them to his house in St Clears, on the way to Laugharne, so that he could examine Dylan. But when the lights came on, Dylan had vanished, probably to the Boar's Head. The doctor went home without seeing him. His mother believed he had a premonition of death; when he left next day, he came back three times to kiss her.*

*Ferris, p.297. Caitlin also disputes this suggestion that Dylan fainted. There was much speculation about Dylan's health when he died so unexpectedly, much of it without any factual foundation. It should be noted that Florence had *always* exaggerated Dylan's ill health, and was just as much a storyteller as her son.

The Thomases left for London the following morning, and probably had hardly any cash between them and little in the bank, for Dent had refused a further advance for the time being. They broke their journey in Swansea to enable Dylan to cash a post-dated cheque with the bookseller Ralph Wishart. They also caught a taxi to see Daniel Jones (there is no special significance in them travelling by taxi; even when he had hardly a penny to his name, Thomas still preferred to use taxis, an attitude that he may have acquired from Caitlin for she has told me in recent years that 'you should never travel anywhere unless you can go first class').

Daniel Jones, who does not mention Caitlin's name anywhere in his book, even when describing occasions such as this, when the couple were together, says that he and Dylan visited several pubs, drinking until afternoon closing-time, and eating:

> Dylan was getting later and later in fulfilling the travelling plans arranged for him, and gave a clear impression that he had no wish to go at all . . . There was a big clock on the wall, and as the hands moved steadily towards the time of Dylan's train I saw his eyes follow them. I read his thoughts perfectly. 'I am *not* going to catch that train. I am determined to be *too late* to catch it. There's always tomorrow.' . . . . As the train moved off, I started first walking, then running to keep up with it. Dylan stood at the open window, waving one hand slightly with exaggerated weakness and smiling an odd little smile.[7]

Why Daniel Jones should have thought there was such urgency is unclear, for the Thomases had arranged to spend a week in London, staying with Harry and Cordelia Locke in Hammersmith. In the end, they stayed even longer. Brinnin sent Dylan's plane ticket to Laugharne, where it arrived after they had left, thus delaying the flight. Thomas sent a telegram to say that he would now be leaving Heathrow on the 7.30 p.m. plane on 19 October.

In London he happened to bump into Fitzgibbon after they had both been to Broadcasting House. This was probably on Thursday 15 October for that was the day Thomas delivered his revised manuscript of *Under Milk Wood* to Cleverdon. As Fitzgibbon walked away from the building, he saw Thomas's familiar figure in the dusk

> headed like myself for The George. I caught up with him – I had not seen him for months – and he suggested that we avoid the BBC pubs and go somewhere where we could have a quiet drink together. We were both

entirely sober . . . how subdued, even sad, he seemed. He told me that he had no wish to go to America so soon again for he was, he said, very tired. On the other hand he was clearly proud that Stravinsky should have chosen him to be his librettist, for Stravinsky was one of the great. He outlined the idea of the opera to me, much as Stravinsky has described it. I only remember one further detail. The tree in the new Garden of Eden . . . was to bear leaves on each of which there would be a single letter of the alphabet. Then when the fresh winds blew and the Tree of Knowledge shed its leaves, the second Adam would recreate for the second Eve, all words and languages.

We talked amiably and calmly, about this and that, trivia mostly, while strangers drifted in and out of the dark bar. He certainly did not seem to me to be at all suicidal . . . I sensed a certain trepidation, which was characteristic, towards the unwritten opera . . . He spoke, I think, of the speed with which he hoped to write it. He invited my wife and myself to spend Christmas at Laugharne . . . he suggested that we go to the other pub. We did. Immediately he was surrounded by the usual people; immediately he became the life and soul of the party, funny, obscene, instant Dylan, quite unlike the man with whom I had just been talking . . .[8]

Cleverdon arranged for his secretary, Elizabeth Fox, to type *Under Milk Wood* on duplicating stencils, so that Thomas could pick up his original manuscript by calling at Broadcasting House on Saturday morning, 17 October.

During the weekend he telephoned me at home, in some agitation, to say that he had lost the manuscript, either in a taxi or in a pub. I assured him that I could get the script duplicated on Monday, and would bring copies to him at the Victoria Air Terminal before he left for New York. I met him on the Monday evening, and to his evident relief, gave him three copies. As we were having a farewell drink before the coach started for the airport, I said how sorry I was that the manuscript had been lost; he replied that if I could find it I could keep it; and he gave me the names of three or four pubs in which he might have left it. A couple of days later I found it in the Helvetia in Old Compton Street.[9]

During that week, Thomas also spent an evening with the BBC producer Philip Burton, who befriended and then adopted the young Richard Burton. They had known each other for some years. Burton produced Thomas's radio documentary *Return Journey* in 1947, and now Thomas was anxious that they should work together on *Two Streets*, which he envisaged as a stage play. Burton recalled:

He talked with affectionate warmth of a new poem he had written about his father, and he talked as though it was likely to be the last of its kind. He said, 'I've got another twenty, or perhaps twenty-five, years to live. I've got to try new things. This is the beginning.'

Before we had been talking long about the play we found it necessary to find a working title for it. We decided on *Two Streets*. My part in the discussion was to suggest how Dylan's vision might best be realised in the physical opportunities of the stage, for the play was to have little resemblance to the normal commercial three-act entertainment. To begin with, there was to be no interval. On this point Dylan was adamant . . . a play must be an unbroken experience, like a film or a symphony . . . the first character to form a link between the families would be the midwife attending the mothers. What a rich, Dylanesque character she would have been! I suggested that the centre of the stage throughout the play might be dominated by the voice of the valley itself, a character who would become different things at different times, a voice that the families sometimes listened to and sometimes ignored; he could be a preacher, a politician, a football-supporter, a recruiting-sergeant, a poet, a cheapjack selling the valley in the depression, a bureaucrat, a multiple-shop owner . . . in this part I saw Dylan himself; he would have been superb . . . In the actual staging of the play his mind's eye had not seen much beyond the opening, and for this he begged with comic fervour: 'Please, please let me have two prodigiously pregnant women.'[10]

After talking solidly for four hours, reading chunks from *Under Milk Wood* and the new poem, *Elegy*, talking excitedly of his collaboration with Stravinsky, Thomas suddenly said

'I feel ill. May I lie down?' Soon he was in a very deep sleep on my bed. When it was necessary to wake him, I found it difficult to do so, but, when he left, he was bouncing with life again and full of the usual promises of a certain future: 'I'll write you from New York, and see you as soon as I get back.'

This last incident has been taken as proof that Thomas had another blackout before leaving London, but it sounds as though he was tired and needed rest. Certainly, he seems to have been fit, but subdued, late in the afternoon of Monday 19 October, when Caitlin accompanied him to the air terminal along with Harry and Cordelia Locke and Margaret Taylor. They stood drinking in the bar, where they were joined by Douglas Cleverdon with his duplicated copies of *Under Milk Wood*. When the time came for Thomas to board the coach for the airport, Locke walked with him, noticing that he seemed 'sober, depressed and quiet'.[11] Thomas sat at the back of the coach. As the driver pulled away, he gave a thumbs-down signal to Locke who returned to join the others in the bar. That evening, Caitlin walked the streets of London in a state of deep depression; she felt the marriage was over.

Liz Reitell met Dylan Thomas off the plane in New York. As they travelled into Manhattan by taxi, he said the days in London had been the 'worst week of my entire life'. There had been constant arguments between him and Caitlin, fuelled by lack of money and her anger that he was going to Hollywood to stay with Stravinsky without being able to make arrangements for her to join him.

Because of the tickets' delay, Thomas lost his reservation at the Chelsea Hotel. Instead of being given one of the best rooms overlooking 23rd Street he was allocated a small one at the rear:

> While he seldom seemed to pay the slightest attention to his living-quarters anywhere, being put into a small dark room when he had become used to the best in the house upset him inordinately and made him sullen.[12]

That night he and Liz Reitell dined at a Spanish restaurant in Greenwich Village and then went off for a rehearsal of *Under Milk Wood*, which was being performed with a cast of actors with him as First Voice:

> he was in a sober and serious mood . . . . To the actors, who not only held him in warm affection as a person but who showed an almost awed respect for his ingenuity as a man of the theatre, his presence was magic. Under his direction the new version of *Under Milk Wood* leaped into shape . . .[13]

Afterwards, the couple went on to the White Horse, where they stayed talking with friends until 2 a.m. What time he managed to get to bed, Brinnin does not say but it would seem that Thomas had been travelling and working for 30 or 40 hours without any opportunity for proper sleep; he had spent a full day in London, travelled against the clock to start a new day in New York, followed by eating out, rehearsing and drinking. Caitlin says that he seemed well when he left London, but could his body cope without normal rest?

Next day, Dylan felt unwell, after a few lunchtime drinks, and said that 'perhaps he had better return to the hotel to rest. Liz accompanied him, sat with him through the remainder of the afternoon, and went out to a nearby delicatessen to get him a light supper. After he had eaten he said he felt he could sleep'.[14] She left him to return to her own apartment. Thomas slept late the following morning, arriving 'sober and professionally concentrated' for the next rehearsal of Under Milk Wood. That evening he ate an 'enormous dinner' and 'mentioned repeatedly, yet without explanation, his immense relief in having "escaped" from London.'

The following day (23 October) he lunched with Liz Reitell at a sea-food restaurant near the Chelsea Hotel, became distressed over the meal 'in an acute state of nervous agitation' and later returned to the Chelsea with a party of film people. When Reitell phoned, she could tell that he had been drinking and went round to the hotel, asking his visitors to leave and persuading Thomas to rest for a few hours until 'he had returned to comparative sobriety and was able to work on new scenes of the play'. That evening, Thomas attended another rehearsal of Under Milk Wood, incorporating extra material that he had written that day. During the rehearsal, he was restless, sometimes too hot and then freezing; all the symptoms of a chill. Later, he 'returned to the Green Room, became nauseated and had to vomit, retching so violently that he lost his balance and fell to the floor . . . . 'I can't do anything more,' he said. 'I'm too tired to do anything.' He lay down on a couch, rambled a bit and said, 'I've seen the gates of hell to-night. Oh, but I want to go on for another ten years anyway. But not as a bloody invalid, not as a bloody invalid . . . I'm too sick too much of the time.'[14] He is then said to have slept a few minutes before opening his eyes and calmly saying, 'To-night in my home the men have their arms around one another, and they are singing.'

So far this dramatic sequence of events, reconstructed secondhand by Brinnin with assistance from Liz Reitell, seems to have a simple enough explanation. Brinnin implied that Thomas was disintegrating, either physically or psychologically, but there seems to have been a simpler explanation; he was tired after his journey and had been working hard since his arrival, and, as always, he was appealing for sympathy. Florence had always fallen for that, and so had Caitlin. And yes, it was Friday night; the end of the working week when the men of Laugharne had their pay packets, went off to the pub, drank well and started to sing, as Welshmen often do. Thomas was being sentimental, far from home.

The next morning, Saturday 24 October one of the friends who had attended the previous night's rehearsal, an architect named Herb Hannum who was later to become Liz Reitell's third husband, went round to see Dylan who appeared unwell.

'How long have you been this way?'

'Never this sick; never this much before. After last night and now this morning, I've come to the melancholy conclusion that my health is totally gone. I can't drink at all. I always could before . . . but now most of the time I can't even swallow beer without being sick . . .'

Thomas now had what he always craved: attention. Hannum, and then later Liz Reitell, listened while he wallowed. They suggested he should see a doctor, and took him to see Dr Milton Feltenstein, whom Thomas nicknamed 'the man with the winking needle' because of his inclination to use injections; he gave Thomas a shot of cortisone, then a relatively new drug with unknown side-effects. That afternoon, there was another rehearsal and in the evening, the first presentation of *Under Milk Wood* with actors reading the different parts.

Brinnin went to the Poetry Center for the afternoon rehearsal:

When the lights went up I could barely stop myself from gasping aloud. His face was lime-white, his lips loose and twisted, his eyes dulled, gelid and sunk in his head. He showed the countenance of a man who had been appalled by something beyond comprehension.[15]

Or was it the countenance of a man injected with cortisone who already had alcohol in his bloodstream and was not adhering to a balanced diet? This seems more likely, for after the performance Thomas went on to a party at Rollie McKenna's apartment which continued into the early hours with Brinnin noting that, 'Dylan grew expansive, talkative, laughed boisterously, much like his normal self' (by then the cortisone would have worn off). The following day, 25 October, Thomas gave a confident performance of *Under Milk Wood*, his best yet, 'suddenly chipper and as full of song as a lark' . . . but Liz Reitell was unhappy because Thomas had given her the brush-off;

Brinnin was maudlin because he felt they 'spoke like strangers', with Dylan wanting to know where he stood financially. Brinnin was also aware that Thomas was close to a decision that would have left no more room for him in the poet's life.[16]

This has such a familiar ring to anyone who has witnessed, as I have on numerous occasions, artists beginning to realise that the time has come for them to shed the business managers, producers and general hangers-on who have been part of their lives until . . . It's always painful, like a divorce – and here was Dylan Thomas on the point of signing that new deal with a lecture agency that would guarantee him $1,000 a week, and make Brinnin's *ad hoc* arrangements a thing of the past.

Brinnin missed the matinée performance of *Under Milk Wood*, which 'was by every report its greatest performance. A thousand people were left hushed by its lyrical harmonies and its grandeur . . . Dylan himself said he had at last heard the performance he wanted to hear.' Instead, Brinnin 'spent the afternoon in withering depression' and that night 'quickly came to tears' when he met Dylan Thomas again at a supper party in Sutton Place. Brinnin claims that

Dylan began to weep, and Liz wept. Speaking half-articulated phrases, we learned that each of us had felt shut off, that each had sensed disillusion with the other, and that the clumsy silence into which we had retreated was the consequence of a sensitivity so acute and of a misunderstanding so vast that only now could we begin to understand it . . . Holding my face in my hands as I attempted to regain composure, I felt strong arms about me. Standing behind me as he held me very firmly, Dylan spoke the last words I was ever to hear him say directly to me: 'John, you know, don't you – this is for ever'.

This maudlin description of their last meeting needs careful consideration. Brinnin was losing Dylan. Of that, there is no doubt – for Thomas did subsequently sign that $1,000 a week contract. Was Brinnin now too emotionally involved in Dylan Thomas's affairs? Was Caitlin right when she said, not only to me but on many occasions, including once on television in an interview with Dan Farson, 'that bloody man was in love with my husband'?

Here, we may be getting to the heart of those last confusing days of Dylan Thomas's life, knowing now that Thomas was fit but tired when he left London for New York; that his marriage was in deep trouble, and that, far from wishing to escape from life or being unable to write, he was busily planning the most important projects of his life – his stage play *Two Streets* with Philip Burton; his opera with Stravinsky; his possible move into world cinema with Michael Powell, and putting his US lecture tours on a far more commercial footing.

As Thomas walked away from Brinnin and Reitell to circulate among the other guests, she told Brinnin that Thomas was 'without any question, the most lovable human being she had ever known'. However, while adoring him 'she knew also that he was a destroyer – that he had an instinct for drawing to him those most capable of being annihilated by him.[16] . . . now she felt she was at breaking point. Tonight she was going to let him know that she could no longer be with him, and that she could no longer take care of him.'

That night, Thomas went off to the White Horse while Brinnin and Reitell returned to their homes. The following day, 26 October, Brinnin says Reitell found Thomas at the Algonquin, talking to a Dutch businessman, already drunk and ordering one whisky after another:

implying that he had been in actual war-time combat, that he had witnessed horrors involving his family, became disconnected, violent, maudlin and obscene . . . ranted on about blood and mutilation and burning and death. In an attempt to calm him, Liz held his hand; he broke into tears and began to sob.

Like so many of Brinnin's hyperbolic descriptions, these need careful analysis. He is discussing something that happened when he was not present, and makes no attempt to suggest what was being discussed. Were Thomas and the Dutchman discussing the wartime air raids on their respective countries, for Thomas had witnessed the bombs falling on London, and had written a poem about a child being killed in an air raid? He had once been sitting in a taxi when a bomb exploded nearby. That Thomas may have become genuinely distressed during the conversation is clear from the Dutchman's comment: 'He is a good man, take care of him.'

This is the constant difficulty with Brinnin's book; the emotional lurches from scene to scene without rooted explanation. And always one is aware that Brinnin *supposes* what others felt, without making it totally clear that he was somewhere else at the time. Occasionally, there are direct quotations that are more revealing than he realises. On 27 October, which was Thomas's birthday (and always an intensely personal time for he had written four birthday poems), Thomas says: 'What a filthy, undignified creature I am . . .' which Brinnin repeats for its face value, without apparently re-alising for a moment that Thomas was quoting from *The Hunchback of Notre Dame*, and clearly ruminating on the passing of another year. Speak-ing of Caitlin, he says, 'I know she's crying, too' – and we now know what this meant. This was one of the few times when they had not been together on his birthday. And birthdays always held a childlike significance for him.

The following day, 28 October, Thomas gave a poetry reading at the City College of New York, and that evening participated in a symposium on *Poetry and The Film* with the playwright Arthur Miller, 'apparently in fine fettle . . . a frequent and serious participant in the discussion'. Later, he joined a party at the White Horse and the following day lunched and dined with friends. On 30 October, he went to a party at Ruthven Todd's home, drank only beer, talked through the evening with 14 or 15 people, and then went off again to the White Horse. On 31 October, Thomas lunched with Liz Reitell and another friend, eating 'next to nothing, merely picking at dishes he had ordered', although the occasion was 'pleasant, even merry'. That evening he went out drinking, and com-plained of a hangover the following day, although he still went off to the White Horse, then to a dinner party, and finally to another party late at night. He was still flirtatious with any woman who would respond, and 'showed every sign that, ill or no, he could still muster the zest of his famous party behaviour':

After midnight Howard Moss invited a group from the party to come to his apartment for a nightcap. As they were making desultory conversation and listening to music there, Dylan said nervously: 'I just saw a mouse. Did you see it?' He pointed to a door. 'It went under there.' Liz and the others did not see it, and sensed immediately that there was no real mouse to see. But Dylan was so obviously distraught that Liz said yes, she had seen it, and he seemed relieved.

What none of them realised was that Thomas had been seeing mice in pubs and at parties for the past 20 years. He saw them in The Mermaid and The Antelope, and frequently running behind girls' legs in the pubs of Fitzrovia and Soho. It was just another game, but they were taking him far too seriously – and he even responded to that, agreeing to read them poetry for over an hour, in the still hours of the night. It was 5 a.m. when the party finished. Another night's sleep had been missed, and Thomas was in pain, having scratched his eye on a rose thorn when he walked out on to a balcony for some fresh air.

The next day, 1 November, Thomas went to the unveiling of a statue of Sir Thomas Lipton by the sculptor Frank Dobson, then had dinner at the Colony restaurant where he met the novelist William Faulkner before going on to another bar. On 3 November, which was Election Day in the United States, Thomas signed the contract that would guarantee him $1,000 a week – and that night visited the apartment of the writer Santha Rama Rau 'where he drank moderately, played with her little son, and seemed quite his congenial self'. Afterwards he called on Frank Dobson at his hotel, but returned to the Chelsea rather than go to the theatre that night:

Dylan's exhaustion seemed as much mental as physical as, hardly able to speak, he fell asleep immediately. Liz sat with him through the evening. Fretfully turning on his bed, he awoke to speak, sometimes in tears, of his wife, the misery of his existence, and of his wish to die. 'I want to go to the Garden of Eden,' he said . . . 'You have no idea how beautiful she [Caitlin] is. There is an illumination about her . . . she shines.' As Liz attempted to comfort him, telling him that he did not have to die, that he could get well, he began to weep uncontrollably.

Again, Brinnin is describing something that happened in his absence. Was Thomas's mention of the Garden of Eden a half-asleep reference to his Stravinsky libretto? Was he distressed because of the troubles within his marriage when so much else was coming right for him?

Later in the night, around 2 a.m. on the morning of 4 November, Thomas insisted on leaving the Chelsea. 'I've got to have a drink,' he said. 'I'll come back in half an hour.' Reitell urged him not to, but he insisted and was gone an hour and a half, returning with the now-legendary remark, 'I've had eighteen straight whiskies. I think that's a record.' Whereupon, it is said, he sank to his knees, reached out his arms, fell into her lap and said, 'I love you . . . but I'm alone', before falling asleep.

Ever since Brinnin's book was published that last remark has attracted comment. Could Thomas really have drunk eighteen whiskies within an hour and a half without an immediate alcoholic seizure? Would he have been able to boast about it if he had done it? Ruthven Todd re-traced Thomas's steps and found that the story could not possibly be true. Back in Wales, friends did not believe it for other reasons – Thomas had never had that kind of drinking capacity, although he was given to exaggerating his drinking (which is not uncommon in Wales).

So what really happened that night? Here, I am indebted to Eric Corbett Williams who wrote in the *New York Times Book Review* (8 February 1981) and the *Washington Post Book World* (12 April 1981) asking readers for any personal recollections, photographs, newspaper accounts, letters, programmes or anecdotes relating to Thomas's visits to America. Among those who replied was an artist John CuRoi, who died in a car crash just a few weeks later – on 14 June 1981. CuRoi said he had met Dylan Thomas previously, accompanied by their mutual friend the sculptor Dave Slivka when they had talked at length of the Spanish poet Lorca. That was in the White Horse Tavern, where

I saw him again on the eve of his death. I had taken a table near the window of the back room for my wife and self on the way home from another activity. Dylan was seated at a table with a few academic types, one of whom was an Asian; one of which looked like a tart. Dylan's eyes were unfocused, he swayed in his chair. His color was horrifying. The man seemed a monster puppet. His condition was clearly a source of amusement and contempt to his companions. The 'tart' progressively dipped thin cigars in one of the eight highballs before him and slid them into his mouth. She finished with three in his mouth. I thought, now all that's needed is a red robe, a crown of thorns and the final casting of dice.

If this account is true (and it does have sufficient detail to give it a feeling of accuracy), then the pieces begin to fall into place. Here was this deeply depressed man, at the height of his powers but afraid that his marriage was finished (with all this would mean to someone of his Puritan background), faced with the greatest opportunities of his life . . . with another group of 'friends' pumping him with drink, as so many had done over the years, knowing perhaps that he couldn't say, 'No', and watching them pile up before him.

What other drugs or drinks might Thomas have taken that evening? His sleep had been irregular, and it is now known that on previous trips he had been observed washing down sleeping pills with whisky when he needed sleep and taking pep pills, particularly benzedrine, when he needed extra strength to cope with his work schedule.

When he returned from his first US tour in 1951, the Thomases spent an afternoon with Vernon Watkins and his wife Gwen at their house on the Pennard cliffs near Swansea. Daniel Jones and Fred Janes were there as well, and Thomas –

boasted of what an uproarious time he had had in America, 'showing off like a small boy'. He claimed to have taken drugs for the first time; no details were given.[17]

During that same tour, David Daiches, who was teaching at Cornell University when Thomas gave a reading there on 14 March 1950, says

he had been almost killed with kindness; round after round of heavy parties had rendered him sick and exhausted. I met the plane on which he was due to arrive from New York but found he was not among the passengers who alighted. I entered the plane and found Dylan fast asleep in his seat. He had been feeling sick, and had promptly filled himself up with sleeping tablets, which he had obtained in New York because of his inability to sleep in the steam-heated hotel bedroom . . . (after black coffee, cold beer and a walk in the clear frosty air) . . . a sudden queasiness overtook him and before I could stop him he had crammed a handful of sleeping pills in his mouth. We hurried home, and he was soon fast asleep.[18]

When Thomas visited the University of Vermont, on the second tour, he was visited at his hotel by Gladys LaFlamme and her husband, where

this strange, familiar, dishevelled, great little man said, with Olympian dignity, 'Will you join me in a pill?' He opened his pill bottle, warning, 'This is going to make you frightfully dry!'
'I know,' said my husband. 'Phenobarb and atropine. I have been here before.'
'Maybe two?' Thomas asked.
'One might-do.'
So, in solemn ritual, and as a sort of armor against the frightening world, they each took a pill.[19]

What other drugs was he taking and for what purpose? In every city he would have had a choice of drugs if he wanted them, for Thomas naturally headed for the looser community of artists, writers, designers, painters, actors and musicians among whom drug-taking was acceptable. Once he started mixing drugs with whisky (he was partial to Old Grandad), the risks were clear. Caitlin told me that when she arrived in New York, shortly before he died, 'there was a lot of talk about drugs'. She did not follow this up, because with his death she saw no point.

Throughout these last months, Dylan Thomas was pulling away from those who wished to help him. His career was changing. He had acquired new status as a writer, and yet couldn't control his other impulses, continuing to draw attention to himself through bursts of self-pity or excessive behaviour. This was nothing new: it had been the pattern of his life in Swansea and London, during the War, throughout his marriage, and in every crisis. What had changed was his audience. The poet was becoming an international figure: great men and women of the day sought his company. But there was no concealing his defects of character. Fame is like that. It sharply focuses attention on every aspect of a person's life.

By the time Thomas returned from the White Horse, and fell asleep in his room at the Chelsea Hotel, it was around 4–5 a.m. Back in Laugharne, he would have had several hours' sleep. There he was always a regular drinker, but seldom a late one.

When Thomas woke he said he needed fresh air, which is a not unfamiliar feeling for those who have had a heavy night. He walked to the White Horse, drank two glasses of beer, and then said he felt unwell. Reitell insisted on calling Dr Feltenstein who gave him another injection of cortisone, recommending a special diet. Two hours later, after more vomiting and similar symptoms to those that followed his first cortisone injection, Brinnin says:

> As Liz almost instantly recognised, Dylan was beginning to go into delirium tremens . . . He indicated that he was 'seeing' something, that it was 'not animals . . . abstractions'. As perspiration broke out on his face, Liz phoned Dr Feltenstein who came to the hotel immediately. As Dylan, raving now, begged to be 'put out', the doctor gave him a sedative.[20]

But was it delirium tremens? And was Liz Reitell qualified to define it?

According to her, Thomas asked her about a friend of hers who had experienced delirium tremens. 'He saw white mice and roses,' she said. 'Roses plural, or Rose's roses with an apostrophe,' said Thomas, who was clearly sufficiently in control of his faculties to play with words, although he now had alcohol, cortisone and that other sedative, morphine, floating around his bloodstream, having apparently been given a dose of half-a-grain by Dr Feltenstein.*

As she was sitting there, holding his hand, Reitell felt Thomas's grip stiffen. She noticed his face turning blue, made another call to Feltenstein, and an ambulance was called to take Thomas to St Vincent's Hospital. It was 2.30 a.m. when Brinnin received a call from her. She was 'shrill, barely controlled'. Thomas had gone into a coma.

There are many conflicting medical, pathological and fanciful accounts of the events that followed at St Vincent's Hospital. A crowd of onlookers gathered in the corridor outside the room where Dylan Thomas lay unconscious. They waited there for several days, with Brinnin coming and going, and various 'friends' calling to see the poet in his coma. After receiving Brinnin's telegram, Caitlin arrived:

> feeling no conscious emotion, just trying to do what I felt I had to do. I was still in a bit of a haze, or a drink haze, probably. The hospital was completely hushed and I could hear my own footsteps as I was led up the stairs to the floor where Dylan was . . . No-one had prepared me for this; until that moment I had had no idea how seriously ill he was . . . and then I saw him, stretched out beneath the bedclothes with what looked like an oxygen tent standing nearby. He was gasping but I couldn't see how he was taking breath. In fact, all I could really see were his hands, resting by his sides. It all seemed so deadly final.[21]

Dylan Thomas died shortly after mid-day, at 12.40 p.m. on Monday 9 November. The primary cause of death was pneumonia, with pressure on the brain the immediate cause. Within his body were found all the usual fatty tissue side effects of heavy drinking, but no evidence of cirrhosis of the liver. He died while a nurse was bathing his body. The poet John Berryman was

---

*Fitzgibbon reported that morphine was the drug administered. Ferris established that the dose was half-a-grain. I have sought the opinion of three doctors, who all confirm that half-a-grain was three times the appropriate dose. This cocktail would have been enough to make Thomas very ill – whatever his bodily reaction to cortisone.

the only other person in the room.
Berryman later wrote to Vernon Watkins

His body died utterly quiet, and he looked so tired that you might once more have burst into tears.[22]

Caitlin brought her husband's body back to Laugharne, where it was interred on 24 November. She thought he had to come home to Wales. The burial was a fitting end, and yet there has been no end. Dylan Thomas left a body of work concerned with Eternity and man's small place within it. His themes of birth, love and death are universal. There remains a deep interest in his curious ambivalence, fuelled by a growing belief that he possessed rare gifts that he was able to shape with the help of a new technology.

It was Edith Sitwell who said

I have never known anyone with a more holy and childlike innocence of mind.

Could it be that the child never really grew up, and that all one could do was love him, or was there an even greater tragedy, as Dame Edith also observed, in his appalling choice of friends?

POSTSCRIPT

YLAN Thomas died just as the world of verbal imagery was changing. For centuries writers had expressed themselves through the printed word, but in his lifetime radio, cinema and television had brought a new technology to the communication of words and ideas. Since his death, the process has further advanced so that now writers who convey their thoughts through recorded sound – the Bob Dylans, Van Morrisons and John Lennons, who are the poets of the new technology – can reach an audience of millions of people through one creative act: the making of a sound.

This sound is their copyright. It embodies words and music, and can be recreated indefinitely enabling people to buy the sound and listen to it in various mass-produced forms; they can hear that sound in their homes through long-playing records, audio cassettes or compact discs, or as part of a world-wide audience that listens to radio. Always, the communication between writer and audience is by the ear. With video, the process has been carried a stage further. The creative artist can now marry what he wants to say with both musical sound and visual image. With some of the finer rock videos, it is as if the works of Picasso had been given movement rather than static form.

Those who create these new artefacts (and conduct their business affairs efficiently, retaining ownership of reproduction rights in all their works) achieve scales of wealth unknown in the history of art or literature. Paul McCartney, for instance, has a gross annual world-wide income of £45m. Lennon's estate was estimated at £220m. Mick Jagger's current assets are estimated at £75m – and Keith Richards' are probably similar for they have both jointly written all The Rolling Stones' major songs. And there are maybe 20 or 30 other artists like Bob Dylan, Michael Jackson, Bruce Springsteen, George Michael, George Harrison, Phil Collins, Eric Clapton and Queen who enjoy comparable wealth, derived from their ability to establish contact with an audience by ear; and often to enhance this initial contact by the personal relationship that comes through live appearances. This, too, is on a massive scale. Top rock artists regularly appear to audiences around the world of 100,000 and more – Pink Floyd's last world tour was seen by 10m people.

In my view, Dylan Thomas was the pioneer, not as a musician, obviously, but as a writer establishing contact with his audience aurally. Many of his followers own few books, but they buy his – and listen to recordings of his poetry, short stories and *Under Milk Wood*. It is not surprising that The Beatles' recording manager George Martin produced the latest sound version of *Under Milk Wood* with contributions from Tom Jones, Bonnie Tyler and Elton John, because it is their generation that was brought up aurally on the works of Dylan Thomas. As a boy, I remember staying up late especially to see Thomas read *A Story* on television; making sure that I did not miss his radio broadcasts; buying *John O' London's Weekly* when it carried an interview with Thomas (as well as my usual copy of *The New Musical Express*). He had an extraordinary impact upon young people of my generation, now in their forties and early fifties, who were at school during those years that radio was the prime means of mass communication.

The relationship felt by a listener is more personal than that experienced by someone reading the same words on a printed page; hundreds of thousands of people flock to concerts by a rock star after hearing his records and reading his lyrics – but few want to HEAR Salman Rushdie or Kingsley Amis. The worlds are different, and yet Thomas, having mastered various forms of literary technique with his father's help, crossed over into this aural world, communicating by sound and personal contact. He handled the consequences far better than might be supposed, because we did not know then of the intolerable strains that modern media fame imposes upon its stars: audiences feel they *know* the artist or even love him – and, given half the chance, try to share his life. Some become fanatical, and the artist has to be shielded from their adulation. For nearly 25 years, most stars appealing to this kind of mass audience have been protected not only by bodyguards but personal staff who make all their travel arrangements, deal with hotel managements, order clothes, arrange laundry, and do any personal shopping; the artists themselves seldom carry cash or even a chequebook.

At its most extreme, fame means the risk of being murdered like John Lennon. No less hazardous for the famous is their need to drink or take drugs either to ease stress or just keep going; the history of Rock is riddled with deaths like that of Dylan Thomas – Jimi Hendrix, Janis Joplin, Sid Vicious, Brian Jones of The Rolling Stones, Steve Clarke of Def Leppard, Elvis Presley, Mama Cass, Phil Lynott, Jim Morrison, Paul Kossoff and the American actor John Belushi would all be alive now if they had not had to lead such unnatural lives.

Dylan Thomas died before modern media technology changed the nature of fame. To be personally idolised is a relatively new phenomenon. Few of the early film stars experienced anything like this because the Hollywood star system shielded them from their public. They were packaged and promoted like the films they made, with their homes and clothes provided for them; and sometimes, even their wives.

All this began to change in the Fifties with audiences preferring stars who were real and vulnerable, with the common touch; which may well be the result of a bonding process that occurs when there is personal contact, either by sound or live appearance, between audience and artist. But there can be a terrible price. The artist cannot escape. If he goes shopping, fans will chase him down the street. He cannot go into pubs or restaurants, because there will always be someone either wanting to take him on (which happened frequently to Dylan Thomas) or ply him with drinks in such a way that he cannot refuse without causing offence (which is partially what happened to Thomas, although he had another real problem; in some situations – particularly when the adrenaline was flowing after a radio broadcast or a stage reading – he couldn't say, 'No'.)

It is difficult for the families of such a performer to adjust to the nature of fame. Caitlin was astonished when she saw him perform for the first time in the United States, because he commanded the stage with authority and held his audience, who listened in respectful silence, responding to every nuance. She was appalled by what she witnessed thereafter: the scramble for personal contact by his fans, with, as she puts it, 'all those girls throwing themselves at him'.

His fame has not diminished in the years since his death. Instead, it has grown similarly to those other icons of the early Fifties, James Dean and Marilyn Monroe, who also died tragically young. The legend has become larger than the man. There is intense interest in every aspect of his life. A cinema film is being made of his life. His home in Laugharne, The Boat House, is now a museum restored with funds provided by the European Economic Community, and there is a market for Dylan Thomas memorabilia of every kind. There are posters, postcards, plaques, mugs, sculptured busts, tableware, thimbles, trays and tea towels carrying either the Dylan Thomas or Boat House motif (or both) as well as a wide array of books, video films and recordings. One entrepreneur even marketed glass phials of what was claimed to be Dylan Thomas's sweat.

His family have had to learn to cope with the consequences. Caitlin tried to kill herself on several occasions and has spent many periods in hospital; at times, his children have found it perilous to live with his memory.

And what does it all boil down to? Maybe twenty poems, especially *Fern Hill, Poem in October, And Death shall have no Dominion, Do Not Go Gentle Into That Good Night, Poem on His Birthday, The Hand That Signed the Paper, After the Funeral, Vision and Prayer, Lament, This Bread I Break, The force that through the green fuse drives the flower, The Hunchback in the Park* and *In My Craft or Sullen Art*; those few autobiographical short stories that are mostly to be found in *Portrait of the Artist as a Young Dog*; the magical *Under Milk Wood*, and a few of the pieces written to perform on radio. Not much in total; but proof enough of what the world loses when fame kills an artist in his prime.

NOTES

CHAPTER ONE

1 'Genius and Madness Akin in The World of Art', *South Wales Evening Post*, 7 January 1933.
2 *Homage to Dylan Thomas*, a tribute written by Dame Edith Sitwell for the memorial concert staged at the Globe Theatre, London, on 24 January 1954.
3 *Conversations with Stravinsky*, Robert Craft, 1959.
4 'Genius and Madness Akin in The World of Art', ibid.
5 Letter from the poet John Berryman to Vernon Watkins quoted on p. 151-2 of *Portrait of a Friend*, Gwen Watkins, 1983. Berryman and a nurse were the only people in Thomas's room when he died.
6 *Soho in the Fifties*, Daniel Farson, 1987.
7 *My Friend Dylan Thomas*, Daniel Jones, 1977, p.6.
8 *Conversations with Capote*, Lawrence Grobel, 1985.

CHAPTER TWO

1 Letter from Caradoc Evans, *Western Mail*, 27 November 1915.
2 Ferris, p.25.
3 *Texas Quarterly*, Winter 1961. This issue reproduced Thomas's answers to a questionnaire from a student seeking help for a thesis. The student was living in Laugharne in 1951. Thomas answered the questions at length and in longhand. It was wholly in character that Thomas, whose humility revealed itself when discussing his values, should be at his most revealing in moments of private kindness.
4 *Dylan: Druid of the Broken Body*, Aneirin Talfan Davies, 1964.
5 Elis Jenkins, *Dylan Thomas Remembered*, a tape issued by the Dylan Thomas Society, 1978.
6 *Texas Quarterly*, idem.
7 *Collected Letters*, p.76-7. Sadly, his father's library did not survive intact. He sold or gave away parts of it when he retired and moved to Bishopston (1937) and from there to Llangain (c.1944), South Leigh (1948) and Laugharne (1949), complaining bitterly that with every move his library diminished. Individual books from it occasionally turn up in secondhand bookshops in Wales, distinguished by his signature on the front endpapers.
8 Fitzgibbon, p.33. This rings true. Caitlin has told me that Florence insisted on calling her husband 'Daddy', which he found intensely irritating.

9 Elis Jenkins, *Dylan Thomas Remembered*, tape, 1978.

10 Daniel Jones later included *His Requiem* in *Dylan Thomas: The Poems* (1971), which he edited, thus publishing many poems that Thomas had chosen not to include himself in *Collected Poems*. The poem was published in *The Sunday Telegraph* as a long-forgotten childhood poem. An observant reader pointed out that it had first appeared in *Boy's Own Paper* (November 1923), written by one Lilian Gard. *His Requiem* was published in *The Western Mail* over Dylan Thomas's name on 14 January 1927.

11 Fitzgibbon quotes another example of plagiarism when Thomas submitted a poem to his school magazine taken from Arthur Mee's *Children's Encyclopaedia*. Fitzgibbon, p.49.

12 *The Fight*, first published in *Life and Letters Today* (December 1939) and then, with some revisions, in *Portrait of the Artist as a Young Dog* (1940).

13 This detail is also contained in *The Fight*. These habits remained throughout his life. When Thomas moved back to Laugharne in 1949, he turned a wooden garage on The Cliff near The Boat House into his workshed, with a coal-fired stove, table, chairs, bookcases and a chest of drawers packed with manuscripts. Photos of all his literary heroes were pinned to the walls.

CHAPTER THREE

1 *My Friend Dylan Thomas*, Daniel Jones, p.11.

2 *Swansea Between the Wars*, Thomas Taig, published in *The Anglo Welsh Review*, Summer 1968.

3 Ferris, pp.33–4.

4 Ferris, p.155. Several of Dylan's letters to his parents are included in *Collected Letters*.

5 *My Friend Dylan Thomas*, p.15.

6 Fitzgibbon, p.15.

7 From a note in Pamela Hansford Johnson's diary, quoted in Ferris, p.42. She and Dylan became pen-friends after they had both won poetry competitions in *The Sunday Referee*. Later, this turned to love and they nearly married. Thomas engaged in a long correspondence with her. He was clearly anxious to impress and his letters are often laboured. Most of his letters have survived, but hers have not. Typically, Thomas did not keep them.

8 So says Jones in *My Friend Dylan Thomas*, p.26. His friend may have had the last laugh. Bram is the Welsh word for fart.

9 *Collected Letters*, p.192. It should be noted that other comments by Thomas on Jones are deleted on this page and also on p.426.

10 Details of Thomas's contributions to the *Swansea Grammar School Magazine* are given in *Dylan Thomas in Print: A Bibliographical History*, Professor Ralph Maud, University of Pittsburgh Press, 1970.

11 His essay *Modern Poetry* (December 1929) was remarkably mature. Fitzgibbon reproduces it in full.

12 His essay *The Films* (July 1930) reveals a detailed knowledge of the better films of the day. Thomas was a regular cinemagoer and later worked in this medium (1944–9), harbouring hopes until the end of his life of being commissioned to write a Hollywood film script.

13 *The Fight.*

14 In his early years Thomas is known to have filled at least ten notebooks with poems. Only four of these survive. They are now owned by the Lockwood Memorial Library, Buffalo, New York. These were analysed by Professor Maud in *Poet in the Making: The Notebooks of Dylan Thomas.*

15 See the two long letters quoted in *My Friend Dylan Thomas* [pp.36–45] and compare these with his other correspondence in *Collected Letters*, which reveal Thomas carefully varying his pitch.

16 Thomas failed every subject in his school Matriculation exams, with the exception of English Literature where legend has it that he scored 98 per cent. This was recalled by a contemporary Philip Smart in the Barclays Bank magazine *Spread Eagle* (April 1954). There is no other verification of this because the school recorded only its successes, never its failures.

17 *Herald of Wales*, 19 September 1936.

18 *Collected Letters*, p.182. This letter was written to his journalist friend Charlie Fisher, who trained with him on the *South Wales Daily Post.*

19 Between 1929 and 1931, Thomas appeared as Edward Stanton in Drinkwater's *Abraham Lincoln*, played the title role in Drinkwater's *Oliver Cromwell*, and the part of Roberts the strike leader in Galsworthy's *Strife.*

20 Thomas appeared in at last two productions for the YMCA Players, *The Man of Six* and *The Fourth Wall* in 1931.

21 His first role with the Little Theatre was in Noël Coward's *Hay Fever* (February 1932), followed by *The Beaux Stratagem* (April 1932), *The Merry Wives of Windsor* (February 1933), *Peter and Paul* (March 1933). *Strange Orchestra* (December 1933), *The Way of the World* (January 1934), *Martine* (February 1934) and *Richard II* (March 1934).

22 This talk was reproduced in *The Listener*, 16 January 1958. Wynford was another great pub storyteller, and I heard him tell this one on other occasions. Many of his stories were so funny that one could never remember them afterwards, and I believe this was the nature of the friendship that Dylan and Wynford had with many of their contemporaries.

23 *South Wales Daily Post*, 2 June 1931.

24 Trevor Hughes was a railway clerk who later moved to Harrow. Thomas maintained a correspondence with him. This can be found in *Collected Letters*, though, once again, the other side of the correspondence is missing!

25 *Dylan – The Eternal Swansea Boy*, an article written by Bert Trick for the Welsh magazine *Country Quest* (Autumn 1960). Another indication that these were very different friendships to most of those he made in Swansea was that Thomas dedicated poems to both of them. This was something he did very rarely. His

only political poem *The Hand That Signs The Paper* was dedicated 'To A.E.T.' (Trick). *Let for one moment a faith statement* was dedicated to Hughes. Both poems are in the notebook Thomas commenced in August 1933, which is now in the Buffalo collection.

26 *Collected Letters*, p.63.

27 *Collected Letters*, p.145.

CHAPTER FOUR

1 Letter from Bert Trick quoted in *The Days of Dylan Thomas* by Bill Read, 1964, p.47.

2 *Collected Letters*, p.12.

3 *Collected Letters*, p.131. This did not stop Thomas sending in more of his work, Orage published three more of his poems during 1934, and an anonymous review of *This Year's Poetry* noted that, 'It has been left to a newcomer, Dylan Thomas, to make the most exciting contribution to the year's poetry.'

4 *Important to Me*, Pamela Hansford Johnson, 1974.

5 *Idem*, p.141/2.

6 *Idem*, p.142.

7 *Idem*, p.142/3.

8 *Idem*, p.143/4.

9 *Collected Letters*, p.138/9. This incident is further discussed in the next chapter.

10 *Important to Me*, p.145. The book to which she refers is *This Bed Thy Centre*, her first novel, published in 1935 which went into five editions in two months. Thomas suggested the title, and later (*Collected Letters*, p.188) offered to 'repeat my usual & my "This Bed" sub-editing' on her next novel *Blessed Above Women*. This suggests that he worked on both manuscripts with her. There are many Thomas touches in *This Bed Thy Centre*, with his characteristic use of adjectival verbs and nouns as adjectives.

11 *Collected Letters*, p.51.

12 There is little point any biographer trying to put these forays into any kind of sequence and then seeking to match dates with specific poems or short stories. Everything overlapped. Thomas had dozens of poems and short stories in different stages of composition and would work from one to the other, often going back over old ones and revising, and he was just as haphazard in his domestic arrangements, staying with many different friends in London between visits back to Swansea. Anyone interested in the sequence of his work is advised to refer to the Maud and Rolph bibliographies, *Poet in the Making: The Notebooks of Dylan Thomas*, and perhaps Robert Coleman Williams's *A Concordance to the Collected Poems of Dylan Thomas*, 1967. They will soon discover that there is no beginning and no end; Thomas used the same ideas, words, phrases and images again and again.

13 See *The Magical Dilemma of Victor Neuburg*, Jean Overton Fuller, 1965, and the essay *The Dylan I Knew* by Runia Sheila Macleod in the Dylan Thomas

Memorial Issue of *Adam* (1953). Thomas's relationship with them is also documented in his correspondence with Pamela Hansford Johnson, *Collected Letters* p.20–187.

14 *Soho in the Fifties*, Daniel Farson, 1987.

15 This first issue is easily distinguished from the second, although they were bound from the same printed sheets; the binding of the first has a flat spine and the second, a rounded spine. Joseph Connolly in *Modern First Editions: Their Value to Collectors* (1987) estimates that a good copy of the first issue of *18 Poems* is properly valued at approx £2,000. A signed copy is much more valuable, especially one inscribed by Thomas to a known friend or member of his family. I recently heard of one signed copy being sold for £8,000.

16 *Collected Letters*, p.85.

17 *Important to Me*, p.143.

18 *Recollections of Dylan Thomas*, an article published by *The London Magazine* (September 1957).

19 *Collected Letters*, p.190.

20 *Collected Letters*, p.207.

21 *The Shade of Dylan Thomas* by Lawrence Durrell, an article published in *Encounter* (December 1957). After this meeting Thomas went on to contribute to all three issues of the magazine *Delta* which Durrell edited in Paris.

CHAPTER FIVE

1 John Donne (1572–1631) was the leading metaphysical poet. George Herbert (1593–1633) and Henry Vaughan (*c*.1622–95), both of Anglo-Welsh extraction, were among the others. All three were frequently quoted by Thomas, almost certainly influenced by his father.

2 BBC radio talk, *Wales and the Artist* (1949).

3 *Caitlin*, pp.63–5.

4 Ferris, p.100.

5 *Collected Letters*, p.171.

6 *Collected Letters*, p.140.

7 *Important to Me*, p.146.

8 Letter to *The Spectator*, 27 April 1962.

9 Ferris, p.98.

10 Elisabeth Lutyens quoted on p.119 of *A Pilgrim Soul: The Life and Work of Elisabeth Lutyens*, Meirion and Susie Harries, 1989.

11 As above, also p.119.

12 The stories that Thomas may have had venereal disease rely upon a letter to Geoffrey Grigson (*Collected Letters*, p.201) and another to Desmond Hawkins (*Collected Letters*, p.236). Neither letter is convincing, and in his own subsequent essay on Thomas which appeared in *The London Magazine*, quoted in chapter four, page 54, Grigson suggests otherwise.

13 *Caitlin*, p.1 *et seq.*

14 *Collected Letters*, p.223.

15 Many of Thomas's letters to his wife were stolen when they were living in London during the War. She thinks she knows who took them, but they have not surfaced again – possibly because ownership would be disputed if they did. These are not the only Thomas writings to have disappeared. I understand that there is still one major manuscript, a playscript, in private hands. There are also several other poems and numerous letters that still await publication.

16 *Collected Letters*, p.234.

17 The Macnamaras had been wealthy landowners in County Clare, owning the whole village of Ennistymon and a large estate. They were Protestant-Irish. Her grandfather was High Sheriff of County Clare. Thomas told her it was 'nice to be sleeping with a bit of class'.

18 *Twenty-five Poems* was published on 10 September 1936, in an edition of 730 copies. Three further editions were printed. See the Rolph bibliography, pp.43–4. This volume was part of a series, all with similar format and binding, which also included poetry by Edwin Muir, Richard Church, Llewelyn Wyn Griffith, Norman Cameron and Conrad Aiken.

19 *South Wales Evening Post*, 22 January 1937.

20 *Collected Letters*, p.180.

21 *Collected Letters*, p.185.

22 *Collected Letters*, p.210.

23 *Collected Letters*, p.212.

24 The impact of that review is mentioned by Fitzgibbon and Ferris, although neither quotes from it extensively. The review was printed in full as an appendix to Henry Treece's *Dylan Thomas: Dog Among the Fairies* (1949).

CHAPTER SIX

1 *Collected Letters*, p.248.

2 *Caitlin*, pp.36–9.

3 This significant letter was uncovered by Ferris, and parts of it are reproduced on p.155 of his book. Caitlin has told me that she was never told of this correspondence by Dylan and never had any reason to believe that his parents were against the marriage.

4 *Collected Letters*, p.249.

5 *Collected Letters*, p.252.

6 Edith Sitwell was thanked for her 'lovely present with which we bought all sorts of things we wanted, from knives and towels to a Garbo picture' which sounds as though she sent a useful cheque. *Collected Letters*, p.257. Thomas would have thought this a propitious moment to write to other friends.

7 *Caitlin*, pp.63–5.

8 *Collected Letters*, p.262.

9 *Collected Letters*, p.275.

10 This explanation, contained in a letter to Hermann Peschmann and reproduced

in *Collected Letters*, p.269, has to be read side by side with the poem. Each is impenetrable without the other.

11 Written to Henry Treece, after Church had suggested that it was 'a little too early' for a book on Dylan Thomas. *Collected Letters*, p.273.

12 *Collected Letters*, p.273.

13 *Collected Letters*, p.277.

14 *The Eye of the Beholder*, Lance Sieveking, 1957.

15 This was the American poetess Emma Swan who was published by Laughlin and had a private income. She apparently sent the money at his suggestion, but Caitlin says Dylan never told her that he was receiving these regular cheques from the United States!

16 A survey of living costs at the time was compiled by Dr Harold Priestley and published as *The What It Cost The Day Before Yesterday Book* (1979). Beer was 3p a pint, whisky 65p a bottle, a 4lb. loaf 4p, bacon 5p per lb., beef 4.5p per lb., pork 5p per lb., sugar 6p, and a pair of men's boots 52¼p. A radio was then a luxury item costing £20. These were national figures; food was generally cheaper in West Wales where it was available straight from the farm.

17 *Caitlin*, p.72.

18 *Collected Letters*, p.402.

19 *Collected Letters*, p.415.

20 *Collected Letters*, p.417.

21 *Collected Letters*, p.310.

CHAPTER SEVEN

1 *Collected Letters*, p.391.

2 *Collected Letters*, p.401

3 *Collected Letters*, p.438

4 *Collected Letters*, p.446

5 *Collected Letters*, p.447

6 *Caitlin*, p.72.

7 *Collected Letters*, p.451.

8 See *Caitlin*, pp.73–5, which describes this one-night affair in some detail.

9 *The Death of the King's Canary* was a satire on the poets of the day. It was eventually published in 1976. The idea had been bubbling away in Thomas's mind for several years, and he had previously thought of writing it with Charlie Fisher and Desmond Hawkins. It is a story about the assassination of the Poet Laureate, set in a country house.

10 *Portrait of the Artist as a Young Dog* was published by Dent on 4 April 1940 in an edition of 1,500 copies. This impression remained in print until February 1948, and there were 2nd and 3rd impressions in March and December 1954. A paperback edition was published by Guild Books in 1949.

11 *Adventures in the Skin Trade* remained unfinished, and he was planning to work on it towards the end of his life when he was given more encouragement by Dent.

In its rough, incomplete state it was eventually published in 1955, nearly two years after his death. The 'novel' first appears in his correspondence in 1940.

12 *Deaths and Entrances* was first published in *Horizon* (January 1941).

13 *Into her lying down head* first appeared in *Life and Letters Today* (November 1940).

14 *Ballad of the Long-legged Bait* was one of the longest poems that Thomas ever wrote, with 216 lines. He worked on it between January and April 1941, while staying with his parents.

15 An early version of *The hunchback in the park* appears in the Texas notebooks, dated 9 May 1932, and a poem with a similar idea to *On the Marriage of a Virgin* in the February 1933 notebook.

16 *Collected Letters*, p.493.

17 *Collected Letters*, p.484.

18 This period is well documented by Fitzgibbon, who worked in the same industry at this period. See pp.244–53, although it should be noted that some of his dates do not tally with Thomas's letters.

19 This wartime work for Strand is summarised in an appendix to Fitzgibbon, and in the Maud bibliography details of several of the films Thomas helped to produce are given on pp.135–40. These included *This is Colour*, a film on the use of ICI dyes; *New Towns for Old*, about post-war planning; *Balloon Site 568*, describing women's work on barrage balloons; *These Are The Men*, an attack on the German war leaders superimposing English speech over German film. *Our Country* was said to be a 'lyrical look at the face of war-time Britain'. Thomas also worked on at least five other films.

20 *Caitlin*, pp.80–1.

21 Aeronwy was born in London on 3 March 1943, during an air raid. Thomas was nowhere to be seen, though Caitlin says that usually during air raids he used to hide beneath their table at Manresa Road. He turned up at the hospital several days later, dishevelled and wearing a dressing gown. See *Caitlin* pp.83–5.

22 *Collected Letters*, p.505. He was probably referring to another Strand film titled *Is Your Ernie Really Necessary!* with its obvious pun. The film was completed in 1943, but suppressed because the Ministry of Information thought it too flippant.

23 *The Doctor and the Devils* was published as a book in 1953, and then filmed over 30 years later in 1985 with starring roles played by Timothy Dalton, Jonathan Pryce and Twiggy, with Mel Brooks as executive producer.

24 *Collected Letters*, p.526.

25 First published in *Our Time* (May 1944). This was a left-wing poetry magazine, and the poem was one of only two directly prompted by the war. The other was *Among those Killed in the Dawn Raid was a Man Aged a Hundred*. In both poems, Thomas sympathised with the innocent civilian victims of war.

26 & 27 Both first published in *Poetry London* (June 1944).

28 *Collected Letters*, p.518.

29 In a letter to Dame Edith Sitwell, Thomas said that he wrote *Fern Hill* 'near the farm where it happened' and that the poem was 'a new joy to me, as real as that which made the words come, at last, out of a never-to-be-buried childhood in heaven or Wales.' *Collected Letters*, pp.582–3.

CHAPTER EIGHT

1 *Twenty Years A'Growing* was the autobiography of Maurice O'Sullivan. It was first published in 1933, having originally been written in Irish, describing his childhood on the Blasket Islands. When it was first published, E.M. Forster wrote, 'Here is the egg of a seabird – lovely, perfect and laid this very morning.' Thomas's unfinished film script based on the book was published by Dent in 1964.

2 Oscar Williams (1900–64), American poet and anthologist, first wrote to Thomas in 1942. They corresponded thereafter and he became a personal friend and a key figure in gaining American acceptance for Thomas's work.

3 *Selected Writings* was published in the US on 8 November 1946, nearly two years after its initial discussion by Thomas.

4 Vernon Watkins and his wife Gwen were married in London on 2 October 1944. Thomas was in London at the time, drinking in a pub, and failed to join them at their lunch beforehand at the Charing Cross Hotel or at the wedding itself where he had agreed to be best man. Three weeks later he wrote to apologise, although the letter was patently false. Caitlin believes he could not be bothered to go.

5 The book was never written, although Thomas had signed a contract with Peter Lunn. See *Collected Letters*, p.523 *et seq.* This became part of a pattern. As Thomas became more successful, he abandoned projects when he lost interest in them – even when he had received payments in advance.

6 When the case came to trial, the officer was acquitted. Dylan and Caitlin were key witnesses. As he blasted off his sten gun, the man shouted 'You're nothing but a lot of egoists.' The court case was reported in the *Welsh Gazette* (12 April 1945) and the *News of the World* (24 June 1945). The *Welsh Gazette* report was reproduced in full in Maud's *Dylan Thomas in Print*.

7 Although *Twenty Years A'Growing* was published in book form in 1964, it has still not been filmed.

8 *Quite Early One Morning* was first broadcast by the BBC Welsh Home Service on 31 August 1945; although based on New Quay it is similar in atmosphere to *Under Milk Wood*, with several of the same characters and house names.

9 *Deaths and Entrances* was published on 7 February 1946 in an initial edition of 3,000 copies. Three further editions were published during his lifetime.

10 *Collected Letters*, p.569 *et seq.*

11 *Collected Letters*, p.545.

12 *Dylan Thomas and The Radio*, an essay by John Arlott, published in *Adelphi* (February 1954).

13 Thomas first picked this poem up from Wyn Henderson before the War,

although it has many variations in nursery rhyme; be continued to use it as part of his pub 'act' for the rest of his life. It was, presumably, one of the party tricks that horrified American academic audiences during his four US tours.

14 *The Growth of Milk Wood*, Douglas Cleverdon, 1969.

CHAPTER NINE

1 *A Personal History*, A.J.P. Taylor, 1983, p.107. The other quotations in the paragraphs that follow come from the same source.

2 *Idem*, p.149, 150.

3 *Idem*, p.184.

4 Sir Henry Tizard was a distinguished scientist who had pioneered aeronautical research during the First World War, and assisted the Government on aircraft production in the Second World War.

5 *Idem*, p.185.

6 *Collected Letters*, p.578. Thomas accompanied this letter with a 2,000-word analysis of 13 poems that Margaret Taylor had shown him, studying them in painful detail, picking out lines and phrases that he could praise.

7 *Collected Letters*, p.585.

8 *Collected Letters*, p.588.

9 *Collected Letters*, p.594.

10 *Collected Letters*, p.612.

11 *Collected Letters*, pp.614–15.

12 *Return Journey* became a highly successful BBC radio programme, repeated many times, and published in *Quite Early One Morning*; nothing came of the libretto.

13 *Caitlin*, p.98.

14 *Collected Letters*, p.635.

15 *A Personal History*, A.J.P. Taylor, p.188.

16 Strangely, this talk was written for BBC Radio Scotland and broadcast by them in their *Scottish Life and Letters* series in June 1949.

17 *Collected Letters*, p.689.

18 *A Personal History*, A.J.P. Taylor, p.191.

19 *Caitlin*, pp.63–4.

20 *Caitlin*, p.69.

21 *Collected Letters*, p.879.

22 *Author's Prologue* to his *Collected Poems*. The poem was written in his workshed at Laugharne and describes the landscape that he could see across the estuary, and how he related this to his concepts of life.

23 Both these extracts are taken from the *Poems on his birthday*, which was also written soon after his return to Laugharne and similarly describes the estuary landcape and the birds that he could see there – herons, curlews, cormorants, gulls and hawks.

24 *Collected Letters*, p.707.

CHAPTER TEN

1 *Living in Wales*, broadcast 23 June 1949.
2 *Caitlin*, p.125.
3 *Collected Letters*, p.709.
4 *Collected Letters*, p.689.
5 All three of these Gainsborough scripts/treatments have since been published in book form; *Me and My Bike* and *Rebecca's Daughters* both by Triton (1965) and *The Beach of Falesa* by Jonathan Cape (1964). All three have also been published in paperback.
6 *Collected Letters*, p.681. It has to be remembered that the average wage for a skilled man was still under £10 per week, and that beer was the equivalent of 6p a pint.
7 *Collected Letters*, p.692.
8 This star-struck side of Brinnin's personality emerges clearly in his book *Sextet* (1982), which dwells lovingly on his relationship with Truman Capote, with endless namedropping and much superfluous description of other people's domestic trivia.
9 *Collected Letters*, p.748.
10 *Dylan Thomas in America*, John Malcolm Brinnin, p.3.
11 *Collected Letters*, p.748 and 750.
12 *Collected Letters*, p.750.
13 *Collected Letters*, p.751.
14 *Collected Letters*, p.757.
15 *Collected Letters*, p.757.
16 *Collected Letters*, p.752.
17 *Collected Letters*, p.754.
18 *Collected Letters*, p.760.
19 *Sextet*, John Malcolm Brinnin, 1982, p.70.
20 *Best of Times, Worst of Times*, Shelley Winters, 1990, p.31.
21 *Dylan Thomas in America*, p.61.
22 *Dylan Thomas in America*, p.42.
23 *Best of Times, Worst of Times*, pp.31–40. Ebsen.
24 *Dylan Thomas in America*, p.43.
25 This reminiscence was provided in writing by the student. It was one of many collected by Eric Corbett Williams.
26 Helen Lillie also wrote to Eric Corbett Williams, after the *New York Times* had published his request for personal memories of Thomas's American tours.
27 Professor Bogorad also responded to Williams' advertisement, enclosing this personal memoir which he had written for *Centaur*, a literary magazine published by the University of Vermont (vol. III no. 3, Spring 1956).
28 Mac Hammond visited Laugharne with Professor Ralph Maud in 1988, and told me of these recollections.

29 *When Dylan Thomas in our local doo-yard bloom'd*, an essay by Roselle M. Lewis, published in the *Los Angeles Times* (19 October 1980) and also collated by Eric Corbett Williams.

30 Personal recollection collated by Eric Corbett Williams.

31 *When Dylan Thomas in our local doo-yard bloom'd*, Roselle M. Lewis.

32 David Lougee interviewed in *Point*, the Fordham University Magazine, vol. IX no. 6 (March 1980). Lougee was a friend of Thomas's.

CHAPTER ELEVEN

1 *Remembering Dylan Thomas*, interview with David Lougee, *The Point*, ibid.

2 *Creation and Destruction: notes on Dylan Thomas* by Dr B.W. Murphy of Silver Spring, Maryland, published in the *British Journal of Medical Psychology*, vol. 41, pp. 149–67. This essay was based on a study of Thomas's American medical files, his autopsy, interviews with the doctors who attended Thomas in his last days, and careful appraisal of what was then known about Thomas's family background; the essay needs some re-assessment in the light of the added information on Thomas's life now available through *Collected Letters* and *Caitlin*.

3 Dr Murphy corresponded directly with Vernon Watkins, among others, and this point is among many that he takes from primary sources.

4 *Books*, the Journal of the National Book League, December 1953.

5 From a letter written by Bill Read to Dr B.W. Murphy. Read visited the Thomases in Laugharne, and wrote one of the best early biographies, *The Days of Dylan Thomas*, 1964.

6 *Dylan Thomas in America*, pp.64–5.

7 *Dylan Thomas in America*, p.75.

8 *Collected Letters*, p.769.

9 *Books*, December 1953.

10 *Over Sir John's Hill* was first published by Princess Caetani in *Botteghe Oscure* (December 1949).

11 *In The White Giant's Thigh* was first published in *Botteghe Oscure* (November 1950); at that time Thomas planned it as part of a sequence of poems with the overall title *In Country Heaven* which he intended to publish in book form, present as one radio programme and also record.

12 & 13 Both these poems were first published in *Botteghe Oscure* (November 1951), although Thomas was a little uncertain about publishing the first while his father was still alive; it was a feeling that he overcame for he included *Do Not Go Gentle Into That Good Night* in his *Collected Poems*.

14 *Poem On His Birthday* was first published in *World Review* (October 1951).

15 *Elegy* was his last poem; it remained unfinished at the time of his death. Vernon Watkins gathered together the work-sheets, and finished the poem in a way that he thought Thomas would have approved. It was first published in *Encounter* (February 1956).

16 *Collected Letters*, p.860.

17 Princess Caetani was a rich American woman married to an Italian prince. She was also known as the Duchess of Sermoneta, and was a woman of noted taste, a patron of the arts, who used her wealth to fund *Botteghe Oscure*, a literary magazine that published the latest work by leading American and European writers. The magazine was published in Rome and distributed internationally, with each issue totalling around 500 pages and reaching exceptional standards.

18 *Collected Letters*, p.813. This study is an important source for anyone wanting to study the origins of *Under Milk Wood*, for Thomas went on to describe the personalities of the characters.

19 This project was being put together by the celebrated film producer Michael Powell, who died in 1990. He was also hoping to persuade Stravinsky to write the music for this project, based on Homer's *Odyssey*.

20 The wording here is vague for good reason. In a footnote to p.813 of *Collected Letters*, Ferris says of this work, which Thomas said he had temporarily abandoned, 'If this is true, the work isn't known.' My understanding is that there were at least two other major projects that remain unpublished. I do not know how far Thomas had got with his work on Homer's *Odyssey*; I corresponded with Michael Powell while researching this book, and he said that he was keeping that for his own memoirs! I also understand that Thomas was working on an idea based on a pub crawl, set in the pubs of Carmarthen. At various times, I have been told that this manusript still survives but I have yet to see it.

21 Fitzgibbon, p.298. Thomas discussed this project in detail with Philip Burton shortly before he left for the United States in October 1953 (see Chapter Twelve); he envisaged it as a stage play with Burton as his collaborator.

CHAPTER TWELVE

1 *Portrait of a Friend*, Gwen Watkins, 1983.

2 *Caitlin*, p.189.

3 *Dylan Thomas in America*, pp.180–1.

4 *Dylan Thomas in America*, p.192. These observations *may* be the origin of suggestions that Thomas was beset by 'creative aridity', as Brinnin puts it. The point was taken up by Fitzgibbon and Ferris, but is wholly belied by what is now known about Thomas's plans at that time.

5 *Dylan Thomas in America*, p.203.

6 *Collected Letters*, pp. 916–17.

7 *My Friend Dylan Thomas*, p. 108.

8 Fitzgibbon, pp. 390–1.

9 *The Growth of Milk Wood*, Douglas Cleverdon, 1969. Caitlin later challenged Cleverdon's right to own the manuscript. She took the case to the High Court in 1966, and lost.

10 This quotation and the next are taken from an essay by Philip Burton in the Dylan Thomas Memorial Issue of *Adam* (1953).

11 Fitzgibbon, p.391.

12 *Dylan Thomas in America;* these quotations are taken from Chapter VIII dealing with the fourth and final tour.

13 ibid. p.208.

14 ibid. p.209.

15 ibid. p.213.

16 ibid, p.215.

17 Ferris, p.255.

18 From an essay by David Daiches which appears in *Dylan Thomas: The Legend and the Poet*, edited by Professor E.W. Tedlock, 1960.

19 *Centaur*, the literary magazine of the University of Vermont, vol. III no. 3 (Spring 1956).

20 *Dylan Thomas in America*, p.229.

21 *Caitlin*, pp.182–3.

22 *Portrait of a Friend*, Gwen Watkins, p.151.

INDEX

This Index relates to the Preface, Chapters 1–12 and the Postscript. Readers are advised to use this Index in conjunction with the Chronology (pp. xvii–xxvi) and the Notes (pp. 183–196). The main events of Thomas's life are detailed in their chronological sequence on pp. xvii–xxvi.